TIBET

THE COUNTRY AND ITS INHABITANTS

TIBET

THE COUNTRY AND ITS INHABITANTS

BY

F. Grenard

Translated by **A. TEIXEIRA DE MATTOS**

GYAN

ISBN : 978-81-212-1519-0(HB)

First Published, 1904

Published, 2018

Published by

Gyan Publishing House
5, Ansari Road
Daryaganj, New Delhi-110002
Phone: 011-47034999, 9811692060
www.gyanbooks.com
E-mail: books@gyanbooks.com

Printed at: G. Print Process, Delhi.

PREFACE

THE book which I am now placing before the reader is a partial reprint of a work entitled "A Scientific Mission to Upper Asia" (Paris: Leroux, 3 vols. 4to. and an atlas fol.), which I published in 1897–1898 under the auspices of the Ministry of Public Instruction. This government publication, important both in bulk and price, is not within the reach of the mass of readers nor, especially, of all those who may need to refer to it. I have therefore thought it advisable to extract from it and to issue in a convenient form all that part which relates to Tibet and the Tibetans, to whom recent events have called general attention. I have omitted only purely technical matters.

The following pages contain first the story of the journey, unfortunately attended with tragic results, which I performed with my regretted leader and friend, the late M. Dutreuil de Rhins, across an almost inaccessible region. If devoid of any other merit, this narrative has at least that of sincerity. I have been to no pains to embellish or in any way to distort it, nor have I ever endeavoured to astonish the reader's imagination by displaying things through magnifying-glasses or to flatter the prevailing taste for romantic exoticism which disguises the true character of countries and men under a conventional veneer. After drawing up in his journal a list of the sufferings and difficulties with which we had to cope, Dutreuil de Rhins wrote:

"We can never forget all these sufferings!"

Far from exaggerating them, however, I have rather extenuated them, knowing how greatly he detested anything at all resembling advertisement and how bent he was upon not appearing to solicit the admiration or pity of others.

The second part of this volume comprises an account of the manners and customs, the social and economic life and the political condition of Tibet, one of the most curious and least-known of countries, which is on the verge of losing a notable part of its originality. This account, although dating some years back, has lost none of its novelty. Of the explorers who came after us—Littledale, Welby, Deasy, Bonin, Kozlof, Sven Hedin, of whom each was very remarkable in his way, while the last stands in the first rank from the geographical point of view—not one was in a position to make a thorough study of Tibetan society. Two men alone—the Hindu pundit Sarat Chandra Das* and the Buriat Tsybikoff, a Russian subject†—have brought us any fresh information in this respect. Among recent travellers who went before us, I must mention, as being in the first rank of those who have added to our knowledge of the people of Tibet, Père Desgodins, of the Foreign Missions,‡ and, above all, Mr. W. W. Rockhill,§ who is to-day the most competent man in this matter. I have been careful not to lay stress upon points which they already had sufficiently elucidated.

F. G.

---

* *Journey to Lha-sa and Central Tibet.* London: 1902.

† *Central Tibet.* An article in the *Bulletin of the St. Petersburg Geographical Society*: 1903, Part III.

‡ *Tibet.* Paris: 1885. A work crammed with facts, but lacking in the scientific spirit.

§ *The Land of the Lamas.* London: 1894.—*Diary of a Journey through Mongolia and Tibet.* Washington: 1894.—*Notes on the Ethnology of Tibet.* Washington: 1895.

CONTENTS

PART THE FIRST

THE STORY OF THE JOURNEY

CHAPTER I

FIRST EXPLORATIONS IN NORTH-WESTERN TIBET AND LADAK

CHAPTER II

MARCH ON LHASA—THE MOUNTAIN DESERT—THE NAM CHO—NEGOTIATIONS WITH THE TIBETAN OFFICIALS

CHAPTER III

EXPLORATIONS OF 1894—FROM THE NAM CHO TO JYERKUNDO

CHAPTER IV

FROM JYERKUNDO TO SINING—DEATH OF DUTREUIL DE RHINS

PART THE SECOND

A GENERAL VIEW OF TIBET AND ITS INHABITANTS

CHAPTER I

A DESCRIPTION OF THE COUNTRY AS A WHOLE

CHAPTER II

THE INHABITANTS: THEIR PHYSICAL AND MORAL TYPES

CHAPTER III

HISTORICAL SKETCH

CHAPTER IV

MATERIAL LIFE: HABITATIONS, CLOTHING, FOOD, HYGIENE AND MEDICINE

CHAPTER V

THE FAMILY

CHAPTER VI

SOCIAL ORGANISATION

CHAPTER VII

ECONOMIC CONDITIONS: CATTLE-BREEDING, AGRICULTURE, MANUFACTURES

CHAPTER VIII

ECONOMIC CONDITIONS *(concluded)*: COMMERCE AND ROADS

CHAPTER IX

RELIGION: SURVIVAL OF OLD FORMS OF WORSHIP—THE PONBOS

CHAPTER X

THE ORGANISATION OF THE CLERGY

CHAPTER XI

ADMINISTRATION AND POLICY

CHAPTER I

FIRST EXPLORATIONS IN NORTH-WESTERN TIBET AND LADAK

From Khotan to the Tibetan frontier—Across the plateau of Upper Asia—Fresh departure from Khotan and fresh ascent of the plateau—The first Tibetans—The old route from Khotan to Lhasa—From Lake Rgayé Horpa Cho to Lake Pangong—From Lake Pangong to Leh—From Leh to Khotan through the Karakoram Pass.

By a decree dated 23 July 1890, the Minister of Public Instruction entrusted Dutreuil de Rhins, who had distinguished himself by a journey of exploration in the Congo and by remarkable geographical works on Indo-China and Central Asia, with a scientific mission to Upper Asia, the expenses of which were to be borne in part by the Ministry and in part by the Academy of Inscriptions and Letters. On the 25th of October of the same year, I was appointed a member of the mission; and Dutreuil de Rhins and I left Paris on the 19th of February 1891.

I do not wish to speak here of our journey across the Caucasus, Russian Turkestan and Kashgar to Khotan, the real starting-place of our mission, which we reached on the 7th of July. In that first year, we were to explore the mountains which rise to the south of Khotan; to discover, if possible, the traces of the route which, according to certain Chinese documents, led straight across those mountains from Khotan to Lhasa in the old days when Kashgar still belonged to the Buddhist religion ; and then, after going as far forward as our resources would allow, to return to Khotan to organise a new expedition which would, in our opinion, lead us to the neighbourhood of the Tibetan capital.

On the 14th of August, we reached the poor Turkish hamlet of Polur, situated at a height of 8,440 feet in the valley of the Kurab. It is the village which, on this side, stands furthest in the mountains. It consists of a single street, or rather a narrow, winding road, meandering through some fifty melancholy, low-roofed, squalid houses built of clay and oozing with damp, while their terraces and their cracked walls are overgrown with rank weeds. Near the houses are a dozen willows and poplars, the everlasting trees of Turkestan, and a few fields of corn and barley, the development of which is very soon stopped by the grey and gloomy hills that rise at the edge of the torrent.

After different excursions in the neighbourhood, we turned to the south and went up the gorge of the Kurab by a very difficult path. At one time, the traveller has to walk in the rapid torrent encumbered by mighty blocks of stone, over which the horses, already shaken by the strength of the current, stumble at every step ; at another, he has to climb the side of a mountain by a path so steep and so narrow that the slightest false movement on the part of his horse would hurl him into a ravine many hundred feet deep. On the fourth day, we reached the summit of the Altyn Tagh by the Kyzyl Davan Pass, which is 16,880 feet high. At the top is one of those heaps of stones by means of which the Tibetans and Mongols mark the highest points of the passes : a proof that this neck, to-day abandoned, was formerly frequented by non-Moslem travellers. Beyond it there stretches a barren plateau, like a huge arena surrounded on every side by snow-capped mountains that stand for tiers of benches. Its soil is of volcanic origin; and near two small lakes are layers of sulphur from which this site derives its name of Gugurtluk. This is the beginning of the immense entablature which separates the plain of Hindustan from the steppes of Mongolia and the sands and oases of Turkestan.

Shortly after, we entered the Ustun Tagh, a mountain-chain perceptibly higher than the Altyn Tagh, whence its name of Ustun Tagh, that is to say, "upper mountain," as against Altyn Tagh, which means "lower mountain." These two mountain systems have very different characters. The Altyn Tagh is very articulate, rugged, bristling with pointed peaks and slashed with deep valleys; the Ustun Tagh, on the contrary, has very large, rounded forms: it contains more numerous and more extensive glaciers; and, while the Altyn Tagh abounds in calcareous rocks, primitive and schistose rocks prevail in the Ustun Tagh.

Climbing up beside the River Kiria, we reached, on the 26th of September, a large, flat and marshy valley, strewn with small lakes, covered with a light layer of snow and bordered on the west by a chain of huge glaciers spreading so wide that they seemed but a few feet high. We were now at an altitude of 17,900 feet and we erroneously believed that we had come to the source of the river and to the Tibetan frontier. The glare of the sun on the snow of the plain, all that whiteness spreading in the quivering air to the distant horizon, with not a detail, not a shadow to relieve the gaze, pained our eyes as though they were stabbed by a thousand needles. When we reached the stage, our men, blinded, with aching heads, declared that they were unable to work and lay down on the ground without pitching their tent or preparing their meals. The next day, we descended the valley again in order to turn our steps to the north-east, towards Karasai, hoping to find on our right a gap in the mountains which would take us, next year, to Lhasa. Vain hope! Dutreuil de Rhins had misinterpreted the old Chinese geographers on this point.

We followed the foot of the glaciers of the Ustun Tagh through a region encumbered with moraines of rocks, intersected with ravines, undulated with gentle hills, furrowed with depressions the bottom of which, although generally dried up, was sometimes occupied by a frozen pool. All of this tract was barren, dull, silent as death and infinitely desolate; and the motionless giants of ice that stood sentry over this desolation made it appear more horrible yet. We had a few very hard days. We had observed as many as 40 degrees of heat in the sun at noon; and then the thermometer would fall to 20 degrees below zero.* In the morning, at starting, we shivered with cold and our hands were swollen and cracked with the frost when we used the compass or the pencil; in the middle of the day, a glowing sun burnt our faces; and, almost immediately afterwards, at two o'clock in the afternoon, a keen, icy wind got up, bringing with it snow and hail. The altitude, which was almost always higher than 16,000 feet, choked us and made the least movement, the least word, painful. At night, buried under thick blankets which were hardly able to restore life to our benumbed limbs, we were often awakened by a feeling of stifling and suffocation which compelled us to leave our tent and greedily to gulp down the niggardly air. Add to this the bad food, poisoned by the smoke, and the bad water, which was salt and bitter. Less than this would have been enough to lay low our attendants. During two days, there were three sound men in all: the others, blinded, attacked by mountain-sickness, harassed by continual physical exertion, their hands bleeding from

* Centigrade.

the tents which they had to fold while still covered with ice and snow, were all unfit for work. The horses were still more unfortunate and were a source of great anxiety to us. During eighteen days, we found no grass that suited them : everywhere were rocks, snow and a few *yapkaks*, a sort of very low-growing plant, with exceedingly hard and deep roots, which we used for firewood, this being almost the only thing that ventured to grow in this terrible country. Our barley soon failed. Exposed to the snow and the cold nights, with insufficient food, the beasts began to die. We gave up to them our bread and our rice and were reduced to eating nothing but mutton. Now sheep that have been fasting for several weeks are neither very fat nor very succulent : ours, to tell the truth, were mere wool and bone. As for game, there was no question of it ; the country is absolutely deserted and not so much as a wing is seen to pass through the sky.

Meanwhile, our road was marked by the carcasses of our horses. To save the ailing survivors, we had to leave the least necessary portion of our baggage behind us and to go on foot, a very painful mode of progress at so great a height. We began to fear that we should not arrive in time in a lower and more fruitful region, that we should lose all our beasts and be obliged to sacrifice all in order to save ourselves ; our men were becoming anxious and thought themselves lost, destined to die in this solitude with no visible outlet. We lengthened our stages, in spite of our ever-increasing fatigue. At last, on the 7th of October, having surmounted a steep mountain-crest which forms part of the Altyn Tagh, we reached the margin of the little salt lake of Hangid Kul, in a valley that opened out a road to the east, a road of safety and deliverance.

On the 8th, we marched until pretty far into the night through the valley of Sarak Tuz. As the moon appeared over the mountains, we came to a spot where grass abounded, near an abandoned gold-mine. The next day and the day after, we descended as rapidly as possible by a terraced slope, carpeted with long and varied grasses, which follows the river and is intersected by deep and steep ravines, cut out as though by a punching-machine. On the 10th of October, night surprised us while we were still marching in the midst of the desert and of a silence broken only by the sound of the waters roaring at the bottom of their gorge. Suddenly, as we were groping our way down the cliffs which embank the bed of the river, we heard men's voices in the dark. They were the people whom the Chinese mandarin of Kiria had sent to meet us with provisions and fresh horses. We were at the end of our troubles for that year. On the 12th, we arrived at Karasai, where a few shepherds and their families live in underground dwellings. This place is at a height of only 10,350 feet and may be considered as outside the mountains. Towards the north there are only a few spurs which run into the desert of Takla Makan.

From there, passing through the meadows which lie at the foot of the Altyn Tagh and exhale a penetrating odour of wormwood, through a barren plain covered first with pebbles and then with sandy downs, we reached the little oasis of Nia. In any other circumstances, the fields, shorn and empty after the harvest, the thinned and yellowing foliage, the dead leaves rolling in the dust of the roads would have given us an impression of sadness. But now the softer light and the varied tints of autumn rested our eyes; and the warmth of the temperature, the life and movement of the bazaar, the voices of men talking and shouting revived and gave fresh spirit to the travellers who had come out of the cold and the solitude.

After a stay at Khotan, the length of which was greatly increased by circumstances which I need not recall here, we set out again on the 18th of June 1892.

On the 16th of July, we saw, for the second time, that poor village of Polur, with its damp, dark houses impregnated with a smell of goats and sour milk. This time that wretched, exiguous corner of the earth seemed to us delightful, because we remembered the rude and wild mountainous desert at the foot of which it cowers so chilly. The population received us cordially, but the sky frowned upon us. It rained: the mountain-paths were broken and impracticable; the swollen torrents were filled with muddy, swift and deep waters; the roofs fell in under the rain; in the plain, the floods carried off trees, houses, pieces of the fields; in the mountains, the slopes streamed with water, the tops became laden with snow. We had to wait, after having already waited too long.

When the rain ceased and the road had been mended, we set out, on the 10th of August. Our caravan numbered thirteen men, thirty-six horses, twenty-two donkeys and thirty sheep, to which must be added reinforcements of sixty men and forty-three donkeys supplied by Polur and the surrounding district. With all this assistance, it was nevertheless no easy undertaking to carry, or rather to drag, six tons of baggage to the summit of a plateau loftier than Mont Blanc. For three days, we marched with the greatest precaution and the greatest difficulty in the gorges and gullies of the Kurab. Oftenest we had the bags and chests carried on man-back. All our measures were fairly well taken; and fortune favoured us to the extent that we had to mourn the loss of only one horse. On reaching the plateau of Suraz Kul, we found the sky and the earth equally melancholy. Grey and lowering clouds hid the mountains from our sight; the snow fell in flakes and covered the ground to a depth of two to three inches. This was on the 16th of August. Everything was so wet that it was impossible to make a fire. When the night was over, our local recruits, flinging themselves on their knees, besought us, with many tears and lamentations, to allow them to go back. The suffering was great indeed. Our eyes were affected by the dust, the sun and the snow; the great height made our breathing difficult, our movements painful, our heads ache and caused all the wheels of the human machine to grate. The natives were ill-clad, ill-fed and without shelter. We therefore sent them away, excepting eight, of whom six were to accompany us for three days more and two for seven.

We resumed our march in the direction of the source of the Kiria Daria. The season was decidedly bad and the heavens capricious. At one moment, the weather was bright, the sun burning; and we would take off our too heavy furs: suddenly, a great gust of wind came, black clouds hastened up and heaped themselves one on top of the other, bringing snow and hail; and once more we would wrap ourselves in our sheepskins, shivering from the effects of this abrupt change. But more serious was that the snow which had fallen in spring and summer now melted and turned the country into a vast bog. The valleys were flooded; the soil of the slopes was muddy and soft. A great plain crossed by the Upper Kiria Daria, on which, in 1891, we had seen only two little bogs, had become one great pool of water. We were obliged to keep as much as possible to the heights, which increased the difficulty of our progress owing to the constant climbings and descents; the horses sank into the ground to their knees, sometimes to their bellies: harassed with fatigue, stifled by the height at which we were, shivering with cold, wanting grass, turning against the barley, which they refused, they wasted away rapidly; and, already, on the 22nd of August, we had lost two. Eight men of the thirteen were ill; the others dragged themselves along as best they could. Dutreuil de Rhins himself was very unwell.

We had meantime come to the foot of the immense and magnificent glaciers where the Kiria River takes its source. We succeeded in surmounting, by a pass at 18,200 feet, the chain of the Ustun Tagh, which was thus crossed for the first time by travellers coming from the north. The water no longer flowed towards Turkestan and we could consider ourselves to have reached Tibetan territory : two days' march further were stones blackened by the fire on which Tibetan hunters had boiled their tea. Unfortunately, the obstacles, far from becoming fewer, increased ; the altitude, which was as high as before, varying from 17,000 to 18,000 feet, the marshy soil, the scarcity of food and the cold nights caused our beasts to suffer from extreme weakness, which was aggravated by the time during which they had travelled and the distance which they had covered. The necessity which ensued of marching more slowly, of going only seven or eight miles a day, instead of thirteen, and the consequent insufficiency of our provisions, which had been calculated for a more rapid progress, obliged us to take a south-westerly direction in order to obtain, in the nearest inhabited regions, the resources which we needed and the indications that would enable us to make for our goal by a more practical road.

As far as Lake Sumzi Cho, we followed, with a few modifications, the itinerary which Carey had marked out, in the opposite direction, many years before. The men from Polur had left us, taking with them our last mail for France, and we now continued our journey alone across those monotonous and desolate solitudes, where the air choked us like a leaden breast-plate, where the cold froze our feet and chapped our hands and faces. We heard nothing but the incessant, harsh, furious whistle of the west wind, which seemed to be the voice of the mountains cursing the disturbers of their perennial rest. We saw nothing but a succession of dismal hills, sometimes whitened with snow, trailing sadly and low as though weary from having climbed so high. Nothing grew on the dry soil save here and there a few hard, short blades of yellowish grass. Nothing moved in the sky or on the ground, except that, from time to time, we saw flying, far, very far in the distance, swift as an arrow, the vague shape of an antelope, a yak or a wild horse. Sometimes, however, a fine landscape aroused the attention, as on the 25th of August, on the banks of the Yeshil Kul, the first great lake that we had come upon. It stretched to the foot of the tall mountains all sparkling with snow, its water of a dazzling and unshaded blue, motionless and as it were sleeping in the absolute silence of surrounding nature, a silence not ruffled even by the sound of a bird's flight.

From that lake, which is two days from the source of the Kiria Daria, the traveller follows a series of long valleys and amphitheatres with a red soil, confined within mountain chains, whose summits and northern flanks alone keep their snowy mantle at a height of 18,000 to 18,500 feet, while behind them, towards the south, appear the tops of the *gangri*, or glaciers, which form a third chain, almost parallel with the Ustun Tagh and the Altyn Tagh.

After skirting little Lake Tashliak Kul and going round the Sumzi Cho, we saw, on the 4th of September, our first Tibetan. He was a hunter, with long, tangled hair and a wild face, and he carried a matchlock of inordinate length. He gave us a quick impression that we had now entered upon a new and strange world. For fear of the authorities of his country, he at first refused to reply to our questions; but as, on the other hand, he feared us no less than the said authorities and as the danger from our side appeared the more urgent, he made up his mind to show us the road to the nearest human habitations, on condition that we did not inform against him. In the afternoon of the next day, we came to an immense amphitheatre of snow-topped mountains, crossed by a deep ravine on the edges of which were scattered seven poor little black tents inhabited by Tibetans subject to Lhasa. This place is called Mangtza, and forms part of the district of Rudok and the province of Chang; it is overtowered by the Mawang Gangri, an enormous rounded mountain, behind which, at three days' march, lies the sacred lake, the Mawang Cho, called Bakha Namur Nor by the Mongols. In a few moments, we were surrounded by the entire population, men, women and children, all with their skins burnt and tanned by the sun, wind, cold and snow, their disordered hair flowing in the wind, their bodies covered with a dirty and ragged sheepskin or woollen gown. Good people, for that matter, quite astonished and delighted at seeing men so extraordinary as ourselves, they gave us an excellent reception and made us go the rounds of all their tents, where they regaled us on buttered and salted tea and grilled barley-meal (*tsamba*), an indifferent fare, if the truth be told, but seasoned with good humour. One of them, whose hair was more bristling, his air fiercer, his tongue more active, his clothes dirtier, his iron pipe heavier and longer than the others', offered to guide us wherever we wanted to go, in consideration of a fair wage, swearing to be faithful to us against all comers. A guide was not enough: we also wanted provisions; and those poor nomads, who live by rearing a few yaks and a few sheep and who send to Ladak for the little barley which they consume, were unable to supply us with anything.

Meanwhile, the news of our arrival had spread, and on the 7th of September, the *goba*, or chief of the canton, made his appearance, accompanied by three men armed with prehistoric muskets and iron swords. Forthwith, our faithful volunteer eclipsed like a star before the rising sun and it was impossible to find him again. The goba spoke to us very politely, informed us that he was ready to serve us and that, if we wanted guides, he would put some at our disposal, except by the road to Rudok, where foreigners were not admitted. We had no intention of going to Rudok, first, because we knew that we should not readily be allowed to pass; and, next, because we should not find the needful supplies in that wretched little market-town. We asked only for a guide to lead us in the direction of the south-east; for we hoped to be able soon on that side to reach inhabited districts, less high up and better furnished with resources than that in which we were. The goba, delighted to rid himself of our troublesome presence, picked out two men to accompany us and recommended them to us as being very trustworthy and as knowing the country perfectly.

These guides led us towards the east, over passable and pretty firm ground, but barren and rarely at a lower altitude than 17,500 feet. We skirted the northern foot of a great chain of mountains, running parallel with the Ustun Tagh, whose snowy summits and glaciers were often hidden from our sight by the brown masses in the foreground. On the 10th of September, we camped in a very wide and almost level valley, covered with gravel and sand and devoid of water or grass, like the bottom of a dried-up lake. Quite near, concealed by a mountain spur, lay the point of a great lake, the Rgayé Horpa Cho, which I was to recognise later. Beyond the lake, on the south-east, rose a majestic icy barrier, across which a cutting was indistinctly outlined. Although Dutreuil de Rhins thought that he had lost his way, this was really, as I have since shown,* the old road from Khotan to Lhasa, which went by the Kyzyl Davan, the source of the Kiria Daria, the Rgayé Horpa Cho, the Mawang Cho and Thakdaoragpa.

* "A Scientific Mission to Upper Asia," Vol. III., pp. 228-237.

Unfortunately, we were in a critical situation. Since leaving Polur, our mission had done twenty-six days of effective marching. Although our men had become better accustomed to the extreme altitudes than one would have expected at the start and although the fatigue was now less great, on firmer ground and under a lighter burden, several men, and those among the best, had been rendered almost useless by pains in the head and stomach. True, the temperature had varied only between 8 degrees below and 32 above zero, nor had the difference on any one day exceeded 31 degrees in the shade, but, at a height of 17,500 to 18,000 feet, with wind, bad food and the physical strain, a man becomes very sensitive to such differences. During the three last days' march, we had lost six horses; on the banks of the Rgayé Horpa Cho, in spite of the rest and the grass, we lost six more. Of thirty-six with which we started we had only twenty-four very tired horses left. The jaded donkeys were no longer capable of travelling stages of sufficient length to bring us to the inhabited regions before the provisions gave out, that is, before fourteen days.

Our losses were bound to increase rapidly in this desert, where the altitude became no lower, where the grass was so scarce and so bad and where the road was barred on the south by glaciers which the surviving animals, in their exhausted state, would not have had the strength to cross. Lastly, Dutreuil de Rhins, who was in bad health when leaving Polur, was now so ill as to cause me serious anxiety, in spite of his efforts to conceal his sufferings.

We therefore turned back. Once more travelling near the Sumzi Cho, we skirted very wide valleys by the deeply-ravined slope of the northern spurs of the great chain of which I have already spoken. Next, instead of taking Carey's road by the Lanak La Pass, we pushed into the depth of the chain through the defile of Chakar Skedogpo, between bare, red hills. On the 17th of September, crossing a watershed and a maze of arid heights, we came, amid wind and hail, to an amphitheatre of snow-capped mountains and glaciers which descended at sixty feet from where we stood. The lower slopes were encumbered with moraines of stones as far as the banks of a great lake, the Koné Cho, which was overtowered on the opposite margin by enormous steep peaks. It looked like a drop of water lost at the bottom of a well; and on its wan and melancholy surface floated great grey clouds. Notwithstanding the gloomy and inhospitable aspect of this spot, as it is situated at the junction of the two roads leading to Ladak and Rudok, we found a few Tibetans who came there in summer to graze their flocks on the lean tufts of grass that grow between the stones. We frightened them greatly, for they took us for brigands. The shepherds ran away and did not return that night; the sheep strayed freely over the mountain; and it took three days to look for them, bring them back and sort them.

Two *aptuks*, or policemen, sent to watch the frontier, arrived, wearing red turbans, armed from head to foot and carrying over their shoulders a copper box containing a sacred image, an infallible talisman against bullets and sword-thrusts. They cherished the purpose, as we heard later, of seizing our horses during the night; but, seeing that we looked like honest people, they changed their mind and thought it more expedient to employ persuasion. They were punished, however, for their sin of intention; for, while they were meddling with our affairs, the wife of the younger of them was kidnapped by some enterprising marauders and the poor husband, who heard of the adventure at breakfast, hurriedly left his colleague to go in chase of the ravishers.

The old policeman, while drinking a few cups of buttered tea with us in the tent of a native, tried to turn us from our road. He told us that the way from the Koné Cho to Ladak was very bad, indeed impracticable; that we ought to make for the Lanak road if our intention was to go to Ladak; that the road to Rudok was closed and that to the Koné Ding forbidden to Europeans; that, if he allowed us to take it, he would be trifling with his life. But, as Dutreuil de Rhins gaily observed, that was no reason why he should trifle with us. We had learnt that, through the Koné Ding Pass, we could go straight to the north-western part of Lake Pangong, which is in Ladak, and our scarcity of provisions did not allow us to indulge in circuitous routes.

"Be it so," replied the policeman. "I will send a messenger to Rudok at once, if you will wait for the answer of the authorities, which cannot take long in coming."

"You can do better than that," said Dutreuil de Rhins. "Go with us as far as the Koné Ding, for I refuse to wait another day. You will see for yourself that I shall not try to go to Rudok and everybody will be satisfied."

"Very well, I agree," said the policeman, who was a decent fellow, "on condition that you pass through my place to take a cup of tea."

On the next day, the 19th of September, we set out together, crossing the great moraines of the glaciers which run down to the western margin of Lake Koné Cho. Our worthy policeman informed us that there used to be many bandits in those parts, but that they had disappeared since his appointment to watch over the public safety. When we reproached him with his colleague's adventure, he replied that it was probably not so much a question of marauders, that women have their fancies and that, when you've got a young wife in your tent, it's wiser not to go travelling the high-roads. This wise and formidable policeman appeared himself to have been a great traveller: he had seen Lhasa, Sining, Sikkim, Darjeeling; he had known Chinamen, Hindus, Englishmen; and, in the course of his peregrinations, he had picked up a certain simple and decent civility. He received us, in fact, in his own dwelling with a good grace that enlivened the wretchedness of his smoky tent; and this good grace was set off by a little touch of irony that was not without pungency.

Our host's tent stood on the west bank of the Koné Cho, not far from the junction of two valleys, one of which opens to the south, is wide and dotted with fairly numerous tents and leads to Rudok in three days, while the other, narrower and deserted, goes up to the Koné Ding Pass on the west. We entered the latter, accompanied by the policeman, who, faithful to his promise, guided us to the Kashmir frontier with all the more alacrity in that he was showing us the way out and not the way in. On the 20th of September, crossing the pass at a height of 17,985 feet, we entered the Maharaja's territory. During all that day, we did nothing but climb up and down by sterile gorges, through which blew a fierce wind, laden with the cold of the glaciers. After passing the Pagrim La (18,000 feet), we descended by an interminable stony and barren passage, 500 to 1,100 yards wide, between mountains 2,000 to 2,500 feet high, with steep sides, bare and red, with enormous black rocks. On arriving at the end of this defile, at 3 o'clock in the afternoon of the 21st of September, we saw, on the brink of a clear stream, a coppice consisting of humble shrubs called *ombu*, in whose branches little birds were singing. This was the beginning of the end. We were now no higher than the top of Mont Blanc. A huge number of hares lived in that coppice. We saw them on every side, basking and dozing in the sun, peaceful and unconscious of danger; for the Tibetans, who loathe the flesh of these animals, never hunt them. We had the cruelty to disturb their security for the sake of varying our ordinary fare; but this sport was really too easy to be very amusing and peace was concluded almost as soon as broken. We took a day's rest at this spot, which is called Niagzu and which seemed to us the threshold of paradise. It was not inhabited at this season of the year, but we saw a caravan of Tibetans encamped there who were carrying on sheep-back a quantity of salt, drawn from the Sumzi Cho and other salt lakes of the region, to Leh, with a view to exchanging it for flour, barley, woollens, cooking utensils, artificial pearls and ornaments. Salt is entirely lacking in Ladak and is sold at its weight in barley. As, on the other hand, there is hardly any barley in the Rudok district, the natives do not hesitate to make the annual journey to Leh, which takes four months there and back.

Although our Tibetan neighbours had left Niagzu a day before us, on the 23rd of September, we soon caught them up in the Gyu La Gorge, which the laden sheep were slowly climbing to the lazy, monotonous singing of the shepherds. The next morning, at six o'clock, came from Rudok four Tibetan messengers, in red turbans, carrying gaudy flags and making a great noise with the bells hung round their horses' necks. Why did they enter a territory which is said to be British from Koné Ding? I do not know; but the fact is that they followed us for some distance, accosted us and tried to turn us aside from the Gyu La and to make us take a road more to the north. They had come to the wrong address; we gave them to understand that we wanted neither their advice nor their company; and, when they rode off, their bells sounded less noisily. The ascent of this Gyu La

Gorge (18,700 feet), the highest which we observed in the course of our travels, is by an easy slope and offers neither dangers nor difficulties. On the other hand, the descent on the west, which is short but steep, may be dangerous or even impossible with snow or ice and is very difficult at any time. The top of the pass gives a magnificent view of enormous slices of mountains separated by transversal gorges, one overtopping the other and all surpassed by the distant white summits of the chain which rises between Lake Pangong and the Indus. We made a quick descent of 3,300 feet, climbed up again to a height of 16,600 feet and again went down some 1,800 feet to a little deserted, sandy, salt beach at the edge of one of the deep bays which cut the shore of Lake Pangong into scallops. This lake stretches tortuously, enclosed by huge rocky mountains, as though between the sides of a gigantic, odd-shaped cup. As Dutreuil de Rhins justly remarked, it reminds one of the Lake of the Four Cantons; but how much more majestic it is and how much gloomier! In the presence of the Alps, man feels at his ease and, so to speak, on Nature's own level, for it appears to him as if the landscape had been created and composed for the express pleasure of the spectator, like a stage scene, or of the stroller, like an English garden. But, in Tibet, he feels too weak before the power of rude Nature, too small before the enormousness of what he sees; he is crushed: the scene appears to him to have been painted for a race of Cyclops.

On the 25th of September, we saw, at a height of 14,200 feet, the first barley-fields and the first vassals of Her Britannic Majesty, who, at Lukong, inhabit wretched narrow dwellings contrived in the rocks of the mountain. It was forty-seven days since we had left Polur and of these we had spent thirty-nine days at a height of over 16,000 feet. It was time to arrive at inhabited places, for, only the day before, we had been obliged to share our provision of rice and flour with our beasts. However, we were no longer anxious about them nor about the fate of the caravan; we were no longer afraid of falling short of victuals; and we no longer had to drink brackish water. We forgot our past sufferings. The traces which these had left on our faces seemed to disappear, such was the change that came over their expression. Our grim foreheads became unknit, our dull eyes grew brighter, our stiff limbs received new suppleness in the genial warmth of hope. Those who had been quickest to yield to discouragement and least brave in the facing of pain assumed a valiant air. All laughed at the past, defied the future and treated the Chang La, which we had still to cross, as a wretched little mole-hill.

One thing, however, spoilt our cheerfulness, which was the ill-health of our leader, who was no longer able either to walk or ride. Always ill, for many days unable to eat anything except a little flour mixed with tea, he had reached such a degree of weakness that, in spite of his wonderful courage in resisting suffering, he had become incapable of attending to the caravan and been obliged to reduce his work to a minimum, that is to say, to taking the astronomical observations and making a few summary notes. His physical pain had been aggravated by his smarting regret at not having done what he wanted to do and by the grave care which the precarious position of the expedition had given him. As far as this, at least, was concerned, he was now reassured : the day of rest was approaching which would doubtless put an end to his sufferings; and the time was passing which, little by little, would dispel his regret.

As we were making our appearance on British territory unannounced and without passports and as a Russian traveller had but recently turned back, there was a danger of our situation being rather delicate. Dutreuil de Rhins sent a messenger to the English resident at

Leh, who returned an amiable reply and gave orders that we were to be well treated on our way.

On leaving Lukong, the traveller enters the long defile of Muglib, which is rocky, wild and deserted. On reaching the end, he sees, perched on a ledge of the mountain on the right, a thick, short tower, with a solitary stunted tree and, hanging from the flanks of the rocks on the left, a chapel with hardly distinguishable walls. Quite at the back, at the bottom of the valley, three or four houses, with a few square feet of lean crops, lie basking in the sun. Round about, a dozen sheep and small goats wander among the rocks, looking for the scarce grass.

The village of Tangtze, at 13,000 feet, is reached on the same day. It consists of twelve or fifteen houses, at the crossing of three gorges, amid a heaped-up mass of rocks and stones. All is pale grey under a sapphire sky, except a clump of young willows which the Kashmir government has had planted to enliven the landscape, to give a welcome shade to summer travellers and also, no doubt, to instil into the Tibetans a taste for trees and civilisation. But the latter refuse to be beguiled : they see in trees a superflous invention, in civilisation a novelty against which it is well to be on their guard ; they are satisfied with the old customs of their fathers, with a few spikes of barley in the valley, with a few tufts of grass on the plateau.

The local lama resides in a very inconvenient dwelling, but one particularly well situated and arranged to attract the attention of future Baedekers. When the traveller is shown this dwelling from the village, with, beside it, the red-painted chapel at the top of an isolated rock, resembling a gigantic shaft of a ruined pillar, he is persuaded that the holy man lives only on what the birds of the sky bring him. As he approaches, he is undeceived and sees a sort of very steep and shapeless staircase, half natural, half artificial, which clambers up the outside or even the inside of the rock and gives access to the lama's chamber, a bare, narrow room, with a hard floor, in which, however, one is as it were wrapped in the peace of the limpid sky and in which one feels nearer to the divine beings, the *lhas*, who hover in the air, while, very far and very low down, he sees the almost imperceptible houses of the inferior and miserably restless race of men.

At Tangtze there is no representative of the Kashmir government nor of the British government. The population is allowed to look after its own affairs in its own way and hardly anything is asked of it save the payment of a fairly moderate and wisely-fixed tax. Nevertheless, we perceived the influence in the country of a people so practical as the English by this fact, that, in order to pay our expenses, it was enough for us to give drafts payable at Leh, which were accepted without hesitation as cash.

On the 29th of September, we camped at the hamlet of Durkug and, on the next morning, we set out at half-past seven to make the ascent of the Chang La. Dutreuil de Rhins, who was prevented by toothache from eating and who was never free from pain, gave way to suffering and weakness. We had to carry him in a litter to surmount the slope of 5,080 feet which leads to the top of the pass, where we arrived at four o'clock in the afternoon. For three hours we marched through snow and ice and then descended, by a steep and narrow path, across blocks of stone, along gloomy precipices, to the village of Daghkar, where we pitched our tent at seven o'clock in the evening.

The village of Daghkar consists of fifteen houses, backed against a huge rock wall, of which they seem to be the natural excrescences. Thence the road leads through the more important and less wild villages of Sagti and Chemdeh. Scarce and thin poplars outline their slender foliage, already turning yellow, against the grey of the rocks; and, in the fields, ploughmen urge on their indolent yaks while quavering a monotonous, dragging chant. The road next emerges on the valley of the Indus, almost opposite the monastery of Himis, one of the richest and most famous in all Tibet and inhabited by a large number of Dugpa lamas. The Indus is here already an important stream, at least as wide as the Rhone in the Valais, and its green and powerful waters are crossed by no bridge. Its valley smiled gaily enough upon travellers who were descending from the desert of mountains, but it must appear morose and ill-humoured to those who come from Kashmir. It is fairly wide, contained within two tall, gloomy, rocky, rugged mountains, with straight sides and jagged ridges, lightly sprinkled with snow. The soil is strewn with fragments of rocks, leaving a scanty space, here and there, for a few fields of corn and barley. For the rest, the spectacle is one well calculated to please the eye. The Tibetans are great handlers of stone and have a genius for the picturesque. At the most unexpected places, on the most inaccessible rocks rise stone buildings: chapels painted in red, little altars shaped like pyramids and known as *chortens*, humble cells of solitary monks, monasteries ruined or still standing, that look like fortresses.

On the 2nd of October, we came to a gravel plain, surrounded by a circle of barren, snow-topped mountains, at whose foot stood the green little oasis of Leh. A very wide wall, which runs along the road for several miles, adorned with flat stones bearing religious inscriptions, leads almost to the entrance of the town, which numbers about 3,000 inhabitants and consists almost solely of the street of the bazaar, a wide, clean street, lined with stone houses with one or two storeys, galleries and terraced roofs. Its appearance is on the whole more agreeable and more imposing than that of the mud towns of Turkestan, such as Kashgar and Khotan. At the end of the street there rises abruptly a steep and rocky mountain, on whose slope is built a large rectangular stone house, less wide than high, which was once the palace of the Tibetan Kings. Right at the top of the mountain, an isolated chapel, with no visible access to it, is almost lost up there, in the blue sky. The descendant of the ancient kings, relegated to an honourable captivity at some distance from the town, is to-day no more than a respected, but vain image.

The administration of the country is in the hands of a vizier, delegated by the Maharaja of Kashmir; and the English, in their capacity of protectors of the Maharaja, keep an assistant resident at Leh, whose special duty it is to protect trade, but also to control the Kashmir administration and to maintain in it certain principles of equity and liberalism to which the English have the good sense to remain firmly attached and to which the growth of their prestige among the peoples of Asia must be in no small measure ascribed.

On our arrival, the British resident, Mr. Cubitt, and the Vizier Argen Nath offered the most cordial welcome to the travellers whom fortune had treated so badly in the course of an expedition, lasting one hundred and six days, which had struck so severe a blow at our leader's health and cost us the lives of half our beasts. Mr. Cubitt placed at our disposal a comfortable little white house, shaded by splendid poplars, where Dutreuil de Rhins was able to enjoy a few days' well-earned rest and recover some of his old vigour.

Leaving Leh on the 20th of October, on the next day we climbed the Kardong Mountain by a very narrow and exceedingly steep path, winding through an extraordinary accumulation of rocks. On the other side, a very stiff slope, covered with ice, leads to the bottom of a gorge. Pedestrians have great difficulty in descending this slope without the Alpine climber's gear; horses slide rather than step down to the foot of the neck; and the yaks alone are able to carry baggage from the top to the bottom without danger to themselves or their loads. We spent the night at the hamlet of Kardong, which stands at the foot of the mountain all covered with masses of stone, among which the twenty stone houses of the hamlet are difficult to distinguish. Thence the road descends by the very picturesque gorge of the little Kardong torrent, enlivened by small shrubs which grow in the interstices of the rocks, and comes out into the stony valley of the River Shayok, which is easily fordable at this season. Below the tiny village of Chati, the Shayok receives an affluent on the right, the Nubra, which we went up. Its valley, which is fairly wide, is considered the most fertile in Ladak. It stretches between two huge walls of over 3,300 feet in height, formed of bare rocks which shoot up their countless grey peaks into the blue of the sky. The bottom of the valley is no less grey and barren than the mountain walls which overlook it and is only dotted here and there with brown patches, sorry oases reddened by the autumn, where a few acres of wheat and barley and a few fruit-trees struggle for their lives amid the stone and sand. The name of Pangmig, which the Tibetans give to one of these oases, describes them all admirably. Pangmig means "eye of verdure." This rugged nature of Ladak does not make existence easy to man: unable to tame it, the Tibetan submits to it, in the same way as he submits to the yoke of his new masters, with the wild gentleness of a captive antelope. Rugged as nature herself in his outward aspect, bristling, dirty and ragged, he is morally weak, indifferent and, like all weak creatures, suspicious and insincere; but he pleases by an unpretentious gaiety which forms a happy contrast with the solemn gravity of the Moslem.

On the 24th of October, we slept at the village of Pangmig, where the caravans stop to buy the victuals needed for the crossing of the desert mountains to Suget Kurghan and to hire yaks with which to climb the passes of Karwal and Sassar La. We were kindly helped in our preparations by the *deba* of the valley of Nubra, who, a rare thing, understood Persian well. On the 26th, all was ready and we went as far as the insignificant hamlet of Ljanglong, where we took leave of the last Tibetans. From there, with the assistance of his yaks, the traveller climbs the mountain wall on the left bank of the Nubra by the Karwal Pass, goes up the gorge of the Tulumbati, strewn with mountain refuse and overtowered by snowy peaks and glaciers, and ascends the glacier of the Sassar La; then, abandoning the yaks, he goes up the gorge of one of the sources of the Shayok and, splashing in the water, passes at the foot of the Kichik and Chong Kumdan glaciers. Our guide maintained that, fifty years ago, there was no passage there, the glaciers touching the mountains opposite, very steep mountains, from whose summits a mass of rocks stands out, resembling the ruins of a very enormous castle, which the Turks have christened the Palace of Afrassiab. Further on, the valley opens out and forms a circle of snow-mountains, in which the River Shayok spreads into a long lake.

Here stands Yapchan, where we camped on the 29th of October. Beginning from here, the general aspect of the country is modified. After leaving Leh, the country had presented a series of wild and deep valleys, separated by high, steep and difficult passes; but the ground was firm and the march offered no danger when there was not too much snow and ice. Beyond Yapchan, the mountains have the same character which we had already observed in the Ustun Tagh: rounded summits, gentle slopes, high, wide, barren valleys, a ground which is soft when it is not frozen and inconsiderable differences of level. This character continues as far as the Suget Pass, starting from which we again find the steep mountains, the pointed summits, the narrow and grassy gorges of the Altyn Tagh.

On the 31st of October, we crossed the Karakoram Pass, the summit of the Ustun Tagh. It is the highest pass on the route (18,300 feet), but not the most difficult, for there is no ice and the rugged portion of the ascent is very short. An inscription, placed at the summit, marks the boundary between the States of the Maharaja of Kashmir and those of the Emperor of China. A little lower, on the northern slope, covered with black rocks and occasional patches of snow, a modest monument has been raised by the care of our fellow-countryman, M. Dauvergne, to the memory of the English traveller Dalgleish, who was murdered in this spot by an Afghan trader.

The portion of the road which lies between the Karwal and Suget Passes is the most arduous because of its extreme altitude, its barrenness, its lack of habitations and its low temperature. We had as many as 29 degrees of cold, and on the same day, the 30th of October, we observed a variation of 35 degrees, from 6 above to 29 below zero. But it would be ungracious on our part to complain, for this same road was being traversed, in the opposite direction, by old men, women and children going on pilgrimage to Mecca. Many of them were on foot and the majority had no tents; when the evening came, strengthened by a handful of maize boiled in water and a cup of bad tea, they squatted down, pressing one against the other and shivering around a poor fire, which soon went out, for fuel is scarce in this treeless region. As poor in intelligence as in purse, these pilgrims, young and old, have only the discomfort of the journey and do not in the least enjoy the charms which it would have for us. They go like their beasts of burden, observing nothing, interested in nothing, their mind never drawn from its torpor by the varied spectacle that unfolds itself before their eyes, which look and do not see. They are content to reach the golden city, there to perform their pilgrim rites and to bring back with them a good policy of insurance against hell-fire.

From the foot of the Karakoram, we passed through a series of amphitheatres of mountains which do not appear to be very high, crossed the principal source of the Yarkand River and, on the 2nd of November, reached the Suget Pass, the ascent of which could, if necessary, be made in a carriage. After descending a very steep and sinuous path, over a thin layer of snow, we soon came down through a gorge of wild and melancholy aspect, lined by great snowy masses laden with mist. We walked ahead alone, eager to leave the desert; we were soon overtaken by the shades of night, which increased the size of the mountains and swelled the uproar of the waters. The veiled and uncertain light of the moon just enabled us to pick our way through a maze of rocks, a long series of rugged ravines and noisy torrents, and to arrive, after twelve hours' march, at the foot of the small fort of Suget Kurghan, constructed lately by the Chinese near the confluence of the Suget torrent and the Karakash River, in order to assert their rights of possession over the surrounding district. This little fort is composed simply of a square yard surrounded by four crenellated walls. Our sudden arrival at this unseasonable hour spread terror among the garrison, which at that time comprised a Kirghiz woman, three boy babies and a lame dog. The woman at first breathed not a word, thinking that, if the importunate persons heard nothing or nobody, they would go their way. But her dog betrayed her and we lustily shook the door, to such good purpose that the unfortunate garrison had to admit the besiegers. Our respectable appearance stilled the alarm: the dog stopped barking, the children laughed, the woman showed us to an empty room, spread out some strips of felt and lit a great fire of twigs, for the cold was keen. Our baggage train did not catch us up until the evening of the next day.

On the 5th of November, after passing through the gorge of the Karakash River, at the foot of the walls of the fortlet of Shaidullah, built by the Kashmirians and long since abandoned by them, we came, at Toghrusu, into the midst of the gay tumult of a Kirghiz wedding. Numbers of horsemen, coming from the four points of the horizon, had met at this spot and pitched their round felt tents. They were holding high festival and singing at the top of their voices. We were treated to a madrigal and presented with a bride-cake and half a roast sheep.

On the 7th, we left the Karakash Daria, the valley of which is impracticable in the downward direction, and began to ascend the gorge of one of its affluents which runs down from the Sanju Pass. Imagine an exceedingly narrow gorge, whimsically tortuous, deeply confined within tall peaked rocks, bare and strangely hewn and slashed and the whole gorge obstructed by flint rubbish. On reaching the end of this gorge, we found ourselves as though at the bottom of a well. With the assistance of some Kirghiz oxen, we scaled one of the walls of the well and thus reached the summit of the Sanju Pass, which is at a height of 16,800 feet. From there, according as one turns to the north or the south, the view offers a striking contrast. In the south is a monstrous chaos of gigantic snow-mountains and dazzling glaciers, which the rays of the sun sometimes cause to look like great blue lakes slumbering amid a polar whiteness; in the north, a few brown hills, beyond which stretches something like a vast ocean wrapped in a shroud of grey mist: this is the Kashgarian plain and its atmosphere laden with dust.

The ascent of the pass was not easy, but the descent was worse. The slope is so steep that, in a league of horizontal projection, one descends 1,880 metres and, for a distance of 800 metres, the slope, at 45 degrees, is covered with a thick layer of ice. The yaks are really wonderful animals which, descending a mountain like this, carry over two hundred pounds on their backs without stumbling. Our horses, although carrying no burden, did three-fourths of the road in some other way than on their feet: one of them slipped so badly that it was hurled to the bottom of the valley and broke its spine.

At the top of the pass, we overtook a poor little caravan consisting of an old man, a woman and two children. Their baggage and all their fortune were carried by a lean, mangy donkey. The old man, whose feet were frozen and eaten away with gangrene, was unfit for anything. The woman saw to everything, led the donkey, fastened the pack-saddle when it slipped, tied up the load when it fell, helped the old man and carried the children in the difficult places. Her air of suffering, her drawn features, her bloodshot and lack-lustre eyes, told of a hard life and long affliction. These unfortunate people, who were returning to Sanju, had exposed themselves to the dangers of this journey and its almost inconceivable fatigues, in the circumstances in which they were taking it, in order to go and visit, under a distant tent, kinsmen almost as unfortunate as themselves, from whom they vaguely hoped for I know not what. Nothing is more extraordinary than the quite mechanical resistance with which Asiatics meet suffering and the dull resignation with which they accept it as a quality inherent to this world, as an inexorable necessity of fate.

From the foot of the pass, one follows a deep, grassy valley, here and there meeting the round tents of Kirghiz herdsmen. Little by little, the mountains grow lower, the valley wider, the grass disappears, the sand shows itself and one sees, between two dusky hills, the trees of the oasis of Sanju. Here there are some thousand houses, scattered on every side, and a considerable amount of ground under cultivation; and it is easy for the traveller to procure all that he wants provided that his wants be modest.

On the 21st of November, we once more entered our good town of Khotan, much saddened by the winter. The flat plain was all carpeted with snow and the black skeletons of the trees stood drearily outlined in the mist; but the kindly welcome of our old friends cheered this desolation. A few weeks of absolute rest and the general sympathy with which he was surrounded restored Dutreüil de Rhins' health, consoled him for his vexations and made him ready once more to tempt fortune.

This winter of 1892 to 1893 was occupied, as was the previous one, with ethnographical, archæological and linguistic studies, which formed part of the programme of our mission. In this connection, I may be permitted here to recall the fact that we really laid the foundation of the archæology of Chinese Turkestan and assisted to renew its history. Many travellers after us, such as Messrs. Klementz, Sven Hedin and Stein, have made remarkable discoveries in this branch of research and have on more than one point confirmed my own conclusions.

CHAPTER II

MARCH ON LHASA—THE MOUNTAIN DESERT—THE NAM CHO—NEGOTIATIONS WITH THE TIBETAN OFFICIALS

We go in search of a new route to Lhasa to the south of Cherchen—We reach the extreme point known to the natives—We cross the Akka Tagh—The Dutreuil de Rhins Chain—Again the mountain desert—We meet our first man after sixty-one days' march—The Tibetans try to stop us—The prefect of Senja Jong—The Nam Cho or Tengri Nor—First envoys from Lhasa—Arrival of the Chinese vice-legate and of new delegates from the Tibetan government—We are refused permission to go to Lhasa—We are given leave to stay at Nagchu.

The problem how to cross the mountain desert which separated us from the inhabited portion of Tibet seemed to us almost insoluble with a caravan of horses which eat too much (4 lbs. a day) and carry too little (200 lbs.); and we decided to procure camels for our expedition of 1893 and to seek a route more practicable than that of Polur for the latter animals.

We thought that we might find one to the south of Cherchen, where we proceeded and where we stayed for three months because of various difficulties and an illness of Dutreuil de Rhins'. Our long stay appeared even longer in this little oasis without a town, without a market, without trade, peopled only by peasants living in scattered farms, seventy-six leagues from the nearest village, a hundred leagues from the nearest town and as isolated in the midst of the continent as is an islet never visited by ships in the midst of the sea. On every side around spreads the ocean of the sand-downs, except on the north, where, along the bank of the river, stretches a belt of forest half invaded by sand, a haunt of deer, wild boar and even tigers. The traveller rarely passes here; no caravans come to enliven the country with the tinkling of their bells, the cries of their camel-drivers, the snorting of their horses, the bustle of their arrival and departure; the news of the distant outside world does not penetrate so far, or, when, sometimes, a small trader brings it with his bales of cotton and spice, it arrives distorted, vague and confused, leaving one and all indifferent.

We made a number of reconnoitring expeditions, which failed to decide the question whether it were possible to cross the chain of the Akka Tagh, which rises to the south of the Altyn Tagh and forms the prolongation of the Ustun Tagh. However, we resolved to start. We had over seven tons of baggage, provisions and stores, not counting the pack-saddles and harness. To handle this enormous, but irreducible load and to attend to our thirty camels, twenty-four horses and ten donkeys, we had only thirteen men.

We had had to renew a part of our staff, not always very successfully, Chinese Turkestan being an unfavourable country for the recruiting of a good exploring staff. We kept the leader of our escort, Razoumoff, a discharged Russian soldier, a willing and well-meaning, but volatile and eccentric man, subject to strange crotchets, and old Parpai, an experienced caravaneer and an amusing type of patriarchal adventurer, who had a mania for founding families wherever he went, hoping at last to light upon an heiress for a wife, whose well-filled money-bags would allow him to put an end to his peregrinations and to rest his weary head. We took as our Chinese secretary a sort of giant, a native of Hunan, a petty mandarin whom life had tossed miserably from province to province and flung into the midst of Turkestan almost without resources: apart from all this, he was serious, well-educated, a good writer and not devoid of firmness of character. We engaged, in the capacity of Chinese interpreter, a certain Yunus, a young man of very good family, tall, strong and with a florid complexion showing every sign of health. But the signs were deceptive. The unfortunate man suffered from heart-disease, which proved fatal to him. A Moslem from Ladak, Mohammed Isa, became our interpreter for the Tibetan language. Six feet high and powerfully built, he was a good servant, well-trained, useful, active, full of spirits as long as he had not to struggle with too-exceptional difficulties; unfortunately, he was unintelligent, self-conceited, a great bouncer and a ridiculous coward. He had as his understudy a half-breed between a Turk and a Tibetan, Abdurrahman by name, a short, slight, diligent and very gentle creature, who was entirely in the hands of his big fellow-countryman, Mohammed Isa.

On the 3rd of September, the expedition started gaily in the sun. The horses, fresh and well-fed, went at a brisk pace; the long string of camels unwound itself majestically in the plain and their tinkling bells seemed to sing the end of the boredom of repose, the joy of action, the freedom of the wide horizons, the hope of fine discoveries. Alas, this music was soon to grow slower and sadder in the weariness of the endless road, the many sounds to cease, one after the other, until the final silence, when the last of those patient servants had fallen exhausted on a desert mound! But who foresaw this future and thought of it then? Who foresaw that even these losses would be as nothing beside those which were still in reserve for us; that a day would come when the entire mission would be dispersed, sacked, almost annihilated without a trace; that of the men now full of strength one of the youngest would die, after a long agony, on the harsh soil of the infidels; above all, that another, the first, the best, would die a tragic death, that the lamentable wreck of him who had been our leader would be sent rolling down the waves of a mountain stream? When we left Cherchen, our imagination described to us a very different future and read in the sky none but happy omens.

On the 6th and 7th, we halted at Tukus Davan, the last inhabited spot, and, on the 8th, we once more set out to cross the Altyn Tagh, which, on this side, spreads in the shape of a fan and presents a different appearance from that which it offers in the Polur district. There lie wild and inhospitable valleys, jealously closed against the rays of the sun and delighting in shadow and cold; here friendly and good-humoured valleys, which open wide and joyous to receive the light and warmth of day. One cannot conceive an easier natural road, leading by a gentler slope to a height equal to that of Mont Blanc. On the way we met our first gold-seekers, returning from Bokalyk. The poor fellows had reaped more misery than gold; and the same men whom I had seen a few months before on the road from Nia to Cherchen, full of spirits and gaiety in the rain and hail, I now saw hanging their heads, dragging their feet, shivering as they held the pitiful rags of their clothes to their emaciated bodies, while the sun shone in vain to warm them, for they had nothing left in their wallets, not even hope. One of them, who was from Kashgar, having not enough left to bring him home, asked us to take him into our service. He little cared that the road was long and rough, that he would have to go through Tibet, Mongolia, China, provided that, the trip done, he were able to return to his household gods.

At a short day's march from Tukus Davan, we left the Cherchen River and, leaving the route of the Pievtsoff Mission on the east, we climbed the main chain of the Altyn Tagh by the Gold-washers' Pass (Zarchu Davan, 15,680 feet), so called because, a few miles to the south, there is a gold-mine, which is now abandoned. The stiff part of this pass being very short, the crossing is easy. From here we went down to a first plateau watered by the Toghru Su, a slow and muddy river, where the donkeys got involved in the mire to such an extent that we had to unload them and laboriously drag them across. This stream is an affluent of the Olugh Su, which, with the Muzluk Su, the biggest and most easterly of the three, forms the Cherchen Daria. Opposite us there rose, above the plateau, an enormous mountain-chain, like a perpendicular wall denticulated with snowy peaks. We were not long in discovering that this threatening obstacle was mere vanity, for the Olugh Su intersects it and the valley of the river offers an easy, wide and almost flat road.

On the 14th of September, we camped on the left bank, not far from the Akka Tagh, whose crests were hidden by the mountains in the foreground. It was useless to take the caravan further before knowing if it could cross the mountains and where; and on the morning of the 15th of September, Dutreuil de Rhins, leaving me in charge of the camp, set out reconnoitring to seek a passage across the Akka Tagh.

On his return, he found the best of our men and the one who had been longest with us, Musa, in bed, attacked for the third time with an inflammation of the chest. He was decidedly not fit to travel on those lofty, icy, wind-swept table-lands. On the sixth day, feeling better, he asked for his discharge, which we could not refuse him. He left us on the 23rd. It was hard for us to part with a man for whom we had always felt a great esteem and it gave us a pain at the heart to see him go off in so sad a plight and not even to feel certain that he could stand the journey. Many months after, at Sining, I had the pleasure of learning by a letter from the prefect of Khotan that he had arrived safely in that town and was living there quietly with his wife and child, who, when all is said, may have counted for something in his illness and his determination to leave us.

Those first days spent at a minimum altitude of 14,400 feet had already given us a disagreeable foretaste of the journey which we had undertaken. The gusts of wind and the snow-flakes had entered upon the scene and, on the 23rd of September, the snow covered the ground, slowly evaporating or more slowly soaking into the earth, without perceptibly swelling the stream. The cold was severe for the season of the year; and, in the tent, we had constantly to hold the ink to the fire before we could write with it. Although the fine weather, the clear sky and the sun had returned, we had only 4 degrees of heat in the tent at one o'clock in the afternoon; at night, the thermometer fell to 15 degrees below zero. When on his reconnoitring-trip, Dutreuil de Rhins had observed a variation in one day of 40 degrees: this was worse than the Ladak route at the same time of year.

On the 24th of September, while the natives who had come with us to carry the supplementary provisions went back with our last mail to the warm and populous plain, we plunged into the cold and desert mountains, alone henceforth in the unknown, with no other support than our patience, already tried by long exercise, and no other guide than our star, of which nothing had as yet occurred to dim the lustre.

I have now to describe the journey which we performed across a region which man had never penetrated. I will not dwell upon this narrative, which, if unfolded at too great a length, would not fail to displease through its monotony. The things which we saw in the course of this long march were things great and magnificent, no doubt, but always the same, so much so that for us the days were distinguished one from the other by the date which we inscribed in our journal; barren and dreary things:

> . . . . . Deserts idle,
> Rough quarries, rocks and hills whose heads touch heaven;

immense countries where nothing passes but the wind, where nothing happens but geological phenomena. If the valiant Moor had had no more interesting subjects of conversation, he would have stood but a small chance of winning the most willing of hearts. I could not, like Othello, enliven these rugged landscapes with marvellous adventures nor people them with strange men "whose heads do grow beneath their shoulders." For sixty days, man attracted our attention only by his absence, thus depriving my description of any other element of variety than our own sufferings and our own miseries, upon which it would be in particularly bad taste for an explorer to enlarge in doleful fashion, seeing that he faces and braves them of his own free will. I shall therefore be brief.

On the 25th of September, our caravan reached the basin of the Karamuren in the first masses of the Akka Tagh, which had already been visited by Dutreuil de Rhins, and, on the next day, we ascended by a steep slope, covered with several feet of snow, that which our leader mistakenly believed to be the chief chain of the system. On the other side, we camped, amid a confusion of blocks and of black schistose slabs, on the brim of a sort of dark funnel, overlooked by a chaos of fantastically shaped mountains which seemed as it were surprised to see us. At night, we experienced 30 degrees of cold and lost two horses. It was a fine start, an eloquent exordium *ex abrupto;* but our resolve was taken, our determination fixed beforehand and our ears closed to all adverse argument. On the 27th, we reached the banks and were not far from the most important and most southerly source of the Karamuren. The springs of this river were now completely discovered. Its valley, which is at an altitude of 17,050 feet, is nearly two miles wide, is as smooth and level as a floor and, like the other valleys of the Akka Tagh, is of a schistose character and absolutely barren and desert: not a tuft of grass, not a trace of animal life, not a bird flying, nothing but a little water flowing swift and clear over the flat pebbles. Near us, on our left, rose a colossal mass of snow and ice, solidly fixed on its enormous base and shooting up its tallest peak to a height of 23,140 feet. This is the highest point not only of the chain, but probably also of the whole region between Turkestan and the Himalayas. It long remained in sight, diminishing slowly on the horizon behind us: at 100 miles to the south, we still distinctly saw its crystal pyramid, which seemed to throne in its immutable majesty over the numerous nation of the mountains.

The next day's march took us to the top of a pass of 18,200 feet on the sky-line of the Akka Tagh. It was with beating hearts that we plunged our eyes down the other side; for, if our good fortune had permitted us to open out a passage across the first of the chains that separated us from Tibet, there was nothing to guarantee, since there had never been a road in this direction, that we should not see a definitely insurmountable barrier rise beyond it. We were reassured when we discovered beneath us a table-land twenty-five miles in width, closed at the south by a line of mountains with summits cut into almost regular peaks, which fringed the sky with a white lace-work, but which had in their midst, straight before us and clearly outlined, a pass that seemed to be awaiting us. We were in a pleasant mood, therefore, that evening, when camping at the southern foot of the Akka Tagh. Nothing could be more characteristic of these countries of Upper Asia than what we saw from our tent, this immense desert plateau stretched between two snow-topped walls. The ground which, seen from above, appears almost flat is, in reality, dented with little hills and hillocks, intersected by ravines, generally without water, and ploughed with a number of depressions in which lie hidden as many muddy pools, the humble satellites of the great, blue, infinitely peaceful lake, which reflects the sun or the clouds and no other thing. The soil is cracked by the frost, brown in colour and only just relieved, at distant intervals, by a patch of snow or a small yellow stain of rough, short grass, while beyond, overtowering all, the huge snow mountains, with their heavy, thick-set shapes, as though overwhelmed by the weight of their glocmy solemness, complete the impression of desolate weariness received from this landscape so antagonistic to life.

At this camp of the 29th of September, one of our camels died and in the empty sky appeared black specks, which, as they came nearer, we recognised as crows of extraordinary size, hastening to the banquet. They were the forerunners of Tibet, the land of the great crows. These filthy marauders, flying from carcass to carcass, make their way everywhere, even to places where no sparrow, eagle nor kite dare venture ; nevertheless, they respect the Akka Tagh, where nothing dies since nothing lives there, the Akka Tagh, which is too wide to allow the smell of dead flesh to reach the keenest scent from one of its extremities to the other. For this reason, on the north of this chain, only the small crows of Turkestan are seen, similar to our own. The Akka Tagh is the most absolute of frontiers, a frontier for the sky as well as for the earth, for birds as well as for men. This dead camel permitted us also to make an interesting note on the moral value of the European and Asiatic dogs respectively. Musa had with him a very pretty Russian bitch, which, at the time of our last start from Khotan, had given birth to a litter of pups. We had kept one of these and had brought it as far as Cherchen in a pannier on horseback. It retained a lively gratitude for the beast which had rendered it this service and it was curious to observe the familiarity and the good intelligence that reigned between the two animals. By a singular effort of generalisation, the dog had extended its affection not only to all the horses, even those not belonging to our caravan, but to all the quadrupeds, including the camels. It could not see one of these animals without going up to it and giving it a friendly lick on its muzzle, which often brought down upon it a pretty severe rebuff on the part of the cross-grained brutes. It had a playmate in the person of an Asiatic dog, the property of one of our men. This latter animal had none of its companion's affectionate gaiety; although well treated by us, it was unsociable and melancholy, dull and indifferent to everything except its food. When it saw the camel lying on the ground, it reflected, like the true Asiatic that it was, that here was a rich quarry which would last it for many a long day, that there was no longer any need for it to follow those fools who were constantly travelling up hill and down dale: it therefore set itself beside the carcass and no efforts on our part availed to induce it to stir. Its companion, on the contrary, followed us without our having to call it. Like man, like dog.

On the 3rd of October, we camped on the same plateau in the hollow of a little vale which was as a smile in the midst of that harsh nature. It was carpeted all over with very short, but almost green grass; a little stream of clear water flowed through it; the tops of the slopes assumed a golden hue under the rays of the setting sun ; the sky, slightly paled, was steeped in a very pure and very soft light. Disturbed by our arrival, two supple fallow antelopes got up before us, swiftly crossed the valley and disappeared in a few bounds. It was not an earthly paradise, yet this momentary relaxation of the austerity of the outside world sufficed to give our men fresh heart for their work. One of them broke into song : a neighbouring hare, startled at this novel clamour, darted from its form and, in the twinkling of an eye, ran up and over the hill.

The next day, we climbed, through a rather rough ravine, the chain which bounds the plateau on the south. On the vexed crest of these mountains, the snow lay thick and the blast raised it in whirlwinds. When descending by a narrow gully, the bottom of which was occupied by a frozen brook, we were almost stopped by a cascade of ice, three feet deep, which hung perpendicularly over a frozen slope. European horses would have broken their necks, I think; ours jumped without any accident. When the camels' turn came, it seemed to us, for a moment, that we should have to look for another road for them, especially as the rocks were extremely close together. However, on taking our measurements, we found the space between to be wide enough and, after half an hour's efforts, we succeeded in making the first camel take the plunge. The others followed, all without misadventure, except one, which broke its leg. As for the donkeys, we had to lift them down.

In the evening, we pitched our tent on the margin of a narrow lake which stretched its gleaming dark-blue waters far to the east between bright-red mountains. The view was unusually striking. Beyond extends a series of large mountainous folds, which, rising gradually one above the other, form a chain descending suddenly, in the south, upon another lacustrine valley, which we reached on the 7th of October. Next came hills and lakes, with here and there one or two conical mountains, once perhaps volcanoes.

On the 10th of October, we climbed a lofty chain on whose southern slope we saw, for the first time, three stones blackened by fire, undoubtedly the remains of a camp of Tibetan huntsmen. Lower down, on the brink of a torrent, in a narrow dale that formed as it were a gulf of the main valley, a grassy vale strewn with great rocks which Nature had carved with a pretty fancifulness and disposed at random for the pleasure and marvel of the eyes, rose a boundary-stone with the inevitable inscription, "*Om mani padmé hum*," and near it, on the slope, according to the Tibetan custom, a small enclosure of dry stones, a hearth and sheep-droppings. These vestiges of a shepherds' camp gave us cause for reflection ; for, if we came upon men so early, we should necessarily be stopped long before reaching the Nam Cho, which lay nearly four degrees further south. However, a more careful examination convinced us that this encampment had been abandoned for several years, that those who had constructed it in these remote parts could have had no imitators, that, in a word, it was an isolated and quite exceptional endeavour ; and, in fact, we marched for many a long day after without coming across any similar traces. This opinion was confirmed by the fearless behavour of the wild animals, which were pretty numerous in the neighbourhood. The antelopes alone refused to let us approach them and kept in the distance, often hardly visible, but recognisable by their great gleaming horns, straight, curved or twisted.

The wild asses, looking like nimble and frisky mules, attracted by our horses, came gambolling by twos and threes near our caravan ; and then, startled at the unaccustomed things which they saw, the graceful beasts stopped and, at the slightest movement, at the least cry, swiftly and lightly scampered away. Families of huge yaks, with long, black hair, watched us pass with a vaguely astonished air and only on hearing a rifle-shot made off at a heavy trot, leaving the oldest of the herd behind them. This patriarch received the bullets with remarkable equanimity, contenting himself with flourishing his tail as though to drive away the flies. One day, we shot seventeen rifle-bullets at a yak and found a dozen at least in his body. The flesh of this stubborn beast was so tough that we were unable to eat it even after several days' stewing. For that matter, we rarely indulged in the pleasures of the chase, which would have interfered with our labours and soon exhausted our small remaining stock of ammunition.

On the 14th of October, we began the crossing of another chain of mountains almost as tall as the Akka Tagh. On its southern slopes, a few wild onions grew at a height of almost 17,400 feet; above that, the barrenness was absolute. The west wind, which had not spared us for the space of one hour since we had crossed the Zarchu Davan, was even more terrible during the two days occupied in crossing this chain. The unwearying infernal tempest—

La bufera infernal, che mai non resta—

rushed through space, furious, merciless, fiercely roaring, with, at moments, a maddened increase of strength, as though it would have bent the impassive summits of the mountains. The sun shone in the sky, lavishly shedding its unimpeded light; but not one of its rays of heat reached us: the hurricane carried them all away and plunged icy needles through our furs into our skin. The horses, whose flanks were exposed to this torrent of air which they resisted with difficulty, were strange to see, with their bodies slanting to the right against the wind, their heads turned to the left for breath, their manes and tails floating horizontally in the same direction. It was a hard business to take the bearings of our route and to compass the horizon in so high a wind and Dutreuil de Rhins never forgot the tortures which he underwent in attempting his astronomical observations in these conditions. On the 14th, we climbed a first pass and a second and higher one which led us to the very heart of the snow-mountains. On the 15th, we resumed our march to cross the southernmost ridge, which, as usual, was the highest (18,470 feet).* Our men, terrified at this endless mountain desert, were seized with an ardent longing to escape from it, to see something different. At each step, we felt that they were becoming more impatient to know what would appear in sight behind that topmost crest, which seemed constantly to retire before them; for, as each summit was surmounted, another rose ahead. Nevertheless, by dint of climbing, we at last reached the final ascent: a few steps more and we should discern from on high a new horizon, a more clement, more human landscape, perhaps a noisy stream flowing through green meadows, with, in a corner, a winding column of smoke. They reached the top, they looked greedily and frank disappointment was pictured on every face. To a distance of many days' march, the view on every side stretched over a gloomy desert of bleak valleys and hills, bounded by glaciers and giant mountains whose imperturbable serenity was not far removed from insolence. We ourselves were almost deceived: the mountain was perpendicular, a real abyss opened under our feet, rendering the valley inaccessible. After wandering for some time on the ridge, we found a practicable descent, although it was very rugged and bristled with sharp, pointed pebbles. It was only with great difficulty that we succeeded in leading our camels to the bottom.

On the next day, the wind having veered round to the north, the temperature fell, the sky was overcast

* I have called this pass by the name of Dutreuil de Rhins.

and snow began to fall in thick flakes and to collect on the ground. The atmosphere was no more than a sea of grey clouds, impenetrable to the eye. This lasted for five days, keeping us in camp. They were five days of mortal weariness, during which we had to remain in our cramped, dark tent, shivering under our heaped-up furs and blankets, our feet aching with cold, our beards and mustaches laden with icicles, ourselves unable to make a fire, or stir, or hold pen or pencil. The horses, frozen by the snow that covered them, vainly scratching the ground for grass, roamed about shivering and dejected. The camels, very different in character, lying motionless in a row, were as patient on the halt as on the march, seemed not to feel the wind that blew through their coats, the snow that gathered on their backs, the want of grass, the hunger that slowly reduced them, and turned the same face upon good and ill, upon poverty and plenty. This prolonged situation was not only fraught with irksomeness, but fraught with peril. There was a danger lest the passes should become impracticable; in any case, the animals were dying off without doing any service, the men were becoming tired of the length of the journey, of that funeral shroud which coiled around them and of that hoar-frost which penetrated to the marrow of their bones. Parpai came to give us notice:

"Give me," he said, "the two donkeys which you condemned and I will undertake to make my way back to Cherchen, however long and rough the road may be. When M. Bonvalot sent me back from Sog (in Eastern Tibet), I had eighty-four days' march to do through desert mountins before returning to Turkestan and I did it very well. Of course, I would rather not leave you; but I am ill, I feel that I have not the strength to go further. Yes, I went a long journey in this same country with M. Bonvalot; but with him we followed a road frequented by the Mongols, where there were traces of caravans every here and there. The mountains were not so high, the wind less violent, the march less painful; and, besides, I was not so old then."

The good apostle had another and a better reason for wishing to return to Cherchen, though he did not tell us of it. He had known a young divorced woman there who had sheep in the mountains and crops in the fields (*koy taghda, boghday baghda*). This was an opportunity which Parpai had long dreamt of finding on his travels: he did not let it slip. This veteran of exploration had long ceased to deserve his name, which recalled divine Achilles swift of foot (*Parpai* means "winged foot"): he had grown heavy with age; but he had still a fine, noble beard, had gained experience and the old fox knew how to catch chickens. After a brisk courtship, he won the lady's hand and heart, her sheep and her crops. The first husband, who repented him of his step, but who, by Mussulman law, could not take back his wife before she had gone through a second marriage and a second divorce, assisted Parpai in his enterprise, hoping that, before his departure, he would give the young person back her liberty. Now neither she nor much more Parpai looked at the matter in this light, seeing which, the lady's family tried to quash the marriage. The family was an influential one and the first husband took the same side; but there was no going back upon accomplished facts: the treble and irrevocable repudiation had been pronounced; from then until the new union the legal period of a hundred days had elapsed: Parpai was the undoubted proprietor. Only, he feared lest the wretched plaintiffs should take advantage of his absence to return to the attack, to work upon the judges, to change the young woman's heart and provoke the breaking-off of the marriage; and that was why our man was restless, ill and anxious to go home. We told him that discipline does not allow a man to abandon his chiefs in the middle of a campaign and we sent him back to his work.

At last, on the 23rd of October, the sun reappeared and we resumed our march through those desolate and endless solitudes, whose sadness cannot be expressed in words. Now as before, every day, we passed through high, rugged valleys, skirted blue lakes or climbed passes covered with snow and, every evening, we saw before our eyes white mountains displaying their majestic, icy forms, valleys stretching wide, gloomy and barren, lakes spreading their motionless blue and evaporating dismally in the sun. Now as before, all visible nature was shrouded in silence and, but for the perpetual whistling of the wind, we should have thought ourselves transported to some old globe dead since centuries, resembling the world of the poet:

Monde muet, marqué d'un signe de colère.

Nevertheless, the country had changed its appearance a little since the first day. Instead of the immense valleys widely open at the east and west, we saw, to left and right, short links of mountains, often very high and running north and south, between which we passed as through a long corridor strewn with lakes and often interrupted by transversal mountains.

This region, which we crossed between the 21st of October and the 3rd of November, is remarkable for its complicated orography, into the details of which I need not enter here, for the yellow or red-brick colour of its soil and for a general altitude much lower than that of the region which extends between the northern slopes of the Akka Tagh and the southern slopes of the chains which we crossed on the 14th and 15th of October. From here onwards, the passes are no higher than the valleys were before. The loftiest, which is situated at the exact southern extremity of the region, does not exceed 16,750 feet. After the 22nd, we camped at a height of less than 15,800 feet and, strange to say, the great peaks which tower over the whole country with their 20,350 feet afforded us a passage, on the 22nd of October, over a wide and easy threshold which did not reach the level of Mont Blanc. The reader must not conclude from this decrease in the height of the ground that our journey was any the less arduous because of it; on the contrary, we never had harder days than just at this end of October. The snow that had fallen still covered all the ground and its rapid evaporation took the form of a thick and heavy mist which made the cold more piercing and breathing more difficult. This mist was not dispelled until the afternoon, under the keen blast of the wind, when the desolation of the world around us came into sight once more beneath its snowy shroud.

Once only, on the 25th of October, did the rent veil disclose a wonder to our eyes. In the pearly and immaculate whiteness of a valley overtowered by dazzling peaks slept a limpid lake, whose deep blue was deliciously paled and softened by the surrounding snows, while the azure of the sky became softer as it descended towards the horizon and assumed an opaline tint where it touched the white crests of the mountains. The conjunction in the pure light of those two only colours, blue and white, which melted gradually into each other, formed a harmony of delicate splendour which defies description and which was rendered yet more perfect by the supreme calm that reigned over all; for the least movement would have appeared like a discord in this picture. Our rough camel-drivers themselves were not insensible to this beauty of things; but the snow exacted a high price for its picturesque effects in the disastrous results which it had upon the eyes of our men, who were completely blinded for some days and suffered intolerable agonies. Dutreuil de Rhins himself was not spared and, one day, I was the only member of the expedition who could see. To the accustomed difficulties, to the scarcity of fuel, for we were always reduced to that produced by the wild beasts, to the frequent lack of fresh water, a deficiency indifferently atoned for by the snow and ice, was added the dampness of our encampments in the snow, in an as yet unequalled temperature of 36 degrees below zero. However, gaining by experience, we succeeded better than before in keeping warm at night and preventing a feeling of frozen feet from interrupting that deep and heavy sleep which is known only in these lofty altitudes and which procured for us an utter oblivion of the disagreeable realities around us. But the awakening was rude. In order to prepare for our departure, we had to get up at the coldest hour of the black night. We left the tent with heavy limbs ; our men came and went slowly, with sleepy movements, groping their way in the darkness ; the animals lazily shook their weary, numbed bodies, all covered with icicles ; the men's voices wore a muffled sound in the sort of moist wadding that enveloped us ; attempts were made to light a fire with ill-dried fuel that refused to blaze up and gave forth an acrid smell. Then a little quiver of wan light made its way through space: this was the dawn, a sorry dawn that served only to make the thickness of the fog visible; and the men loaded the beasts with their customary dreamy listlessness, lingering by the fire to catch a breath of warm smoke. We had constantly to be after them to stir up their torpor, without, however, losing sight of their real sufferings, their hands smarting from the touch of the frozen iron or blistered by handling the stiff cords and the sense of suffocation produced by physical exertion in the rarefied atmosphere. At last we set out, finding our way as best we could, with the aid of the compass, through the dense fog which rendered keener our sense of the weight of the silence and made the solitude almost tangible. Amid these floating vapours glided confusedly, like a procession of dumb phantoms, the camels with their monotonous swinging gait and the horses hanging their heads and carrying on their backs the motionless figures of men in fantastic wraps.

However, many signs announced the propinquity of inhabited spots. The grass became gradually more abundant, the plentiful game more timid ; here and there, hunters had left traces of their camps. On the 27th of October, after passing the threshold of which I have spoken above, we saw a sheepfold which must have been occupied that summer. We pitched our tent not far from there, on the bank of a river whose water, frozen only at either brink, flowed swiftly and to a depth of two feet. In the stern and narrow valley of this stream, sparrows and partridges kept the crows company and, in the short brushwood, called foxwood in Tibetan (*waching*), played countless hares. The Tibetan hares, not being looked upon as animals to be trapped and eaten at will, are not so timid as ours nor so difficult to catch. Mohammed Isa had hardly left the camp in search of wood, when he returned carrying one of these hares, sound of body and bright-eyed, which he had seized by the ears. This is the most noteworthy feat of hunting that our expedition accomplished; and I mention it here so that, should its author ever boast of it, he may not be regarded as a greater braggart than he is.

Until we came to the source of this Hare River, our road had deviated but little from the due southerly course ; afterwards, we inclined towards the west, a direction in which the country is better known, with the intention of discovering how much truth or probability lay in the famous hypothesis of the direct route from Khotan to Lhasa, but we saw absolutely no vestige of it.

On the first of November, we encamped near a salt-water lake, which had a fetid smell and taste, like ammonia. In the tall mountains that rise on the western margin of this lake, we saw a gap that seemed to offer a relatively easy passage : this is probably the way by which Captain Bower passed in the important journey which he had recently made from Ladak to Sechuen, a journey of which we had not at that time heard.

The next day and the day after, we crossed two passes which led us to an immense grassy valley, running indefinitely towards the south-east and stretching between the southern slope of the mountains which we had left and a magnificent snowy chain whose peaks rose out of sight, gleaming and drawn up in line like a troop of cuirassiers under arms. This recalled in a striking manner the view of the Transalay Mountains as seen from Sarytach, but with something much more imposing about it. The snow and mist had at last disappeared and we saw remains of camps lately abandoned. This provoked a great sigh of relief and yet all was not over. The altitude was still considerable, between 14,500 and 15,800 feet ; the cold did not decrease ; and the plentiful grass was not relished by the horses, which found it too hard, and was of no use to the camels, which are able to eat only long grass. We had already lost sixteen of our beasts and the survivors were pitiful to see. The very proximity of human beings was a source of anxiety: not that we had the least fear for our safety, but we knew that they would try to impede our passage.

Following the valley, which abounded in game and was frequented also by herds of wild horses, we came, on the 7th of November, to the brink of a torrent where we discovered a fire-place with hot ashes. And, at last, on the next day, two months exactly after leaving the last inhabited spot in Turkestan, we met our first Tibetan, a meeting both dreaded and longed for. He was a herdsman seated with a look of despair beside his sick goat. His wild and rugged face, black with the sun and dirt and lost in the unkempt brushwood of his hair, did us good to see. I will not go so far as to say that the poor herd experienced the same sentiment at the sight of us : to use a Chinese expression, he looked as startled as a new-born calf. He took us for devils from hell or, at the very least, for brigands. He was too much taken up with his goat's illness and too much taken aback by our sudden apparition to give us the smallest information.

At some distance in the pasture-land, we saw several shepherds who, on catching sight of us, collected and hurriedly drove away their herds of yaks and sheep. However, one of them came up to us and we endeavoured to enter into conversation. He put on an air of good-fellowship, but was careful to say nothing that would be likely to interest us. His replies were either vague or untruthful, or else, when he was driven into a corner, he suddenly pretended to be foolish and ignorant and assumed the face of one fallen from the clouds. It would have been amusing had it not been vexing. We wished to find out about Nakchang, which is mentioned in Chinese geography and which was supposed by Dutreuil de Rhins to be a town situated at no great distance from where we were. We had the greatest difficulty in making our interlocutor understand what we wanted. He first opened wide eyes, then a wide mouth and, at last, stood with swinging arms and his looks lost in space. We were ready to throw up the game, when, suddenly, a flash of intelligence seemed to light up the rustic's face :

"Oh, yes," he said, "a place with men as big as the stars !"

We answered yes, thinking that this might be a poetic way of describing public officials and that we were about to receive the desired information.

"*Ooh! Yo ma ré!* (there isn't one)," exclaimed the Tibetan in a sing-song voice, like a Provençal, but peremptorily.

We learnt later that Nakchang was the name of the district in which we then were and that its capital is Senja Jong, to the south of the mountains.

We camped at a place called Gadmar, or Red Cliff, near a fairly large lake, which is known as the Ringmo Cho, or Long Lake. Several black yak-skin tents displayed their spider-like silhouettes, to use Père Huc's very accurate comparison. Three men and a woman came to see us: their types and clothing were very similar to those of the Tibetans whom we had met at Mangrtse, except that the woman's hair was differently dressed and divided into a number of tight plaits, each as thick as the middle joint of the little finger. For that matter, they had a very peaceful appearance, but were exceedingly distrustful of us, as they had guessed us to be Europeans, a fact which surprised us, for we did not know that Captain Bower had recently passed that way. While the men were curiously examining anything that we cared to show them, the woman began to speak frankly, with no notion that she was doing wrong, of the things that interested us, of the roads, of the Nam Cho or Heavenly Lake, of Senja, the residence of the great chief, of Nagchukka, the trading district. But her husband soon went up to her and said, bluntly:

"Hold your tongue; you know nothing."

Then, filling his long iron pipe and crossing his legs, he sat down on the ground and, carefully drawing his sheepskin coat under him, said:

"I do not know if the women are like that where you come from; but here they are always talking at random: what she has been telling you is all rubbish! Ask me what you want to know and you will be told."

Thenceforth, it was impossible to learn any more. Evidently, since Captain Bower had been there, these worthy people had received severe and terrible orders.

The next day, a man appeared, similar to the others in every respect, except that he had a sword stuck in his belt. He was grave and ceremonious ; when accosting us, he took off his huge fur hat, which he had put on for the express purpose of being able to doff it, pinched his left ear, showed a tongue as big as a man's hand and began in these words :

"Revered lords! If it depended only on myself, I would not come to trouble you ; but the formal orders which I have received from our venerable master, the lord lama of Senja Jong, compel me to address a prayer to you. . . . You see," he added, after a short hesitation and suddenly dropping all solemnity, "if you go any further they will cut off my head and, if you have no objection, I would rather keep it on my shoulders."

"My dear fellow," replied Dutreuil de Rhins, familiarly, "these orders do not concern me. I have a letter from the Emperor which I am going to present to His Excellency the Imperial Legate at Lhasa." And, raising his voice and frowning, "There is no objection, I hope!"

"My lord . . . I am at your orders! *(Lalaso, kuchog, lalaso!)*"

And the worthy man withdrew backwards, with his tongue hanging in the air.

On the 11th of November, having taken our astronomical observations, we continued our road and perceived a few armed horsemen who followed us and watched us from afar. Three of them rode up to tell us that the *deba*, or chief of the district, was on the point of arriving and begged us to wait for him. Dutreuil de Rhins, who was suffering from a relapse of rheumatism, received them very curtly and warned them not to show themselves within a radius of two hundred yards. As a matter of fact, the wretched herdsmen were very far from wishing to employ violence: they were performing police duty with extreme reluctance and they felt the unpleasant sensations of one who is placed between the anvil and the hammer. On the 13th, we camped on the shore of a large fresh-water lake, the Chargat Cho, which lay at the bottom of an amphitheatre of snowy mountains that bathed their feet in the bright-blue, perpetually roaring waters. The view was very fine and Dutreuil de Rhins compared it with that between the Bosphorus and the Dardanelles, after a snow-fall, on a fine winter's day. The next two days, we followed, along a narrow path, the side of the prettiest lake imaginable, straitened, sinuous as a sapphire snake, shining in the sun and shivering in the breeze, close-cased between marble walls, gliding into fantastically-scalloped creeks, rounding curious clean-carved promontories and stretching out beyond the rocks that seemed to confine it. This would have been a delightful walk had the cold been less bitter. On the 16th, we again found ourselves amid one of those earlier desolate landscapes, in a large valley, covered with saline efflorescences, with, at the foot of the great, pale mountains, a salt lake, coated with ice, which spread into the distance, infinitely mournful and gloomy. This was the first frozen lake that we had come upon and also the largest that we had yet seen. It is called the Kyaring Cho, a name which it deserves by its exceptional length of over 40 miles. It was on its southern bank that Captain Bower was stopped and turned back. On the north rise tall hills, behind which lies a more habitable valley. We went in this direction, over a rugged, cracked, gullied ground, strewn with frozen pools, covered with saline efflorescences and schistose stones, which sometimes formed a sort of ruined embankment or wall. One of those hideous breezes was blowing, violent, ice-laden, sharp as a sword's point, which made us repeat the cry that was torn from the heart of Père Huc:

"Really, Tibet is a very detestable land."

However, after observing the country from the top of a steep hill, we discovered that we were losing too much time in attempting to go by the other valley and we slanted off to the south-east, towards the lake. On the 20th, after crossing on the ice a considerable river running down to the lake, we halted at the foot of some perpendicular bare rocks, put together in a curious way and hollowed out by natural grottoes, one of which resembled the porch of a gigantic mosque. Continuing our road, we reached the bank of the same Kyaring Cho. It was snowing and we were wrapped in a thick fog through which we guided ourselves by the compass.

We started in this way to cross the frozen lake, but cracks, accompanied by a trembling of the surface, made us hurriedly retrace our steps and, after much groping caused by the impossibility of clearly distinguishing between the frozen water and the dry land in the white darkness that surrounded us, we passed over the ice of a pool, crossed some hills and came to the foot of the great chain, in a green valley, where we saw the black outlines of several tents and of the living wall formed by a large herd of tame yaks. This place, which we reached on the 24th of November, was called Tagstapu.

Meanwhile, the horsemen who had begun to follow us at Gadmar had not lost sight of us. Their deba had joined them and their number had swelled considerably, but they still maintained a respectful distance. They repeatedly tried to enter into a parley with us, to gain time or rather to make us lose it. On the 24th, they again invited us, with redoubled persistency, to stop, informing us that the lama-prefect of Senja was to arrive the next day and that he wished to have a conversation with us, assuring us that, if we would comply with this wish, we should not fail to be pleased with the interview and promising to supply us, in the meantime, with all the provisions which we could need. Dutreuil de Rhins was convinced that, if he stopped, we should soon be surrounded by two or three hundred mounted men, who would block our road to the Nam Cho, which he wished to reach at all costs, and finally oblige us to take the road to Sining, going through uninhabited districts, for the lack of victuals would place us at their mercy. Our provisions were, in fact, nearly exhausted. On the 20th, we had put ourselves upon rations and the flesh of our remaining sheep had not only become almost uneatable, but had decreased to such an extent that two sheep now gave less than did one at the beginning of the journey. At Gadmar, the women, bribed with some small trinkets, had persuaded their husbands to sell us a little butter and a sheep. This went but a very short way. We meant to try to obtain better results at Tagstapu and we contrived to halt there on the 25th, knowing that, in any Asiatic language, "to-morrow" stands for "within an undecided number of days" and that, therefore, the prefect would not appear on that day. We also made our arrangements to break up our camp immediately, in case that honourable functionary should surprise us by being punctual, and we sent our interpreter to the tents to buy what he could. The natives refused to sell anything, having been strictly forbidden to do so.

"But, since we are staying," said our man, "we must needs be supplied with victuals."

The others referred the matter to the deba, who, seeing that, in fact, we did not go away, withdrew the prohibition. In this way, we procured four excellent sheep and enough tsamba for four days ; but we found nothing for our animals.

On the 25th, the prefect had made no sign; and, on the next day, we decamped at break of day in order to cross the chain a little further towards the east. About mid-day, as we were entering a deep gorge, we saw behind us about sixty horsemen, with, in their midst, on a caparisoned horse, a Chinese yellow-silk jacket. The lama had come. We pressed forward, leaning as much as possible towards the south, so as to cross the chain with the least possible delay. Just as we were turning into a very narrow and difficult ravine, the Tibetans called out to us:

"You are going the wrong way; the road is to the right!"

Dutreuil de Rhins was convinced that, if the Tibetans told him that he was wrong, he must needs be right and he went straight on. His argument was not correct. The ravine led us to a high, rugged mountain, covered with snow, which lay to a thickness of several yards at the summit. The ascent cost us three camels and a horse. At six o'clock in the evening, we arrived, in the already complete darkness, at the bottom of a precipice, into which we had to lower the animals one by one, holding them by the head and tail. The prefect took good care not to follow us on this side: he crossed by the right road and, on the next morning, we found him installed in front of us in the valley. If he had been strong in either numbers or character, we should have been caught in a trap. We set out on the march as though there were nothing amiss. On coming abreast of the Tibetan encampment, we saw the prefect come forward with only two or three men, an evident sign of his peaceful intentions. He was a youngish, beardless man, with a placid face and a hesitating air. He entreated us, with tears in his voice, to stop: they would cut off his head if we went any further; if, on the other hand, we vouchsafed to grant his prayer, he would supply all our needs and would use his influence to induce the Lhasa government to let us go whithersoever we pleased. Dutreuil de Rhins replied shortly that he could not stop in the middle of the snow-fields; that his instructions obliged him to go at least as far as the Nam Cho; that he intended to treat directly with the central power; that, besides, he had a passport from Peking; and he passed on.

The lama, alighting from his horse, seized mine by the bridle and once more struck up his doleful litany, almost going on his knees. I urged on my mount, to get rid of him; but the poor emaciated beast, which already had a drop of blood at its nostrils, caught its feet in the countless holes with which the ground was hollowed and fell. This ludicrous incident, at which the prefect seemed quite abashed, delivered me forthwith from his entreaties. I went on and saw him, for a moment, with a tearful air, waving his enormous yellow sleeves like a bird fluttering its wings. At bottom, he was perplexed, not knowing exactly the terms of our passport; and, being a well-bred man as well as a timid official, he was more afraid of going too far than of not going far enough. But it was possible that he might repent of his weakness and get together a more numerous escort, which would allow him to act with greater decision; and, in order to guard against this eventuality, we marched rapidly all day, until night fell at seven o'clock. Then we lit fire and made tea, while waiting for the moon to rise. We were in a large and fairly populous valley, the short grass of which was covered with white dust; on our right stood snowy mountains in which a gap seemed to be marked near our bivouac. At nine o'clock, the moon, which was full, rose above the mountains and we took advantage of its light to set out again; but the paleness of this light, which created illusions and uncertainty, made us abandon the idea of crossing the pass which we had seen and we continued to follow the foot of the heights. We had hardly eaten all day and our weariness soon made itself felt. In the midst of the cold, the silence and the monotonous lullaby of the bells, we were invaded by torpor; our beasts let their heads drop forward in short nods and raised them, from time to time, with a sudden start, when their feet knocked against a stone or sank into a hollow; our men, incapable of reaction, slept as they walked and led the animals into the shallows. At last, at three o'clock in the morning, we considered that we had gone far enough to baffle the lama and we encamped in the valley of Pisang, near some native tents.

Europeans were unknown in this spot. We were taken for Mongols on their way to perform their devotions beside the Heavenly Lake and in the Holy City; and, on our departure after a short sleep, we received the salutations of good people whose prejudices and fears did not dim their good-humour nor their gay smiles, for the Tibetan carries within himself all the gaiety that is lacking in the scenery that surrounds him. A little further on, Dutreuil de Rhins entered a tent to warm his hands and drink a cup of milk; when he came out, an old woman bestirred herself to help him on with his cloak and to hold his stirrup for him while he mounted, saying:

"*Tachi chig, tachi chig!* (May you be happy! A prosperous journey!)"

To cross the chain that still separated us from the Nam Cho, we first climbed a rather steep mountain which, on our left, was quite perpendicular and bathed its feet in Lake Pam Cho, 1,000 feet below us. We next crossed a series of steep hills and narrow valleys, the ground of which was dug out with a multitude of holes full of snow and dented with as many protuberances covered with blades of grass hard as stakes, which wounded the soft feet of the camels. This is the common type of the pasture-land of North Tibet. The fairly numerous inhabitants whom we met, continuing to look upon us as a band of pious pilgrims, received us kindly.

At last, on the 30th November, from the top of the last slope, we beheld the Heavenly Lake, the sacred and revered lake, whose sombre and peaceful blue made a violent contrast with the dazzling whiteness of the mountains with their thousand points, like the waves of a turbulent sea, that stood on its southern shore; and those waves, rising one on the top of another, seemed to be climbing to the assault of a huge mass that sprang up above them, quite black, for its sides were so steep that the snow obtained no hold; and the ruggedness, the gloom, the enormous size of this mass, which was Mount Chari Maru, gave it a very formidable air. In the east, the chain of snowy peaks stretched far beyond the lakes; and all were overtopped by the distant and splendid pyramid of the Samtan Gamcha, the Glacier of Contemplation. This mountain, which, secluded in the midst of this almost dead region, seemed not to deign to see this low world from the height of its cold and impassive serenity and to be trying, with its sharp top, to penetrate and to absorb itself in the heavenly void, was indeed the visible emblem of the Buddhist soul, which strives to isolate itself and to collect itself in the contemplation of eternal things and of absolute perfection, to strip itself of all that which, good or bad, attaches it to this perishable and troubled existence, hopes and fears, pleasures and sorrows, hatreds and affections, which aims at suppressing within itself every need, every sensation, every movement, and at becoming one, in the infinity of silence and of space, with Nirvana, the only absolute and perfect life, which does not feel, nor suffer, nor change, nor end.

We had reached the goal; but our men, in the face of the melancholy of this new and yet unchanging spectacle, felt a disgust mingled with stupefaction at this obstinacy on the part of the icy mountains in pursuing them for three months; and for us, better informed, it was striking to see, in the latitude of Alexandria in Egypt and so near to the capital of Tibet, a country like this, in which the manifestations of inanimate nature were as mighty and grand as those of animate nature were feeble and rare.

On the 1st of December, we followed the northern bank of the lake, a hilly bank, intersected by valleys sinking between the uplands and by promontories projecting far into the waters, which were hemmed by a narrow fringe of ice. There were still no trees, but only, growing in the clefts of the rocks, little juniper shrubs (*chugpa*), whose smoke is regarded by the Tibetans, by the Mongols and even by the Moslem Turkomans as agreeable to the divinity. In the matter of game, we saw hardly anything but hares and partridges; and human civilisation was represented solely by a few wandering herds, nibbling the short, hard grass, and by a few wretched tents, cowering in the corners best protected against the wind and serving as a shelter to the no less wretched serfs of the chief lama of Tachilhunpo, the lord of these parts.

We camped at a spot called Zamna, five miles from the eastern extremity of the Nam Cho. A sort of brigadier of police, wearing a red turban, who had come from Lhasa to meet us, asked us to stop where we were until the early arrival of the officials dispatched to us by the central government. He promised us, moreover, using the stereotyped formula, to procure for us anything that we needed. Now we had been unable to renew our provisions in a country whose population was too scattered, too poor and too distrustful; we had been on rations for the last eleven days; we had not an ounce of flour left; we had emptied our last bag of rice and killed our last sheep. Of our sixty-one animals, thirty-six had perished and the melancholy survivors, to which we had not a grain of barley to give, exhausted with fatigue, hunger and cold, staggered on their four legs and rolled like ships as they went ; their sides, in which the ribs stood out in vigorous relief, were, in spite of the low temperature, wet with fetid sweat ; beads of blood reddened their nostrils ; their backs were covered with sores. Dutreuil de Rhins therefore accepted the proposals that were made to him and wrote to the Imperial Legate in residence at Lhasa to ask for his authorisation to go to the Holy City to rest and to reorganise his caravan. When his letter was written he summoned the brigadier :

"Here," he said, "is a message for the Chinese amban* of Lhasa."

"What Chinese amban ? There are no Chinese at Lhasa ; not one!"

"What ! You dare tell me that there is no representative of the Emperor at Lhasa, no grand amban ?"

"Oh, I was forgetting. . . . He is quite a little amban !" and he affected a very scornful tone.

"Well, big or little, send him this packet and see that it reaches him within four days ; if not, I shall lodge a complaint."

The tone of the other changed forthwith ; he had a horse saddled on the spot and dispatched the letter, which was, in fact, at Lhasa four days later.

There was another reason, in addition to the bad condition of the caravan, that prompted Dutreuil de Rhins to listen to the request of the Tibetan government. He had attached essential importance to reaching the Nam Cho, which was the limit of the known districts. After that, one enters what is called the Tibet of the towns, a country whose main geographical

*A Mongolian word which the Tibetans and Turkomans, as well as the Mongols, use to denote Chinese officials.

lines are pretty well known, a country, therefore, in which it is interesting to travel only on condition that one has the leisure and quiet necessary for serious studies, that one can make exact astronomical or other observations, visit the towns and monasteries, converse freely with the inhabitants, the officials and the lamas, collect books and curiosities of all kinds. For this the assent of the government was necessary; and it appeared to Dutreuil de Rhins that the best way of obtaining this assent, if, indeed, there were any means of obtaining it wholly or in part, was to make a show of the greatest deference to the authorities, to prove his good intentions by the correctness of his conduct and, in his intercourse with the Chinese agents, of whose power he was well aware, to make the most of the peculiarly flattering terms of his official passport and of the friendly relations which he had till then always maintained with all the Chinese functionaries. True, there was no room for any illusion as to the result of purely official negotiations; but it was important that these should be conducted correctly from start to finish, in order that we might give an exact account of the degree of resistance, of the nature of the real or apparent reasons which the Tibetan government and the representatives of the Emperor of China might offer; it was important that the experiment should not be vitiated in any way, that no surprise, no act of bad faith or violence on our part should furnish our adversaries with easy arguments against us, arguments invented *ad hoc*.

One matter embarrassed us: this was the affair of the prefect of Senja, to whose summons we had refused to surrender. We foresaw the objections that could be raised against us when we wrote to the Imperial Legate that an individual, claiming to be an officer of the government, had endeavoured to stop us in the midst of the desert; that, as we had no proof of his real quality and as, in any case, he was not furnished with full powers from the central government, we felt that we neither could nor should enter into parley with him; that, lastly, he had dared to take my horse by the bridle and had caused it to fall, a grave insult for which we demanded apologies, if that man were really an official person. Now the prefect had been able to think of nothing better, in order to obtain his pardon for allowing us to pass, than to accuse us of wounding him in the arm with a pistol-shot. He was summoned to Lhasa, where it was shown that he had lied and his trick turned in our favour. The government made us an official apology; and an incident which seemed to us capable of weakening our argument served, on the contrary, to strengthen it.

Gradually, a few armed men came and installed themselves near us; but it was not until eleven days after our arrival, when the first delegates of the government made their appearance, that a troop was collected of sufficient size to oppose a serious obstacle to our progress. If, therefore, we had thought it necssary or useful to continue our march, nothing would have been easier than to push on to the village of Dam, on the other side of the southern chain, and even there we should not have been stopped except by the lack of provisions and the weariness of our beasts. Supposing that our plan had been to advance at all costs as near Lhasa as possible, we should have taken our measures accordingly: at the end of October, instead of turning towards the west, we should have turned towards the east, so as to gain the few days indispensable to our project. Besides, I consider, speaking from experience—and I say this for the instruction of future travellers—that, with a better marching method than that adopted by us, it is possible at the same time both to spare the animals more and to cover more road. As a matter of fact, prolonged halts are of no benefit to the animals in these high-lying countries, where there is practically no grass, at least in the season during which we travelled; there is no reason for stopping except on the days required for astronomical observations and when the weather becomes absolutely impossible. On the other hand, the day's march should in no case exceed seven hours, nor should the horses nor, especially, the camels be forced to increase their pace in the smallest degree: for the poor pleasure of pitching camp half-an-hour earlier, the beasts whose rate of speed is hurried are subjected to a considerable additional fatigue which has the most grievous consequences. By strictly and patiently applying the system which I have described, it is possible to cover on an average twelve miles a day, allowing for stoppages. In this way and without altering our route, we should have taken about seventy days, instead of eighty-five, to go from Tukus Davan to the Nam Cho and our caravan would certainly have been in no worse plight than that in which it was two months after leaving Cherchen. Well, imagine a traveller possessed of resources sufficient to get together a caravan able to carry an ample provision for a hundred days for about twenty-five men, half of whom would have been trained and carefully-picked soldiers. He would have gone beyond Dam without difficulty, reached Pumdo Jong and would there probably have found in face of him only an insufficient troop, whom the resolute bearing of his men would have overawed and whom the fear of consequences and responsibilities, even more than cowardice, would have prevented from going to the length of an armed conflict; for the watchword given to those who are instructed to stop Europeans is: in words firmness, but in action prudence, prudence and again prudence. In this way, I believe that he would not have been definitely stopped before reaching the very gates of Lhasa and the twenty and so many days' provisions which he would still have left would allow him to enjoy at his ease the mortal terror into which his presence would throw the monkhood of the country.

Our intentions, as well as the conditions of our caravan, were different and we awaited the arrival of the negotiators from Lhasa without undue impatience. Two of them came first: a monk who was honoured with the title of *rdjetsum*, a lama in attendance on the Rinpocheh Gyabang, or Dalai Lama, and a layman, the *midpon* or prefect of the town of Lhasa. The latter, who was of mature age, had thin lips, bright eyes, movements which were quick for an oriental, wore handsome rings in his ears and on his fingers and was the spokesman of the embassy. To see his trick of pushing forward his head when he was about to speak, his contented and self-sufficient air, his triumphant gestures was enough to make one feel that he was convinced that his eloquence would overthrow every obstacle on the instant. While he gave vent to the abundant flow of his discourse, his colleague, the lama, a young man with a placid and prepossessing countenance, listened in silence, smiled softly from time to time and never ceased telling his beads, praying, no doubt, for the success of the negotiation. The midpon, presenting us with the traditional *katags*,* told us that, on hearing of our arrival, the government had sent both of them to present its respects to us, to inquire into our needs and to satisfy them, to point out to us the safest and easiest routes: in short, to assist us to continue our journey under the best possible conditions. We replied that we were very grateful to the government for its attention and care and that we thought it our duty to go and thank it in the capital itself.

---

* The katag is a scarf which is presented as a mark of honour and respect.

"Certainly," replied the midpon, "we should be profoundly honoured and charmed to welcome at Lhasa guests so distinguished as yourselves; but the law of the country, which is founded on a secular tradition, is opposed to your admission to Tibetan territory: we can only, to our great regret, help you to leave a country which you ought not to have entered."

"The law of which you speak was made against your enemies; it is not pertinent to invoke it against your friends. You can have no doubt that we belong to the latter: the correctness of our attitude, the deference which we have shown towards your government are proof enough of this. We stopped so soon as its emissaries asked us to and, although you yourselves did not appear at the time fixed, we did not take your unpunctuality as a pretext for going further; and yet this would have been easy for us to do, seeing that there was no obstacle before us. We had the feeling of confidence, which you would not like to shake, that the recommendations of the Court of Peking, the obvious purity of our intentions, your own good sense and equity would serve us better than artifice or force. No apprehension can advise you to expel us; your own interest should dissuade you from that course. The journey which we have undertaken is a work of science and peace alone and conceals no political or religious object, no plan connected with trade or lucre. We belong, moreover, to a nation whose power and ambition can give you no umbrage, for it is very distant from your frontiers and its sole desire is that you should live peacefully in your own country. Since you have no reason to mistrust it, clearly your interest must lie in conciliating its goodwill, in case your security should be threatened from another side. Instead of suggesting these wise ideas to yourselves, you had the clumsiness, not long ago, to set public opinion in France against you by not offering a better reception to two of our most considerable and considered fellow-countrymen ; and you will end by alienating it completely, if you to-day hold the same conduct towards two official travellers who ask leave only to go and rest from their fatigues in a spot less cold, less unhealthy, less devoid of everything than that in which we now are. This is a request which would cost you nothing, which it would be advantageous to you, on the contrary, to grant, a request which the humanity and charity enjoined by your noble religion do not permit you to refuse. No doubt you are free to act as you please in your own country : every man's house, as we say, is his castle ; but, if he lives like a savage, if he snubs everybody and closes his gate against all comers, friends and foes alike, none will be interested in him and, if misfortune ever threaten him, everyone, so far from coming to his assistance, will applaud his ruin. Well, by knocking at your gate to-day, we give you an opportunity of retrieving your past errors. It is probably the last : do not let it escape you !"

"We do not," replied the midpon, "contest the accuracy of your observations; we fully understand their importance and it seems to us that there would be every occasion to show them the greatest respect, if only we were free to do so. But each people has its own customs. As you have so well said, every man's house is his castle; and now the householder says to you, 'The castle is mine: you must go !' The instructions given us are formal ones ; we cannot change them, however much we would like to be agreeable to you."

This time the conversation went no further. Three days later, the midpon returned to the attack :

"When do you propose to leave ?" he asked. "We are ready to do all that is necessary to assist you in your preparations. It is time to make up your minds."

"I am in no hurry," replied Dutreuil de Rhins. "I have written to the Imperial Legate and am waiting for his answer."

"The Imperial Legate has nothing to say in this matter. He is sent to Lhasa to honour the Holy City with his presence and to show the respect due to His Precious Majesty the Dalai Lama in the name of the Emperor. He never interferes in the government and our powers are absolute, within the limits of our instructions. We can no longer wait your good pleasure, for a period of time has been fixed beyond which we are not authorised to go on any pretext."

"I am sorry, but I will yield only to force: employ it if you dare. I am ill, I cannot leave this spot, except to go south, to a better climate. If you insist, you will endanger my life and, if anything happens to me, you will be held responsible."

The two negotiators looked at each other with a perplexed air and withdrew for a moment to confer together in a low voice, after which the midpon said:

"We are much distressed that you should have taken our entreaties in bad part; we had no intention of being disagreeable to you. In proof of this, we will dispatch a messenger immediately to Lhasa to inform the government of your proposals and to ask for fresh instructions."

On the next day, the 17th, the imperial vice-legate arrived, accompanied by a numerous retinue. He was a Manchu, still a young man, who had been secretary of embassy in St. Petersburg, where he admitted that he had picked up a few words of Russian with which he brightened his conversation, here and there, to please us. As for Chinese, he spoke it with an easy, fluent and abundant eloquence and with the clearness of pronunciation peculiar to the natives of Peking. He had an agreeable appearance, an easy gait, under his ample Chinese dress, and visible pretensions to elegance: at every turn, in and out of season, he would produce a fine cambric handkerchief, of irreproachable whiteness; but he made the mistake of sniffing noisily and of spitting on the ground with a great crash. His pleasant smile and courteous manners served admirably to cover the intrinsic haughtiness of his character, in the same way that his display of cordial frankness disguised to a certain extent his diplomatic skill. He had a supple and resourceful mind, affected a great freedom from prejudice of every kind and was clever enough to allow us the same superiority over other men which he attributed to himself. With him came two secretaries of the legation and three officers of the Chinese garrison of Lhasa.

In addition to these, the King, or rather the Viceroy of Tibet, the Bod Gyatsab, had sent a lama styled a *djopa*, who was one of the two supreme judges, or *chagpons*. Short and fat, with a round, smooth face, a mild and sanctimonious expression, lack-lustre eyes, which often gave a sly, upward glance, and a slow and staid voice, without tone or accent, he was almost immovable in his serenity, which was enlivened only at rare intervals by a pale and fleeting smile; he seemed alien to what others said to him and to what he said himself; sometimes, only, a sudden gesture, a louder note in the voice of one conversing with him would draw him from his inner contemplation and make him open great astonished eyes to think that any man could take so impassioned an interest in the things of this world. It would have been as great a mistake to consider him a hypocrite as to believe him to be unconcerned or disinterested. He was capable of dissimulation and was not loth to resort to stratagem; but he did so with a free conscience, in view of a lofty cause. He was a worthy man at bottom, not without a certain simplicity and a little weak and timid: he often readily made a promise out of kindness which his weakness prevented him from keeping. He was accompanied by three rather boorish and dull-witted lamas, who seemed as though they had come only to listen and to act as wallflowers with their yellow jackets: in reality, they had deliberative votes in the embassy, for they represented the three great monasteries in the neighbourhood of Lhasa—Sera, Drebung and Galdan—which have a preponderant influence in the government. Lastly, the two jongpons, or prefects, of Senja and Nagchu had arrived, so that, on the 17th of December 1893, there were fourteen officials on the bank of the Nam Cho, of whom six were Chinamen and eight Tibetans. Around them were gathered four hundred long-haired musketeers, but yesterday herdsmen or peasants, similar in dress, but different in type, some of them being hardly distinguishable from certain Indo-Europeans by their slightly almond-shaped eyes, others resembling the Mongols with their wide, round, flat faces, others again recalling the Redskins of North America by their tall stature, their long, square, bony faces, their large, hooked noses, their wide, thin-lipped mouths, their strong teeth, their hardy muscles, while differing from them, however, in the height and narrowness of their foreheads and a gentler expression of face.

The officials at once came to visit us in great state. They were clad in splendid dresses, dainty silks, soft and exquisite furs and this brilliant finery made a rather amusing contrast with the wildness of the landscape and with our own attire, which was greatly neglected, through no fault of our own. Stripped of all its polite forms and rhetorical superfluities, the speech which the vice-legate addressed to us might be summed up in the phrase with which certain slanderous tongues pretend that the Genevese are wont to receive their guests:

"My dear sir, I am delighted to see you! How soon are you going?"

He handed us the visiting-card of the chief of the Chinese mission, who, in welcoming us to the country, begged us to forgive him for not replying earlier, as he had been prevented from doing so by having pressing matters to settle on the Indian frontier. He regretted not to be able to give us a favourable reply to the letter with which we had honoured him, in spite of his keen desire to be useful and agreeable to visitors whom he regarded as friends of the Empire and even as personal friends of his own. We must be assured that he would be pleased to accede to all our requests, with the exception of that asking to be admitted to Lhasa. We were no doubt aware of the strictness of the usage of immemorial antiquity which prohibited Europeans from entering Tibetan territory; there was no precedent of a man coming from Europe who had ever been allowed to visit the capital of the country and he was sure that we would be the first to understand that it was impossible to make an exception in our favour.

We protested that, in the seventeenth century, French missionaries had resided for many years at Lhasa; that, in the eighteenth century, Orazio della Penna had written a narrative of his journey to Tibet and his stay in the Holy City; that, in 1810, Thomas Manning, the English traveller, had remained for a whole year at Lhasa; that, lastly, less than fifty years had elapsed since our fellow-countrymen Huc and Gabet had spent several months there. We therefore claimed only the application of the common right, founded on an ancient prescriptive usage which had never been interrupted.

The vice-legate cried out: he had never heard of all this and questioned the Tibetans present, who all displayed a touching unanimity in their ignorance; and, surely, if the facts which we alleged had really taken place, none could have known better than they, which showed that our credulity had been played upon by impostors. To endeavour to correct their wilful ignorance would have been time wasted; but, in the course of our subsequent conversations, we could not resist the pleasure of frequently mentioning the relations enjoyed by our predecessors and of often insinuating some such phrase as, "One of our fellow-countrymen, who stayed at Lhasa fifty years ago, says . . ." whereat our auditors would adjust their countenances and affect a stern and impassive attitude. They were the more embarrassed inasmuch as it was impossible for them to deny the accuracy of the facts quoted, our illustrious forerunner and fellow-countryman having had a general care for truth which his detractors have not always displayed.

Nevertheless, on one occasion, Père Huc was disapproved of, in connection with the microscope. When we described the curiosity aroused by this instrument among the exalted dignitaries of Lhasa and told how, Père Huc having asked for some extremely small object, such as an insect, for the purposes of his demonstration, one of the principal lamas present had at once put his hand into his clothes and offered the experimentalist a proper-sized flea, the vice-legate could not help laughing and the lamas showed by their attitude that they looked upon the thing as quite natural; but, when we added that, the flea having perished amid the general eagerness to admire it under the magnifying glass, the noble onlookers had been scandalised and dismayed at this ruthless killing of a living thing, our audience protested that one was not expected so greatly to respect an animal which contains so insignificant a particle (if, indeed, it contain one at all) of the human soul: the only thing being that one must crunch it between the teeth and not crush it between the finger-nails.

We repeated to the vice-legate, adopting the Chinese point of view, the arguments which we had put forward in our conversation with the first envoys from Lhasa. We laid especial stress upon our character of disinterested travellers : we were not political agents, nor religious missionaries, nor seekers after adventures or lucrative enterprises against whom the Chinese government might have more or less well-founded reasons to protect itself ; but what motive could possibly be alleged for impeding the progress of scientific explorers, bent, above all, upon remaining foreign to any kind of intrigue and scrupulously respecting the laws, the customs and the authorities of the countries through which they passed ? Could it be that the geographical labours with which we were entrusted and the maps which we were making were causing them anxiety, as being able to serve as a basis of operation for a military expedition ? But European Powers had waged successful wars in regions the geography of which was no better or even less well known than that of Tibet is to-day (in saying this, Dutreuil de Rhins was thinking of Tongking). And, for that matter, we were prepared to dispel any suspicions in this respect by undertaking to execute no geographical labours except within those limits where we should be authorised to do so. In short, our one wish was to go to the only neighbouring town where there were proper resources and where the climate was endurable, in order to rest from our fatigue, to restore our shattered healths and to reconstitute our caravan so that we might set out again as soon as possible. At the same time, Dutreuil de Rhins gave the vice-legate his map of Tibet. The mandarin seemed greatly pleased, examined the map, which he understood how to read, and particularly the roads which he knew between Lhasa and Chamdo and

Darjeeling, declared that it was the most accurate map of Tibet which he had yet seen and thanked Dutreuil de Rhins effusively:

"You must not think," he said, "that we entertain the least anxiety as to your geographical studies; on the contrary, we look upon them as very useful to ourselves," and, turning to the Tibetans, in an imperious tone, "You will take care not to interfere with these gentlemen in any way in their astronomical observations or topographical surveys; you must help them as far as in you lies and, if they ask you for the names of the districts through which they pass or the neighbouring places, inform them with sincerity and accuracy."

The Tibetans bowed low and the vice-legate continued:

"We are entirely at your disposal for the reorganising of your caravan; you can do that here quite as well as at Lhasa, whither the terms of your passport do not authorise you to proceed. Nor, for that matter, have you any great reason for regret. Lhasa is a horrible place, where the sky is inclement, the men savage, the houses uncomfortable and the soil infertile. Nothing grows there but barley and peas and, even then, each grain sown gives only four in the reaping. Since we Chinese have settled there, we have endeavoured to improve the country, to introduce fresh crops, wheat, rice, vegetables, fruit-trees; but our efforts have been foiled by the uncouthness of the population and the ruggedness of nature. We have with great difficulty succeeded in planting a few puny and stunted trees, in sowing two or three fields of corn which produce hardly anything. You would waste your time in going to look at a country like that. You seem to think that a fear of political intrigues is at the bottom of our refusal to accede to your request. You are mistaken: we have nothing to fear and, if your hypothesis were correct, we could not but yield before the excellence of the arguments which you have unfolded. We were convinced beforehand that your visit, had it been possible, far from causing the slightest inconvenience, would have had none but the best results. To tell the truth, it is the Tibetans who are responsible for this refusal : we are not their masters, but simply their councillors. They decide as they think fit and not only are they very obstinate and jealous of their independence, but you can see for yourself, from the functionaries whom their government has sent to you, how very uncivilised this nation is and how incapable of understanding. You and I, on the other hand, know the Li, the code of international politeness, and, if you had a passport for Peking, I should be pleased to take you to Lhasa through every obstacle : if necessary, we would call out the whole garrison of the city to cause the Emperor's orders to be respected."

If we next turned to the Tibetans, they, with great humility, would declare that they were acting only in accordance with the instructions of the Chinese authorities :

"The amban is the master," said the very men who had pretended that he had nothing to say in the matter ; and, in fact, they were very tiny people in his presence and kissed the dust beneath his feet.

We disclosed to them what the vice-legate had told us, that, if we had a passport for Lhasa, he would take us straightway to the foot of the Potala :

"We propose, therefore," we added, "to send to Peking for this passport which, in view of the close bonds of friendship that exist between China and France and of the impossibility of raising any serious objection, will certainly not be refused ; and, in this way, we shall soon be visiting the Dalai Lama."

They were greatly shocked and replied that, even if we had an order for Peking, they would not allow us to pass. It was useless to insist upon the inconsistency of their language and the incompatibility between their words and the vice-legate's; it was vain to say to them:

"At least, agree among yourselves!"

They did not feel the need for any such agreement nor did their mutual contradictions cause them the smallest embarrassment:

"We are convinced," they said, "that you mean us no harm and we have the highest opinion of you; but, according to our religion, your presence would contaminate the sacred soil."

"But, after all, you admit Moslems and Brahmins; and, if it be sufficient to be a Buddhist to have the right of admission, we have plenty of very sincere Buddhists in France. Would you receive these if they applied to you?"

"No doubt, any good Buddhist has the right to go to Lhasa; but we should always have reason to suspect the good faith of a European professing Buddhism. As for the Moslems and others, we tolerate them because they are of no importance; the Piling (Europeans) are the only people that need be considered."

This betrayed their secret and showed us that fear was the guiding principle of their policy, a fear which had increased at the same time and in the same proportion as the British power in India. They reflected that, although we, who were scientific travellers and Frenchmen, might not be dangerous, the English, who were disseminators of intrigue, discord and conquest, would enter by the door which we should have opened, without counting that, behind us, they saw those Catholic missionaries whose zeal greatly alarms the lamas on the Sechuen side of the country.

Meanwhile, the days were passing by and our situation was far from enviable. There was not much snow, but a keen wind blew; the lake had been frozen since the middle of the month; the temperature varied between zero and 33 degrees below zero, according to the time of day; and we were still in our tent without fire. The altitude of about 15,000 feet was hard to endure, even for the people from Lhasa, who complained bitterly; as for the Chinese, two of them were so ill that they had to be sent back to the town: it is true that both of them were opium-smokers. The Changpa, or men from the north, on the contrary, seemed quite acclimatised and we often saw them, burdened with the weight of their arms, climbing hills at a run and shouting, without losing their breath or discomfort of any kind. As for us, who had been living for nearly four months at a similar or loftier height, our organs had become resigned, but not reconciled to it. The heart-disease from which our Chinese interpreter was suffering had grown much worse and the poor man's face was terribly swollen. Dutreuil de Rhins was in a sad physical plight: he suffered from rheumatism and attacks of painful coughing ("This cruel cough which shatters me," he writes) and he was subject to sudden fainting-fits. One day, when he had gone a few hundred yards from the camp to measure the principal peaks around us with the theodolite, he swooned away and we had to carry him back to the tent.

Our sore-footed beasts, finding no edible grass, were unable to recover. The horses, staggering on their legs, hovering like rags in the wind, roamed about in a disconsolate way: the tamer ones came and sniffed in our pockets and raised the hangings of our tent to ask for the food which we were unable to give them; they no longer had the strength to chew their barley and, every day, one of them, suddenly struck motionless and looking fixedly before it with its glassy and watery eyes, would begin to spin round and fall never to rise again. The camels lay kneeling, solemn and impassive, while great crows settled on their backs and drove the hard horn of their beaks into their open sores, with the quiet satisfaction of an honest burgess sitting down to his dinner; and it was as much as the tortured victim troubled to do, from time to time, slowly, to turn its long neck with a grunt. It availed little to drive away the black monsters: they constantly returned. In the end, all our beasts died, with the exception of two camels. The neighbourhood of the camp became a charnel-house infested with crows and even more horrible huge vultures, through which we had to make our way by flinging stones at them. They would then move off by fluttering heavily away and settle down again at three paces from us, whence these filthy carrion-birds, which looked like hunchbacks, with their long bare necks tucked between their shoulders, sat watching us with their dull and stupid eyes.

Our men, who already had had as much as they could endure of the journey and its sufferings, were stirred up by the stories of Parpai, who told them how they could get back to Kashgar in two months, and came to ask for their discharge. I regret to say that the Russian was at their head. He acted, I have no doubt, as he did from impulse and green-horn stupidity rather than from ill-will. Our Chinese secretary himself, who had been roundly rated by the vice-legate for assisting us and for writing, on behalf of Europeans, a much too well-turned letter and who had come back from his blowing-up filled with irritation against the Tatsus,* nevertheless took advantage of the first opportunity to pack up his trunks and go. Only three men remained faithful: Yunus, who was too ill to dream of leaving; Mohammed Isa, who was not a Chinese subject, who was less mad than the others and who saw, in staying at his post, an excellent

*The name contemptuously given by the Chinese to the Mongolian and Manchurian barbarians, the Tartars.

means of distinguishing himself and obtaining an increase of pay; and, lastly, Mohammed Isa's shadow, Abdurrahman. The Chinese secretary was the first to return to the fold, upon the intervention of the vice-legate, who was delighted to be able so cheaply to prove his good feeling towards us. A short time after, the others came to beg pardon; but Dutreuil de Rhins was too angry at their dastardly conduct and refused. The Tibetans and Chinese, on their side, strenuously opposed the men's departure; and, after much vain and annoying discussion, Dutreuil de Rhins yielded with a bad grace and took back his men, with the exception of the three worst, whom he sent back by the road taken by the Mongolian pilgrims.

These incidents did not cause him to lose sight of the course of the negotiations. The delegates from Lhasa, who were being bored, tried different artifices to persuade us to weigh anchor. The vice-legate told us that the Nam Cho was full of terrible monsters, that an old woman had just been eaten by a bear, that the wolves could be heard howling at night and that he himself dared not sleep without his sword by his side. The long-haired musketeers sometimes went through their military drill in an ostentatious manner, uttering blood-curdling yells. One day, they thought out a solemn farce; while we were at the vice-legate's, all the lamas entered in a body and threw themselves on their knees to beseech His Excellency to rid the country of the foreigners. Their prayer was urgent and a little insolent. His Excellency, turning to us, said:

"You see! It's a difficult situation and we must not strain it any further."

"I can quite understand," said Dutreuil de Rhins, "that you are tired of remaining in this horrible wilderness; I am no less tired than you. Why do we not all

6

go to Dam, beyond the mountains? We can there talk much more at our ease."

"It is quite as impossible to go to Dam as to Lhasa."

"Well then, we must wait for the reply from the government."

The reply came at the end of the month. Not only did the government forbid the foreigners to go to Lhasa, or even to Dam, but it ordered them without delay to return by the road by which they had come, adding that, if these orders were not strictly executed, the negotiators would be flung into the river with hands and feet tied. When giving us this news, the Chinese and Tibetan delegates seemed painfully afflicted:

"We have done what we could for you," they said, with a pitying air, "but all in vain."

I need, perhaps, hardly add that we did not see the smallest paper signed by the King or the ministers; but it was clear that it would serve no purpose to insist. Dutreuil de Rhins declared that, if the reply of the authorities of Lhasa was not wise, perhaps, nor consonant with their best interests, that was their affair; that he, as a peaceful traveller, considered himself bound to defer to their wishes; that, therefore, he gave up his plan of going further south; but that he did not think it contrary to the spirit of the instructions to ask to be allowed to go by the road to Sining, in accordance with the terms of the imperial passport, and to stay, on that road, at the village of Nagchu for the length of time required for the restoration of his health and the reorganising of his caravan, for he considered that no self-respecting government would, under any pretext, allow official travellers to be left hanging about in the midst of the desert.

"This is my last word," he said and broke off the interview.

The next day, we went to see the vice-legate, who had something grave and mysterious in his air. When the page had served the tea and handed round the pipe of hospitality, the mandarin gave him a sign to go, made sure that no one was listening outside and, after a silence intended to enhance the effect of what he was about to say, informed us, in a deep and impressive voice, that the Tibetans would not listen to reason ; that, say what he might, they were determined to turn us back forthwith and by main force along the road by which we had come ; that he was powerless openly to prevent them from executing their designs ; but that his great and sincere affection for us had suggested to him an expedient calculated to baffle their scheme : he would place at our disposal two of his Chinese officers, with some trustworthy servants acquainted with the country, who, leaving with us that same night, so soon as the Tibetans were asleep, would take us in the direction of the road to Sining, so that, by the next day, we should be far enough away to discourage them from pursuing us. This scheme was not without danger for himself, but he was glad to run any risk in order to be of use to us. Suppressing a roar of laughter that tickled his throat, Dutreuil de Rhins burst into protestations and declared that he felt touched to tears at so precious a proof of devotion :

"I expected no less," he said, "from so firm a friend as yourself. But you must confess that this flight under cover of darkness would be inconsistent with our dignity ; we must and shall act only in the light of day. Grant me also that our last proposals contain nothing that is unacceptable or opposed to the instructions from Lhasa. There can be no question of making us return by the exact same road by which we came, because nobody in the world knows that road except ourselves. In ordering us to retrace our steps, it is evident that the government meant in a general way to make us go back north, instead of allowing us to go down further south. We agree on this point and, in order to comply with this wish, I select the road to Sining, because my passport allows me to travel by it, because it is that which my instrúctions tell me to follow and, lastly, because it is that which will take me soonest out of the Lhasa territory. The village of Nagchu is on that road and, as I must needs stop somewhere to make my preparations, you may as well authorise me to stop there as here. You will thus have the satisfaction of seeing me further away from Lhasa and I shall have the advantage of finding a house that will better permit me to restore my health than my worn-out tent, which is in urgent need of repair. You cannot refuse me anything so insignificant as this or so necessary to myself, nor can you force me to travel without being prepared, in the month of February, a time at which the roads are almost impracticable. You have never, for that matter, ceased to promise me, in agreement with the Tibetans, that you would do everything to assist me to continue my journey under good conditions; and I am relying on your promise now. As for what you tell me of the obstinacy and ill-will of the lamas, I venture to believe that you are too modest, that you do not attach enough value to your methods of persuasion and that you underestimate the power of the Emperor."

The vice-legate put on an air as if he thought that Dutreuil de Rhins was a terrible man, whose opinion it was not easy to shake. We quite well knew how much to believe or disbelieve of the cunning diplomatist's talk. Those lamas, who, if we had listened to him, were at the bottom of all the mischief, were, when one saw them in private, the most amiable and compliant people and at the same time the most respectful to

Chinese authority. They were made to play the part of bugbears in spite of themselves.

"Well," said the vice-legate, "I will send for the Tibetans and you shall hear what they say."

When they came, there was but one voice—against our proposals: we were all the more wrong in insisting inasmuch as there were no houses at Nagchu.

"No houses at Nagchu?"

"Ask the prefect himself!"

That honourable functionary was fetched and, on arriving, bore loud witness that he had never seen the smallest house in the whole Nagchu district, although he had lived there for several years.

"Then you live in a tent?" we asked.

"Just so."

It was as though the prefect of Seine-et-Oise were to declare that there was no palace at Versailles. The lie was too gross not to defeat its own object. We persisted in our demands.

"In point of fact," the Lhasa delegates ended by saying, "this is none of our business. The prefect of Nagchu is master of his own district and responsible for what happens there. Let him say whether he will or will not have you."

The official referred to rose and, in the tone of a schoolboy saying a lesson, made a little speech which ended with the words:

"I draw the conclusion that it is not expedient to grant the foreigners' demand."

The game of tennis was now being played with three racquets. The vice-legate stated that an idea had come to him which was capable, in his opinion, of bringing everybody into agreement: it was certainly impossible to oblige travellers whom the imperial recommendation made worthy of the highest respect to stay in a spot as unhealthy as that where we now were; he had learnt that there was not far from there a place called Changchalam,* which had been described to him as very agreeable, sheltered from the wind and the cold, containing running water and good pasture-land; they would there fix us up a good tent and send us the animals, the food, the stores and even the workmen of whom we stood in need. This place was not on the Nagchu road, which would satisfy the Tibetan authorities; on the other hand, it was situated on an easy road which would lead us straight to Sining and which, being unknown to that day, would please our taste as explorers. Dutreuil de Rhins replied that, out of consideration for the representative of the Chinese government and to show that he was guided in his conduct not by any vain obstinacy, but only by serious reasons, he would send me to examine the place in question; that, if I considered it satisfactory, he would move on there; but that, if not, he would go to Nagchu and nowhere else.

On the 8th of January 1894, I set out, escorted by a Chinese officer and thirty mounted Tibetans. The road in question was, in fact, very easy, in that part of it, at least, which I saw; but it was not unknown and did not lead to Sining. It was the road to the Lob Nor, which the Mongolian pilgrims follow and which M. Bonvalot and Prince Henry of Orleans had taken. The vice-legate was not a little ingenuous to imagine that I should not recognise it, the more so as I had with me a man who had been in those travellers' service. As for the spot known as Changchalam, situated at 23 miles to the north-west of Zamna, it possessed no advantage over our encampment on the Nam Cho. On my return, on the 10th of January, Dutreuil de Rhins said to the vice-legate:

"I am very sorry not to be able to accept your proposal; you must make up your mind to have us at Nagchu."

* Meaning simply the high-road to the north (*Byangrgyalam*).

The next day, two of our men, who had gone to fetch fuel, were ill-treated by armed Tibetans. This was the last attempt to intimidate us; it was also the boldest and the clumsiest. We politely, but firmly declared that we demanded, as a satisfaction for this unjustifiable act:

1. The punishment of the culprits;

2. A prompt settlement of the Nagchu question in accordance with our wishes.

A few poor devils, who perhaps had had nothing to do with it, had their legs broken and our diplomatists, who had been dancing attendance on us for more than a month in one of the most inhospitable spots on earth, in the middle of the winter, at a height equal to the top of Mont Blanc, and who were growing restless at the approach of the New Year's festivities, which demanded their presence at Lhasa at the beginning of February, lost patience and granted in a few moments what they had been withholding so long. After a few conversations on points of detail, a convention, drawn up in three languages and in triplicate, was signed and sealed, on the 10th of January, by the vice-legate, the chagpon and Dutreuil de Rhins. It stated:

1. That we were to go to Nagchu by the shortest road;

2. That a good house should be placed at our disposal there for a month from the date of our arrival;

3. That our baggage, as well as the provisions and stores ordered by us at Lhasa, should be carried to Nagchu on the same conditions as the baggage of Chinese officials travelling in Tibet, that is to say free of charge or at a greatly reduced price;

4. That any disputes which might arise between our men and the inhabitants should be settled in concert between ourselves and the local authorities, according to the rules of equity;

5. That the authorities at Nagchu undertook to procure for us, at the usual price, the necessary food and animals, to give us generally every facility needed to allow us to continue our journey to Sining, by the most direct route, under good conditions and, in particular, to give us the indispensable directions as well as guides to the frontier ;

6. That no obstacle should be placed in the way of our scientific and geographical labours ;

7. That we should respect the usages and customs of the country.

Shortly before the signature of the convention, the chief lama, despite his air of detachment from worldly things, had timidly manifested a keen desire to know what curious things we had in our boxes and what presents we were going to make him ; but we took care to postpone the distribution of gifts until after the conclusion of the treaty. The lama appeared very much pleased with his share and especially with a very fine musical-box, which he would be glad, he said, to present to the Dalai Lama in person, who would thank us for it. Certainly, although the skittish Majesty of the latter had kept us at so strict a distance, it was a pleasure to us to think that this infidel toy might for a moment distract the boredom of this young god exiled upon earth and that the profane frivolity of a comic-opera tune would sing something of the joy of life to a child of eighteen, condemned from his swaddling-clothes to enforced holiness and perpetual meditation, imprisoned for life in his austere dignity as in a narrow cell, removed from the pleasures of his age, solitary in the midst of the dreary respect of the crowd, hedged in by show and endless ceremonies, an unbending and superhuman idol at the same time as a frail plaything of human ambitions which take him from the cradle to set him on a pinnacle, keep him in leading-strings, suggest all his thoughts to him, dictate all his words to him, arrange all his movements for him, keep watch jealously lest his personality should emerge from its immortal sleep and, lastly, when they are tired of him or feel that he is weary of the existence which they have created for him, deliver him from his revered slavery by helping him, from pity, no doubt, as well as from prudence, to be born again under a suppler and more docile shape.

On the 19th of January, all the officials and lamas called upon us, in solemn state, to take their leave. They were amiable, smiling, flattering and caressing and never was bride on her wedding-morn more complimented and congratulated than were we that day. To thank these gentlemen for their graciousness, we exhibited a collection of lithographic prints, which had a great success. They went the round of the company, one after the other, and not one came back to us. The chief lama himself, while piously telling his beads, retained on their passage two fair and pink, delicate and sentimental beauties, of the type which the English love ; he was enraptured and dazzled by them and asked to be allowed to have them for a keepsake.

The next day we left Zamna, fifty days after our arrival. The vice-legate offered us a stirrup-cup in the form of a dish of buttered tea and, suddenly displaying a more extensive acquaintance with Russian than he had yet done, found a number of excellent phrases in that language in which to express his friendship for us and to wish us a good journey. Had he known Italian, he might, when thinking of the little comedy which he had played together with the Tibetans, have repeated what Pius IX. said to M. de Grammont, our ambassador :

"*Buffoni! Buffoni di quà, buffoni di là! Noi siamo tutti buffoni!*"

I am not reproaching him. Let that diplomatist who has never concealed anything and who has a heart pure of all artifice cast the first stone! His knavery, on the whole, was very innocent and he atoned for it by much politeness and by the good-humour with which he seasoned the dinners, necessarily somewhat scanty, which we ate together and enlivened our long talks, which did not always turn on thorny questions of business. In the concessions which he made us, he went to the extreme limit of his powers and of our own hopes; and perhaps he kept us waiting for the desired solution only to make us appreciate it the more.

CHAPTER III

EXPLORATIONS OF 1894—FROM THE NAM CHO TO JYERKUNDO

From the Nam Cho to Nagchu; the sources of the Salwen—Nagchu—We set out for Sining—Basin of the Upper Salwen; an unknown route from Lhasa to Tasienlu—The Ponbo Tibetans—Sources of the Blue River—Sources of the Mekong—Tachi Gompa; hostile monks; a great Tibetan fair—The exploration of the basin of the Upper Mekong continued—Jyerkundo; hostility of the monks; the agents of the Chinese government.

WHILE Dutreuil de Rhins proceeded towards Nagchu by the direct road, I set about accompanying the chief lama to the foot of the Dam Larghan La. This was a slight favour which was not obtained without difficulty and the risk of reopening the whole question; but we had insisted on it in order to be able to connect our route exactly with that of M. Bonvalot. I camped, in the evening, at the extreme point reached by the latter traveller. All day long, we had horrible weather, heavy mists on the mountains and the lake, hail, snow, a biting wind and a penetrating cold.

"See!" said the lama. "The spirits of the lake are weeping because you have troubled its serenity!"

"No," I replied, "they are weeping over our departure."

He deigned to smile at my poor joke. This chief lama, for that matter, was a good, gentle, easy-going creature. We talked long and far into the night. He told me that he was happy to have met us, because people who knew each other better learnt to esteem each other more; that the prejudices which nations entertain against one another disappear with their ignorance of one another; that he had now a better idea of what Europeans were like; that he would keep a kindly remembrance of us and particularly of Dutreuil de Rhins, who was a little plain-spoken, it was true, but who, it was easy to feel, had an excellent nature at bottom. He next indulged in a dream of a journey to Europe and France and asked me for information: how he would have to set about it; how many days the voyage would take; whether he would be well received in France, notwithstanding that Tibet had closed its doors to us:

"It is not our fault," he said; "custom is too strong for us. It is a pity; I should have liked to take you with me to Lhasa to see the New Year's festivities and you would have seen what a beautiful country Lhasa is."

I observed that the vice-legate, on the contrary, had drawn a far from attractive picture of it.

"That is because he is a foreigner," said the lama. "One cannot fully appreciate the beauty of any country but one's own. It is, nevertheless, the case that at Lhasa there are large numbers of white houses, hills crowned with temples with golden roofs to them, a limpid river, flowing through the plain shaded by tall trees and green with gardens and crops, and that the soil produces all the necessaries of life: rice, wheat, barley and fruits and vegetables of every kind. While the people work, we lamas pray that rain may fall when the earth needs it; we bring back the sun when the country wants heat; and that is why this land blessed by the gods is fertile and prosperous."

I reminded him of two promises which he had made us: to send us, at Nagchu, two rare and interesting volumes on the history of Tibet and to propose to the government council that it should no longer, in the future, oblige travellers who appeared at the frontier after an arduous march through the desert to remain for long days at a time in uninhabited spots, but instead, to offer them hospitality, for a limited period, in the nearest village. The lama saw in this a simple question of humanity, which could have no religious or political drawback, and promised us to support this suggestion at Lhasa. He renewed his promises, but, alas, they were all blown to the wind. And that wind of Tibet is so terrible!

On the 21st of January, I set out again to join Dutreuil de Rhins, accompanied by a respectable escort commanded by the *tongyig** of Nagchu. This tongyig combined the functions of prefectorial secretary, clerk of the court, collector of taxes and chief of police. He was a jolly companion who tried to put on a serious air, a difficult thing with his pointed and tolerably bald pate, his huge red ears sticking out from the sides of his head, his small goggle eyes, gay or dull according to the time of day, and his large, bony, brandy-blossomed nose. In his family, as he explained to us, a man became a tongyig from father to son, in accordance with the Tibetan custom, and he was as proud of the ink-horn that hung from his belt as a nobleman of his sword. He was, conjointly with his two brothers, the partial husband of a lady of Gyangtse, his native city; on the other hand, at Nagchu, he was the sole proprietor of two wives. When, in order to draw him out, we told him that, according to our ideas, it would not be considered correct thus to divide one wife among several, while, at the same time, having several wives for one's self alone, he grew angry and replied that our ideas were the ideas of barbarians, who knew nothing about morality:

---

* *Drungyig*, or secretary.

"Brothers have nothing to refuse one another!"

"So that, if your brothers came to Nagchu . . ."

"There is a distinction! It is quite another thing. My wife at Gyangtse lives on our common, indivisible, paternal property; she herself, therefore, shares those qualities of the property. On the other hand, my wives at Nagchu live on my personal and private effects and they are my private and personal property, with which my brothers have nothing to do. That is logic."

He had under his orders a few fashionable young men, with panther-skin borders to their tunics, handsome silver rings in their ears, turquoise and coral ornaments in the plaits of their hair. At one time, they would gaily urge their horses onward; at another, they would make them paw the ground beside the caravan, flinging to the winds the notes of some profane song, while old men of sixty or sixty-five, their long grey hair floating over their shoulders, went their peaceful little gait, saying their prayers in a snuffling voice, which now rose loud and solemnly and again dropped suddenly to a confused muttering. It is curious that very distant and very different peoples should have agreed in considering a snuffling tone to be that most agreeable to the divinity. The Roman Catholics sing Latin through their noses; among the perfections introduced into religion by the Puritans, the intensity of their snuffling was one of those which made the most noise in the world; the Moslems would think that they were insulting the sacred word if they did not pronounce it through their noses; I have spoken of the Tibetans; and the Chinese actors, when they want to rise to the sublime, take pains to pass the sounds through their olfactory organs.

To return to my old men, they had good, simple, smiling faces; they were kind and eager to be useful to me. At the halting-place, they arranged the tent, saw to it that the fire blazed, that the tea boiled, that nothing was wanting, came and went, still brisk in their somewhat bent old age, walking with short, quick steps on the uneven ground and wriggling their haunches in the Tibetan fashion. No, indeed: the people of this country have none of the shy rudeness with which our imagination so readily endows them; but do not press them with questions, for they are persuaded that their masters have given them speech to disguise the truth from foreigners.

We crossed on the ice a tributary of the Nam Cho, the Chakartsang, 80 yards wide. Our horses were not rough-shod, but did not slip for a moment during this crossing. Asiatic horses are generally firm-footed on the ice: this was not my first experiment and, to quote only one, I had several times, on a horse which was not rough-shod, crossed the frozen river Yarkand, about 800 yards wide,* without encountering the least mishap. After crossing the little Setalaghlagh Pass, which was difficult only because of the snow which covered it at the time, I joined the mission, on the 22nd, in a large grassy valley beside a lake which ran out of sight towards the north-west. This was the Bum Cho, which corresponds with the lake entered on Dutreuil de Rhins' map under the Mongolian name of Buka Nor. Upon my arrival, I saw that the lama-prefect of Nagchu and Dutreuil de Rhins were on excellent terms and talking familiarly without understanding each other. Laughingly, the lama, with his air of a good country priest, tried to thrust different Buddhist prayers into his interlocutor's head :

"You see," he said, "religion is necessary to men. Come, say after me, '*Om mani padmé hum!*' . . No, not '*pedmé:*' '*padmé,*' through your nose. . . . That's it. . . . You say that ten thousand times a day and you will be all the better for it."

* At the spot where it is crossed in winter and counting the turns which one is obliged to take.

Until Nagchu, the country is undulated by small mountains, generally rounded in shape, grass-grown and separated by valleys which extend freely and give the easiest road that one could wish for to Tibet. On the 24th of January, we passed abreast of Lake Bul Cho, so called after the borax that abounds on its shores; on the 26th, we crossed to the Black River, or Nag Chu, which is no other than the Upper Salwen and comes from the Amdo Cho Nagh. Its bed stretches to a width of 200 yards, but, at that time, only 40 yards were occupied by the frozen water of the river. On the 27th, we reached the plain of Nagchu, surrounded by long lines of low hills, covered with the wintry grass like a thread-bare, discoloured carpet. In the middle were gathered about sixty square, whitewashed stone houses, each consisting of one floor alone, so that the convent of Kyabten timidly overtopped them all with its solitary upper storey and its flat roof adorned with many-coloured streamers. The size of the plain made this poor group of houses appear still smaller and flatter. As we entered the village, the dirt and wretchedness of the dwellings, the silence and solitude of the alleys frequented by lean dogs, base and sullen devourers of the dead, the absence of any flowers or plants, of any picturesque rag of stuff, of any bright colour, of all that interests or gladdens the eye gave us an impression of shabby dreariness, which impression was increased by the monotony of the surrounding landscape, a monotony hardly relieved by a modest convent of women* on the slope of the western hill and by the appearance in the south, above the bare knolls, of the highest summits of the snow-mountains, which the distance and the intervening strips of foreground deprived of their grandeur. The inhabitants have no resources beyond their herds and their pasturage: no husbandry,

*Ané gomba. Ané means aunt and, by extension, woman in general.

no trade ; they have to go to fetch the wood necessary for the construction of their houses at twelve days' march, on the banks of the Sog Chu, a little to the north of its confluence with the Nag Chu. However, the caravans going to or from Tasienlu and Sining pass through this place and give it some little movement and importance. A few days before our departure, we saw a caravan sent to Tasienlu by the Pangchen Rinpocheh of Tachilhunpo: it was led by three noble lamas and consisted of a hundred armed men and seven hundred beasts of burden; we caught it up on the road and met it again at Jyerkundo. During the fine season, the movement is greater and the herdsmen of the surrounding districts come in from a distance of several days, or even a month, to sell their wool and their hides and to buy the tea and flour which they need.

Such is the principal town of the province of Nagchukka, a very large province, although numbering no more than 10,000 inhabitants. It is governed by two prefects, a monk and a layman, according to the Tibetan custom, which prescribes that, in the majority of administrative offices, the religious and lay elements shall reign side by side and mutually watch over each other. The two prefects are supposed to take all their decisions in concert; and, as a matter of fact, the layman has no difficulty in agreeing with the monk, for he approves of all that his colleague does. On the occasion of the stay in this spot of two persons as dangerous as ourselves, the Lhasa government took an additional precaution : it sent a new prefect, who was to replace the one in office after our departure and, in the meantime, to watch over him. He was picked from among the monks of Sera, who are the most masterful, the hardest against the people, the most intolerant and the most hostile to Europeans of all the monks of Tibet. He locked himself up in the convent, held no communication with us and, every day, cross-questioned the prefect about us:

"What are they doing? What do they say? What do they ask for? When are they going away? Above all, be discreet and show no weakness!"

The Lhasa government understood very well and even exaggerated a little the importance of the concession which we had wrung from it. We had created an embarrassing precedent by striking at the sacrosanct principle of the inviolability of Tibetan territory; for not only the capital is forbidden to Europeans, but the whole extent of Tibet and chiefly the towns and villages, that is to say all the places where the Europeans are supposed by these maniacs of distrust and fear to be able more easily to keep up relations with the population, to carry on intrigues, to sow the seeds of discord and revolt. Since the time when this principle became an absolute dogma of Chino-Tibetan policy, all the travellers who, like ourselves, had succeeded, by surprise, in penetrating more or less far into the country had been rigorously shown out again; they had never been allowed any right except that of leaving as quickly as possible, by the most deserted road, and the authorities had carefully avoided permitting them to pass through any town or village. If, occasionally, they had stayed for a few weeks or days at any point in Tibetan territory, this had been only a state of fact, which the government had always declared to be unlawful and at once exerted itself to bring to an end: the principle, therefore, had not been encroached upon. We were the first to obtain, by a treaty in due form, the right to stay on the forbidden territory, in a village which was the capital of a prefecture, in a house that was not an inn, under the shadow of a sacred monastery. The government was obliged to carry out the convention signed by its plenipotentiaries, but it meant to keep us strictly to the limits which the convention fixed, to prevent us from abusing it in order to establish any relations with the population other than those necessary to our revictualling and the preparations for our journey and to put every possible obstacle in the way of the accomplishment of our supposed plans of espionage. For the rest, it relied upon the unpleasantness of our stay in this wretched and remote place to discourage any one from imitating our example and it did not reflect that explorers find their pleasure wherever there is anything to see, that a small village is often as fertile in information as a great city and that our annoyances would be quite wiped out by our satisfaction in having opened in the wall of Tibetan prejudice a peep-hole of which our successors would make a window.

As a signal mark of favour, the prefect gave us the best house in Nagchu. It comprised, in all, three rooms on the ground-floor, opening by as many doors into a court-yard, sixty feet square, surrounded by walls four feet high. A rampart of dried cow-dung flanked the right of the building and set off its architecture. Inside, a great heap of the same material constituted the most noteworthy ornament of our new lodgings, which were floorless, dirty, overrun with vermin, smoke-ridden and dark. Outside, the wind roared, the snow whirled, the thermometer registered 30 degrees below zero. Our abode had no chimney, it was impossible to light a fire and we began to think that, in spite of the bad weather, it might have been more pleasant to start at once; but it was necessary that we should stay the whole month to enforce our rights. We thought of building stone stoves: we set to work and, in two days, all was ready and the fires were blazing merrily in these impromptu receptacles. We had reckoned without the wind, which smoked us out, and we found no way of warding off this inconvenience. Luckily, our two chimneys, having separate outlets, did not smoke at the same time, for the wind changed according to the time of day: in the morning, driven from my room by irritating clouds of smoke, I went to call on Dutreuil de Rhins, who enjoyed a pure atmosphere at that hour; and he returned my visit in the afternoon. Although our experiment in masonry had not answered all our wishes, it nevertheless attracted a great crowd of people. The prefects and their suite admired the ingenuity of the Europeans; our landlord, a worthy old man of seventy-eight, who endeavoured to make up for lost time by ardently spinning his praying-wheel and interlarding his least speeches with prayers and litanies, praised our architectural efforts and sent in a claim for damages. Our interpreter, who was a wag in his way, replied that he ought to be ashamed at his age to occupy himself with such trifles, that he had better take care not to migrate into the skin of a dog or a rat and that, in all justice, he ought to contribute out of his savings towards the improvements which we had made in his property. He consented at last to let us off paying, provided that he were not asked to pay himself: it is true that he received from us, for a month's rent, more than a Tibetan would ever have paid him for a year.

Two things consoled us for these discomforts, namely, that the prefects were worse lodged than ourselves and that they were amiable and obliging. I have not presented the lay prefect to my readers, but this estimable magistrate, a short, thin, spare man, with his tuft of grey beard on his chin and his glittering diamond on his finger, was a very discreet person, who loved to stay quietly and peacefully in his corner, and we thought it right to respect his modesty. He and his colleague did not omit to call on us on the first day of the Tibetan year and to present us with their compliments, with scarves of honour, jugs of foaming *chang** and different presents. They and the members of their suite had put on their best clothes and washed their faces for the occasion. We became aware of the latter detail through the fact that their necks were as black as on the other days of the year, while their cheeks shone with an exceptionally bright, vermilion radiance. The lama told us that he regretted that the festivals were not very splendid at Nagchu, that this poor village could not, like Lhasa, offer us a spectacle worthy of our contemplation; and he described to us the gaieties celebrated in the capital in the course of the first month of the year: the solemn blessing of the people by the Dalai Lama; his banquet to the Chinese and Tibetan officials; the dance of axes performed by a troop of young men; the feast of lanterns and the exhibition of bas-reliefs in butter; the review of the troops which march three times round the Jokang Temple and which, to drive away the demons, discharge numerous volleys of musketry and fire off the big cannon, which is a thousand years old and which is redoubtable not only because of its age, but also for its inscription: "I am the destroyer of rebellion;" the horse-races; the foot-races; and, lastly, on the last day of the month, the theological discussion between the devil and the advocate of the Dalai Lama, a discussion in which the Spirit of Darkness, falling short of arguments, proposes a game of dice to settle the question, but, as he infallibly throws blank, he takes fright and runs away, pursued with gun-shots, mocked, howled at and beaten by the crowd of lamas and laymen. At Nagchu, we saw none of these diverting things; we had only the story of

*A sort of beer which is manufactured as follows: grains of barley are boiled; when cold, a yeast is added composed of flour, ginger and bonga (aconite?); the whole is left to ferment for two or three days; then water is added. When carefully prepared, this makes a pleasant, more or less effervescing drink; but it does not keep.

them, like Don Cæsar reading another's love-letters to the smell of dishes that were not for him.

The severe cold and the snow-storms that raged throughout the month of February were very painful to us. The altitude, although lower than it had been, for it did not now exceed 14,600 feet, appeared to us, because of the dampness, as difficult to support as those above 16,400. The relative rest which we enjoyed, coming after a period of extreme and continuous fatigue, so far from being favourable to our health, injured it by, in a measure, relaxing the springs of our constitution. Sickness is a person that loves ease, calm and idleness ; it hates bustle and flees those who march, act and toil unceasingly. Dutreuil de Rhins' bronchitis became chronic as it grew worse : as for myself, I suffered from complete loss of voice, a very inconvenient complaint for an interpreter in constant practice ; but all this was not dangerous. The case was different with our interpreter Yunus, whose condition grew daily worse. A lama doctor deigned to come down from the convent to attend to him ; he felt the patient's left pulse for five minutes, his right for as long and then explained to him at length how there were in the human body three cardinal humours, to wit, the phlegm, the bile and the wind, which in Tibetan is called *lungpa*, each of which is sub-divided into five kinds ; that from the derangements arising in the circulation of these three humours spring the four hundred and four maladies recognised by the faculty ; that the examination which he had just made of the patient's pulse enabled him to establish the diagnosis of a disorder of the lungpa or wind humour, in consequence of which he proposed to administer an appropriate remedy ; that, if the sick man were destined to be cured, he would not fail to get better ; but that, in the contrary case, his life would be in jeopardy. This doctor was an old man of eighty years, whose face blooming with health, together with his air of gentle gravity and simple conviction, strengthened the impression of confidence inspired by the wisdom and the authentic science of his language. Our poor Yunus was comforted by it and had hardly taken the first remedies prescribed by the faculty before feeling relieved; nevertheless, he did not neglect his soul and, when not sleeping, piously read a little book containing prayers out of the Koran. He had asked to remain in the common room with his fellows; and, one day, the 19th of February, just three years after our departure from Paris, passing outside the closed door, I heard on the other side a sneeze, followed by a loud and merry burst of laughter. I went in and saw Yunus on his knees, in the midst of the laughers, with his head on the ground; I went to him and, raising his head, saw that he had ceased to live. Dutreuil de Rhins wished to send for the doctor to certify the death; it was difficult to persuade him that, according to Tibetan notions, this would have meant offering a mortal insult to that worthy man.

We arranged for a funeral according to Moslem rites. The prefect was good enough, notwithstanding the contrary Tibetan usage, to permit the body to be buried at some distance from the village; and, on the morning of the 21st of February, in a storm of wind and snow, we accompanied our unfortunate fellow-traveller to his last halting-place, on the side of the hill. The hard earth refused to open to receive the sad remains and we had to be content to lay them in a natural crevice. One of the men, who was more or less of a clerk, having read the prayers for the dead and pronounced the sacramental words, "We are God's and to God we shall return," we covered the body with heavy stones to protect it against the starveling dogs which had followed us, with gleaming eyes, and which hovered around us, yelping with greed.

Meanwhile, we were busy making our preparations and collecting information as to the route to Sining from people who had travelled over it. On the 5th of February, they brought us a man who had five times, on foot, made that journey of about 1,600 miles there and back. On his last journey, which he had finished a month before, his feet had been frost-bitten and gangrened; hideous sores had formed and the front portions, almost completely severed, hung down like horrible rags. This poor wretch enumerated the names of the eighty-eight halting-places where the yak caravans are accustomed to camp. This was the actual trading road followed by Père Huc; it crosses the Yangtze (Chumar in Mongolian) at the Seven Fords (Rabdun, or Dolan Olon in Mongolian) and passes through the village of Jung, thus making a rather wide circuit towards the north. Now according to the Chinese documents there must be another and more direct road, whose existence I did, in fact, establish later, although the merchants and peaceful travellers have abandoned it because it is too much exposed to the incursions of the Golok brigands. It coincides with the other during its first portion, but separates from it before reaching the Yangtze, which it crosses below Chumar Rabdun, and then passes between Lakes Kyaring and Ngaring Cho. This is the road which Dutreuil de Rhins wished to take. He cross-questioned all who knew anything about the country lying between Nagchu and Sining and many who knew nothing; he turned them inside out; and he ended by having to admit that this route had been abandoned for a very long time, seeing that the very memory of it seemed to have died out.

It was most difficult to obtain information, no one consenting to speak without a formal authorisation from the authorities, which gave rise to rather amusing incidents. The prefect had sent to us, to tell us about the road to Sining and, if necessary, to accompany us, a rather shrewd young man who answered to the name of Dongdhub Tsering, which was the name of the famous warrior who, setting out from Khotan with a Mongolian army, invaded Tibet, by the road followed later by M. Bonvalot, and took Lhasa in 1717. In the matter of roads, he knew none besides the ordinary one, but we succeeded, one day, in making him tell us some interesting things about the social condition of the country. The next day, Dutreuil de Rhins, wishing to clear up an obscure point in the itinerary and seeing Dongdhub near the door, called to him; but the other, instead of approaching, ran away and, the louder he was called to, the faster he made off, shouting:

"I will go and ask leave of the tongyig."

They had questioned him as to his interview with us, he had confessed his indiscretions and they had blown him up and forbidden him to say anything without being authorised to do so. He came back to us with the tongyig, who received a tremendous scolding at our hands. He protested that Dongdhub was a fool, that he had never been told not to speak, and, turning to him, angrily apostrophised him and commanded him in future to tell all that he knew, all! Dutreuil de Rhins turned the tongyig out of doors and button-holed Dongdhub, who was greatly perplexed what to do with himself and his tongue: he got out of the difficulty thanks to an attack of partial amnesia.

We and our men finding ourselves in need of tailors, the prefect put two at our disposal, who worked for several days in our court-yard. They were excellent workmen, natives of Lhasa, whence they had been banished for unruliness and for airing their opinions. When they were together, they were secret as the tomb; but, so soon as one of them was gone, the other would talk open-heartedly and betray fairly revolutionary ideas. According to him, the lamas were tyrants whom everybody hated and whom nobody had ever known to do the least good:

"If we could be rid of them, it would be a great relief for all Tibet. They prey upon the people with their tithes, collections, sales of indulgences and amulets, usury and monopolies. The government is their accomplice, sells justice, makes the people work for it without paying them, compels them to sell to it for tenpence what is worth twenty and to buy of it for twenty pence what is worth only ten and what they have no use for. The lamas of Sera are the worst of all. Twenty years ago,* the monastery of Galdan contrived a plot against the Dalai Lama. More than one person of importance was poisoned in spite of the price which he had paid for his platter;† the people took up arms, but the monks of Sera put on their war-trousers‡ and, descending into the plain, restored order. Since then, they are the masters . . . What the devil have you done with my thread?" he exclaimed suddenly to his returning companion. "I have been looking for it this last half-hour, without finding it; if you keep on going out so often and so long, we shall never get done; and they are in a hurry!"

The work that had still to be done being much for the eight servants that remained to us, we obtained

---

* To be exact, in 1872.

† Every Tibetan carries on his person a wooden platter or porringer which he uses to eat from and which he entrusts to nobody. Some of these platters are worth as much as 80 rupees, because they are supposed to possess the virtue of rendering poison innocuous.

‡ The lamas wear a gown without sleeves and a shawl, called *zangos*, which serves to cover their naked arms. When exceptional circumstances oblige them to take an active part in an armed struggle, they turn their zangos into breeches.

leave to engage for two months two Tibetans, one of whom bore the blissful name of Tachi Norbu, the jewel of happiness. This jewel of happiness was a very poor devil, whose property, as they say in Tibet, consisted solely of the smoke from his fire (*dhubapa*). As a child, he embraced the religious state, went through his noviciate and already saw in perspective an easy and certain life, with plenty of tea and plenty of butter, when he allowed himself to be tempted by a pair of bright eyes, was caught, soundly flogged and expelled.

"And that," said the unhappy, forcibly unfrocked monk, "that is how the small pay for the great! Do you think that the big-wigs stint themselves? Not they! You can indulge in sweets to your heart's content, if you have money; and for the lamas whose purses are full their colleagues have eyes and see not and ears and hear not. They catch only the small fry, from whom the convent expects to gain neither honour nor profit."

After we had repaired our plant and our tent, we thought of introducing an improvement into our campaigning-installation by constructing a small portable stove. The comparative success of our stone chimneys had given us a taste and stimulated our creative faculties for this class of work. We discovered an old iron bucket, fitted a grid to the opening, planted it on three feet and made a circular hole in the bottom, to which we fixed a flue which we happened to have. This improvised instrument, simple, handy and light, never failed to fulfil its functions with the most scrupulous exactness and rendered us at least as much service as the most perfect, shiny and highly-recommended English travelling-stove could have done. We regretted only that we did not invent it sooner.

As for our travelling-provisions, of which we needed a considerable quantity, our flour and rice came from

Lhasa, while Nagchu supplied us with sheep, barley and tsampa. The reader will understand our weariness at counting and checking the quantities, when he learns that there is no other measure used in the country than the *deh*, a sort of square box, with no lid, which, when filled to the top, contains a pound at the most of tsampa. The person engaged in measuring has a wooden rule with which he levels the contents and he counts the successive measures aloud, repeating the last number several times in a different note, so as not to forget it, and suddenly raising his voice at each tenth number.

Lastly, there remained the question of the beasts of burden. Of the animals which we possessed on leaving Cherchen, we had only two camels left ; and these poor beasts had been unable, in this wretched country, to find a grass that suited them : emaciated and exhausted, they dragged themselves sorrily on their shaking legs. We kept these old servants only from pity, hoping to be able to take them to a more clement country, where they would regain their strength. We had, therefore, to make up our caravan afresh. We needed a considerable number of animals to make the journey to Sining, for, on the road which we intended to take, the traveller finds no resources and has to carry everything with him. On the other hand, Dutreuil de Rhins no longer had enough money left to be able to depart from the strictest economy. He had to resign himselt to starting on his new campaign with yaks, which are much more economical than horses. In fact, while carrying the same load as a horse—I speak of the Tibetan horse, for the horse of Turkestan carries more —the yak requires neither grain nor bran, but feeds itself entirely on the grass which it finds on the way ; moreover, it is much cheaper to buy. Whereas a middling horse cost us about 80 rupees, a good yak came to 20 rupees. Unfortunately, the disheartening slowness of these beasts was destined to be the chief cause of the disaster which struck the mission, by preventing it from going straight to Sining without taking in supplies on the road.

The bad weather had obliged us to prolong our stay at Nagchu a little beyond the fixed time. The two prefects began to grow impatient and anxious and to tremble for their places ; for the Lhasa government is not a tender one. Accordingly, when, on the 6th of March, the weather grew a little better and we announced our departure for the next day, they felt relieved of a great burden. Our relations, which were threatening to become strained, grew easier ; frowning brows were unbent ; eyes looked bright and merry ; words became gentler and more amiable. The next morning, our two friends had the pleasure of accompanying us to the first halting-place, with an escort of about thirty horses. On leaving us, the religious prefect made us a farewell speech filled with ecclesiastical unction, while his colleague nodded approval at each word. He told us in elegant terms how agreeable our company had been to them during the too short weeks which we had spent together ; how they regretted to see us start so soon on a long and difficult journey ; and how, nevertheless, they approved of our wisdom at not prolonging a stay which might have caused them so much embarrassment. He hoped that we would not take it unkindly of them that they had shown some impatience and ended by calling down upon us the blessings of the gods, which we had earned, he said, by our loyalty and our courage. We replied to these compliments as prettily as we could and, after an interchange of small presents, the Tibetan officials left us, delighted to have acquitted themselves so well of the knotty task which their government had laid upon them. The government hastened to remove them.

I do not know what became of the layman, but the lama was appointed to an important post in the central government: this was a means of rewarding him for his services and, at the same time, of preventing him from coming into fresh contract with other European travellers, towards whom he might, perhaps, not display all the impartiality desirable.

As for us, we felt as though we saw disappear, with them, Tibet itself, with its desert mountains, its snows, its icy winds, its privations and wretchedness. No doubt, the road which stretched before us was full of more rough mountains and more vast solitudes where the wind reigned and the cold; but it was the road back. At its further end, our imagination saw, as in a mirage, under a beautiful and warm sun, rich plains, populous cities, comfortable houses and green trees. The foretaste of this approaching future smoothed all present asperities. And so we gaily once more donned our explorer's harness, in spite of our shattered healths; for Dutreuil de Rhins' chest was torn with a persistent cough and he had grown visibly thinner, while I myself was in no much better plight.

The prefects had left, for our escort, a score of mounted men, under the captaincy of the tongyig. It was curious to see them, with their long hair, their big caps and their great matchlocks, carelessly dangling their heads as they trotted on their little horses and incessantly turning their praying-wheels and mumbling endless litanies to beguile or at least to sanctify the weariness of the road. On reaching the halting-place—and we were obliged to halt very soon to leave the yaks time to feed—they spent their leisure in swallowing an incalculable number of cups of buttered tea and in playing at dice or some other game of hazard. Ardent gamblers that they were, they uttered little quivering and passionate cries to mark their joy or their anger at the different turns of the contest. Still, we never saw them come to blows or quarrel violently. At nightfall, the tongyig lit his lamp and a few joss-sticks, placed them on a little bench between two vases of symbolical flowers and, with curious inflexions of his voice, droned out a never-ending prayer. Often we chatted; and our conversations, strewn with unexpected words and ideas, helped to make us know and understand this eccentric people, lovable despite its faults and its rudimentary civilisation.

From Nagchu to the Tachang Pass, the appearance of the country is monotonous and devoid of picturesqueness: fairly wide plains stretch their long, flat outlines between the low mountains; the soil is covered with a short grass, which gives to the whole landscape a yellowish tint, except where its uniformity is broken by a few patches of snow, a black tent or the blue ice of a lake. The surface of the ground, which, in the distance, looks level, is, in reality, dented all over with protuberances the size of mole-hills, having between them hollows a foot deep, often full of water or snow. This sort of ground is very common in North Tibet and is very difficult to march on. On the 11th of March, we camped at the southern foot of the Tachang La, in the gloomy little valley of Dhuglong, which already is outside the territory subject to the Lhasa government. Beyond this spot, the country is under the authority of the Hortsi Gyapeko, a Tibetan prince residing at Pachen, in the valley of the Sog Chu. He himself is under the Chinese Imperial Legate at Lhasa, but is absolutely independent of the Debajong. The majority of his subjects belong to the sect of the Ponbos, whose religion is to-day regarded as a schismatic form of Buddhism, although, in reality, it is quite different and much older.

On the 13th of March, we crossed the Bhumcha Mountains, the first big mountains since Nagchu, by the Tachang Pass, 18,000 feet high, the crossing of which was made rather difficult by snow and bogs. Beyond, at the end of a very wide valley similar to many which I have already described, is the place known as Chunagkang. From this point, the Chinese geographers give two different roads, both leading to Sining. Our Tibetans swore that they knew of one only, the more westernly, which crosses the Kamrong La, at whose foot we were, and the Tang La. This is Père Huc's road. It is true that, as the latter had not made a topographical survey of it, it would have been interesting and useful to go over it again; but the eastern road, apart from the fact that it had never been covered by a European, offered this advantage, that it passed nearer the probable sources of the Mekong, which we wished to explore. However, the tongyig, the men with him, the people of the country and everybody knew nothing of the existence of this road. When we questioned them, they gravely listened to our explanations, studied the map attentively, reflected at length and invariably ended by replying:

"*Ches gu ma ré* (we do not know)."

Dutreuil de Rhins had almost resigned himself to taking the road to the Tang La, when he saw a caravan enter a gorge which at first had seemed to him to be too narrow for a road to lead through. This was the caravan of a young Hutuketu* lama, who was going from Lhasa to a convent of Dergyeh. We followed in his traces, despite the protests of the tongyig, who assured us that this road led not to Sining, but to Tasienlu. Dutreuil de Rhins refused to believe him, for it seemed unlikely that people coming from Lhasa should go so far out of their way to the north in order to go

*Incarnation of Buddha.

to Tasienlu; but he was soon obliged to modify his opinion and yield to the weight of evidence on meeting caravans coming from that town or going there. This roundabout route is naturally explained by the fact that the straight road, which goes through Gyamdo, Lhari, Shobando and Lhasa and which was followed by Père Huc on his return journey, is very bad at all times and almost impracticable at this season of the year. For that matter, in all likelihood, the road which Dutreuil de Rhins had determined to take was bound, for a certain time, to coincide with that of which he was in search. If, however, this hypothesis were not verified, if we missed the fork and if the road led us too far eastwards, we could always turn to the north. We had done more difficult things than that; but circumstances were destined to make us alter our plans.

The gorge upon which we had entered was that of the Charong Chu, an affluent of the Chag Chu, one of the principal sources of the Salwen, the others being the Nag Chu and the Sog Chu. It is very narrow and deep and runs between perpendicular mountains. We went where best we could, on the left bank or the right, on the mountain-side or on the ice of the river itself. On the 17th of March, we left this gorge and, on the mountains on the left, climbed to the plateau of Tsagni, where the chief of a native tribe, the Atag Mema, had pitched his tent. He was a Ponbo and appeared to us a very decent man, hospitable and obliging. He showed us a paper which Captain Bower had given him when passing this way, praising him for services received at his hands. We thought it well to stop here for three days, both to collect information concerning the country and to allow our yaks to feed and rest. They needed this, for they had had a wearying march through the gorge of the Charong Chu and had found but a meagre pittance there.

At our next encampment, near Lake Ngongkar Cho, on the 22nd of March, we took leave of the tongyig and the men of Nagchu. We rewarded them generously for the trouble which they had taken in coming so far and for all that they had done or could have done to make themselves useful and agreeable to us. There was no reason for their further presence. In the first place, they did not know the district well enough to give us the names of the places or any information concerning the surrounding country ; in the second place, whereas a man like the tongyig of Nagchu would have served as an excellent recommendation for us in an orthodox region, he was deprived of all credit in these heretical parts. We could reckon only upon the sympathy of the Ponbos, among whom we were, nor did we look for it in vain.

On the 23rd of March, I went, accompanied by a single interpreter, to pay a visit to a camp of Tibetans a few miles from our tent. At four or five hundred paces, as usual, an avalanche of dogs came rushing down upon us, barking furiously, showing fierce teeth and rolling blood-shot eyes. My intrepreter, who had been telling me how, alone and armed with a mere lance, he had killed several wolves in the snows of the Karakoram, began to tremble like a leaf and tried to hide behind me, but in vain, for he was much taller and stouter. It was enough, however, to pretend to pick up stones to keep the barking brutes at a distance and transform their attack into a platonic, though noisy demonstration. At last, the Tibetans came out and all the noise ceased. They greeted us with respectful cordiality and led us to the chief of the three tents, which contained a gathering of several persons. In the first place, there were two women with their cheeks covered with *toja*, that hideous black glaze which the Tibetan women use to protect themselves against the bite of the wind: they received us with a merry smile which for the moment lit up that blackness. One was churning butter; the other, standing before the stone stove, was boiling tea in a great pot. A tiny little girl, holding on to her sheepskin dress, threw hesitating and timid glances at the strangers. Other children, not quite so small, looked at us with great round eyes of astonishment and stood motionless, with their hands before their half-opened mouths. A few trifles which I distributed among them changed their surprise into joy and they began to laugh silently with all their teeth and all their eyes, through their disordered hair.

Seated on the ground in a corner was a Ponbo lama, with long, grey hair, who went on reading his prayers in a low voice and turning his praying-wheel. His attention did not swerve at our entrance and he did not even reply to the few short words which I addressed to him, for the majesty of him with whom he was talking did not permit of any sharing of the conversation. At last, asking me to sit down, they spread at the upper end of the tent a small piece of felt, the best, no doubt, that they were able to find: alas, it was very much worn and eaten by vermin, but it still served to soften the hardness of the soil. The five men present sat down in their turn and filled their pipes; the women served the tea and conversation began. It was full of cordiality and good humour. They talked of those strange nations of the west whose marvellous inventions come so near witchcraft and whose fame, young and vague as yet, but ever increasing, has a lively effect upon the simple imaginations of these nomads lost in their solitary mountains. They talked of the recent travellers, of M. Bonvalot, of the French Prince, of the "Captain" (Captain Bower), of Mr. Rockhill; they admired their courage, their powers of endurance, their generosity, their spirit of courtesy and equity.

"But," they added, "seeing that among you there are so many people bold enough to undertake such long journeys, why do you not come oftener? We would receive you with open arms. No doubt, the Lhasa government does not look favourably upon you; but we ourselves are not friends either with the people of Lhasa. They have overthrown our once powerful religion and keep it in a state of inferiority from which we are unable to raise it, for we are few and weak. Anything that displeases them is calculated to please us."

Then they made a very violent attack upon the Dalai Lama and the Debajong and jeered at the cowardice and folly of the population, which allowed itself to be eaten up by a heap of deceitful, greedy and hypocritical lamas, who displayed an austere manner in public and enjoyed themselves in secret.

"And the Chinese?" I asked.

There was a short silence, for the question embarrassed them:

"The Chinese," said one of them, at last, shaking his head and clearing out the bowl of his pipe, "are too good for the people of Lhasa; but the amban of Lhasa is a great man: he is our chief and does us no harm."

Returning to what they had said before, I declared that, in travelling through these parts, we had no slightest intention of creating difficulties for the Lhasa government; that we were journeying under the protection of the Emperor of China and that we owed the same consideration to all his subjects; that, nevertheless, we could not but feel a very lively and special sympathy for those who had given us such a good and friendly welcome. I insisted on the gratitude which I felt towards them and I ended by asking them for a guide. Two of them immediately offered to accompany us. The next morning, just after we had broken up our camp, the men came with the children to wish us a prosperous journey:

"Above all," they said, "remember that we shall always be pleased to see you and your fellow-countrymen."

After crossing the valleys of the Peh Chu and the Pom Chu, we ascended the narrow gorge of a little torrent, the Gema Chu, overtopped by tall, snowy peaks. We followed the slope of the mountain to reach the summit of the Sog Gema La, at 16,850 feet. The soil, which was very much broken and intersected by ravines full of snow, made our progress very difficult. The camels, especially, proceeded only with the greatest difficulty. The camel-driver, seeing an almost flat field of snow, took it into his head to lead the camel which he held by its leash that way. After a hundred paces, the thick, soft snow yielded under the weight of the huge brute, which sank deeper the more it struggled to extricate itself. Soon nothing was seen of it but its head and the tips of its humps. It was impossible to clear it and the man could think himself lucky to be able to make his way back. The descent of the northern slope was no easier and this day of the 25th of March may be reckoned as one of the hardest of the journey. We encamped beside people of Zachukka, returning from Lhasa. Our cook, who had a difficulty in lighting his fire, went to ask them for some. They replied that they did not wish to hold any intercourse with Europeans. This gave us a good idea of the politeness of the people of Zachukka; but we did not then think that we should later have to become more closely acquainted with them.

The next day, after descending 2,000 feet in less than four leagues, we came to the banks of the Sog Chu, the most important river that we had yet seen in

Tibet. It is 135 feet wide. As it was frozen only on the surface—to a great enough depth, however, to bear the weight of a caravan—we were able to make holes in the ice to measure the depth of the stream, which is under three feet at this time of year. The valley is very narrow and gives hardly any flat surface; it is contained within high, snow-capped mountains, which, especially on the left bank, are very steep, slashed by dark gorges and bristling with pointed tops, rising 4,000 feet above the river. It is inhabited by the Sogdema tribe, which belongs to the Ponbo religion and is under the Hortsi Gyapeko, whose tents stood at two days' march below our encampment of the 25th of March.

When we asked some Tibetans who had come to see us the name of the spot where we were, they gave us a very complicated name; but an old man with a rough beard and a crabbed look said, curtly:

"You don't want to know the name of this place, which has nothing remarkable about it. Better put down on your map the name of that confluent just there, where you can see that red-washed chorten. Anyone passing this way after you will be able to recognise it. It is Wabeh Sumdo."

Surprised at this observation on the part of a native, we thought at first that we were, perhaps, in the presence of an agent of the Indian government; but not only were we unable to discover anything suspicious either in his person or his manner of speaking, but everybody seemed to know him as a man of the country. When we tried to make him talk, he said that he must go home and that he had no time to waste in fine speeches. We asked him if he would sell us some yaks to replace two of ours which were diseased in their feet. He said yes, if we would go to fetch them and pay him a lot of money for them. And the old eccentric turned his back on us and went away, spinning his praying-wheel.

Shortly after came a rather elderly woman, accompanied by a very good-looking boy of about fifteen: he had the reddish-brown complexion of Raphael's madonnas and wore an odd-looking gilt-cardboard helmet. He executed a few gambols and asked us for food. He told us that he was the son of a Ponbo lama who had died leaving him alone with his mother and unprovided for. He himself was a lama like his father, but he was too young still and the trade did not pay. We proposed to take him as a guide at a decent salary. His mother consented, on condition that he did not stay away too long. He accordingly went off with us. The cold was still very bitter and the wind was keen. The poor boy, who, like many Tibetans, wore no breeches for lack of the money to buy them, shivered and was obliged to fasten his dress round his knees with a string so as not to admit too much air. He was very zealous about informing us. He invented names for the smallest mountains and, anxious to give us plenty for our money, invented them very long: he seemed to think that we measured the price by the yard.

At less than three miles from our encampment on the Sog Chu, we perceived the bifurcation of two roads. The one on the left, which was known as the road of the Goloks, was evidently the road to Sining; the other was the road to Tasienlu, but, knowing that it passed by the sources of the Mekong, we preferred it to the first. The crossing of the huge chain of mountains which separates the basin of the Sog Chu from that of the Dam Chu is very difficult. On the 28th of March, we went over the steep pass known as the Gyring La, at 17,000 feet; on the next day, after crossing a field of ice at the foot of the Damtao La, we encamped at mid-height in three feet of snow. On the 30th, crossing the pass, our caravan descended the northern slope, which was very steep and thickly covered with snow, in which the yaks sank up to their necks. On the following day, we reached the watershed in the pass of Nyaka Marbo, at 16,250 feet. After that, the mountains no longer have the rugged and storm-tossed aspect which they present on the Sog Chu side. They descend with a gentle slope towards the Dam Chu, forming a sort of hardly undulated plateau, which is hemmed in, in the distance, by flattened hills. The Tao Chu, which is the southernmost branch of the sources of the Yangtzekiang, here spread its frozen waters to a width sometimes exceeding 2,300 feet. Also, the valley of the Dam Chu, of which it is the affluent, although farther from the watershed than the valley of the Sog Chu, is much higher than the latter (15,600 feet, as against 14,750). Looking backwards, there is a fine view over a long row of peaks of the Damtao La Chain, peaks which, on the north side, appear to be wrapped from head to foot in a mantle of snow, whereas on the south side, they have only a white cap pulled over their heads. The country ahead is flat and dismal. On the 1st of April, while a snow-laden fog, which the squalls were unable to dispel, hung drearily over the monotonous landscape, we reached the first tents of the Dungpa Tibetans. This tribe is dependent upon the Nanchen Gyapo (Rgyalpo), a very venerable and lazy king who pitches his camp in the basin of the Mekong, between Jyerkundo and Chamdo. We were now within the territorial jurisdiction of the Imperial Legate of Sining.

We halted for two days because of the bad weather. On the evening of the first day, we saw two or three men arrive, armed with matchlocks or lances. They remained in the tents of the natives without speaking to us. At our departure, they were still there and began to follow us at a short distance. We pulled up to ask them what they wanted. They replied that they had come in search of some lost, or probably stolen yaks ;

unfortunately, they had failed to find them and were going home. In reality, they wanted to know who we were and what our plans were. We told them that we were travelling with the authorisation of the Emperor and under the protection of the amban of Sining. They at once showed themselves eager to serve us. Camping near their tents, at Kamrug, we entered into a parley with them for the purchase of yaks; for already some of ours were good for little and it was clear to us that not many of them would last as far as Sining. But we had nothing but gold and the Tibetans wanted silver, for gold does not pass current as cash: it is a commodity which is marketable only in the important villages. In every other respect, these good people of Kamrug were very obliging and their leader himself offered to guide us as far as the territory of the Gejis, a numerous and powerful tribe, he said. The Dungpa are greatly inferior to them. They possess no monasteries and this is probably the reason why we were not ill-received by them, although they are orthodox Buddhists. They also keep up pretty good relations with their Ponbo neighbours, the Sogdema and the Kongkiema, notwithstanding their reciprocal thefts of horses and yaks. The Gejis, who are a very thieving tribe, are further off and therefore less to be feared. Consequently, the Dungpa, in their wide valleys well supplied with grass, could feed their herds in peace and prosperity, were it not that, five leagues further west, their flat and unprotected country is intersected by the famous road of the Goloks. These horsemen with the shaved heads are formidable brigands and sometimes come in numerous bands to make raids in the district, when all those who have not been warned or have not taken their measures in time see their tents overturned and pillaged, their children, their young wives, their herds carried off without pity and think themselves lucky when they are not themselves killed for attempting an impossible resistance.

On the 6th of April, we crossed the Dam Chu, or Muddy River. We were unable to ascertain if its name is well-deserved, for the water was frozen; but, the wide, flat valley offering only a very slight slope, the river divides into seven arms, the most important of which measures 260 feet. When the snows melt, a sort of great muddy lake forms there to a width of some miles. On the banks of this river, three days' march up stream, at Damsarchaho, lives the great chief of the Dungpas. He occupies a tent, for there are no houses in the district.

On the 8th of April, at nine o'clock in the morning, we had the satisfaction, in crossing the Zanag Lungmug La, to achieve one of the objects which we had set ourselves to accomplish. From this pass, which is 16,760 feet high, runs the Lungmug Chu, the most westernly of the sources of the Mekong. The joys of discovery, which are enough to make any good explorer forget the sufferings of a journey, were increased two-fold for us by the fact that this humble stream of water, now motionless under ice, but soon to flow over mountains and plains to French territory, established an imaginary and yet a real communication between ourselves and the motherland of which we had heard nothing for so many months. By holding one end of this stream, of which France holds the other, we felt nearer home and we ceased to notice the rugged desolation of the surrounding scene, the gloom of those silent, gaping clefts, the melancholy of those bare, red mountains, covered here and there with a thin, dull layer of snow.

The Lungmug Chu takes the name of the Zanag Chu after its junction with the Norpa Chu. Its valley, generally straitened between steep mountains and inhabited by a few scattered Geji Tibetans, led us to the confluence of the Zagar Chu, starting from which the river takes the name of Za Chu, which it retains throughout Tibetan territory. Now that the sources of the Mekong were clearly settled, Dutreuil de Rhins no longer proposed to go lower down the river. It would have suited him to go north through the Zagar Chu Valley, to seek a passage over the mountains which stand at the source of this river and beyond them to meet the road to Sining. But the yaks had gone more slowly than we had expected and had not resisted fatigue so well as we had been led to hope. Since leaving Nagchu, we had covered on an average not much more than six miles a day, allowing for the halts necessary both for resting the animals and for astronomical observations. At this rate, we should need nearly a hundred days to reach Sining by a road which was desert almost to the end; and we had provisions for barely fifty days. On the other hand, in spite of all our care to take spare yaks at the rate of one to every three, the number of invalids proved to us that, long before reaching our destination, we should not have a sound beast left. We must therefore procure victuals and animals somewhere, without, however, going to Jyerkundo, which would have taken us much too far out of our way. Our Dungpa guides had left us soon after crossing the Lungmug La and none of the inhabitants of the country had consented to take their place. Chance made us fall in once more with five young wandering lamas whom we had already seen a few days earlier walking bravely through wind and snow, stick in hand and sack on back. Natives of the Amdo country and of Kansu, they had been to Lhasa to present themselves to the Dalai Lama and were now returning home through Jyerkundo and the country of the Horkangtze. Carrying all their goods on their shoulders, clad in thin woollen gowns, they walked on, braving the rigours of the atmosphere, the asperities and the length of the road, sleeping in the open air in one another's arms for warmth, living on what was given them for charity or in return for a few prayers to ward off the devils and bad luck. They had no reason to congratulate themselves on the generosity of the Gejis, who were unbelievers, they said, careless of religion and harsh to poor people. During the last three days, they had been given nothing except a dead goat, of which they had already eaten half among the five of them; fortunately, thanks to the coldness of the temperature, the other half still smelt quite fresh and would allow them to walk another two days and a half to Tachi Gompa, where the other lamas, their brothers, would doubtless replenish their sack. They told us that Tachi Gompa, or the Monastery of Felicity, stood on the banks of the Za Chu, that it numbered nearly three hundred monks and that, in two or three days, a great fair was to be held there. Dutreuil de Rhins resolved to go to it, hoping to be able to buy what he stood in need of.

Immediately after the confluence of the two torrents, the Zanag and the Zagar, the river becomes suddenly confined and forms a rapid; its waters, free for the first time and only for a moment, in the deepest part of their bed, rush bubbling between two banks of ice. The path, which follows the foot of a very steep mountain on the right bank, is interrupted by a great rock which overhangs the river. We were obliged to pass over the ice-bank, which, at that time, attacked by the beginning of the thaw, was very narrow. Our men had to unload the animals and, with the greatest caution, to carry the packages by hand to the other side of the rock. We tried to make the yaks pass one by one. But they were unmanageable: they flung themselves against one another, pushed and crowded and, so soon as one of them had extricated itself, it rushed through the narrow passage, slipping on the ice and knocking itself against the rock. I once again wondered at these animals, which, notwithstanding their heavy and clumsy appearance, are, in reality, nimble and sure-footed, for, in spite of all this disorder, none of them fell into the water. In this way, we took an hour to cover a distance of a hundred yards. At that day's camp, we lost two sheep, poisoned by the bad grass which they had eaten. We were told that this was not an uncommon accident. Still, it is curious that nothing of the kind happened on the journey to either our yaks or our horses.

Two days later, on the 15th of April, we witnessed some natural phenomena that to our eyes seemed almost miraculous. The river had thawed and its waters, which were carrying blocks of ice, filled the valley with a dull, but loud roar, which was increased by the echoes from the rocks. On the slopes of the hills grew a few tufted dwarf-willows, poor shrubs scarcely two feet high; but their feeble branches, together with the music of the waters, aroused in us both distant memories and the speedy hope of reaching gentler climes. Nevertheless, nature seemed bent upon contriving contrasts; and snow-flakes and hail-stones obliged us once more to turn up our collars, to pull our caps over our ears, to tighten our belts. The one camel left to us, exhausted with cold and fatigue, sorrowing over the death of its last companion and despairing of this ever implacable country, through which it had now been travelling for so long without finding the long grass which it loved, knelt down on the ground and refused to rise again. It was at that time the oldest in our service of any of our beasts; it had a year and five days' campaign behind it, had covered nearly two thousand miles and, for seven months and six days, had had hardly any grass to eat.

We pretty frequently met pilgrims going to or from Lhasa, Mongols or Tibetans from the Koko Nor, poor people who to the direct, but deserted route preferred this long, but inhabited road which passes by Jyerkundo, the country of the Horkangtze and that of the Goloks. The Tibetans, generally, carried in their eyes and on their brows something that reflected a thinking and anxious mind; whereas on the rude, flat and almost shapeless faces of the Mongols, for the most part Khalkas, was depicted a simplicity that came near to being the stupidity of the brute. Of the immense journey which they had made on foot from Urga to Lhasa, a journey of 700 leagues as the crow flies, they retained only the names of Sining and the Koko Nor. They spoke to us of the Russians, whose traders often come to their country; themselves had been to the Russian frontier-stations. In the course of this contact with Slav civilisation, they had learnt to esteem the recent masters of the north for their fine boots and their good brandy. This is all that struck their imagination in European culture, all that they knew of it, nor did they feel the smallest desire to know more. The smallness of their intellectual needs, while depriving them of any idea of raising themselves above their present condition, enabled them to be perfectly contented with it. They had worn out the soles of their feet on the dry wastes of Gobi and on the rocks of Tibet; they suffered hunger and cold; they fed oftenest on dead meat and fresh water; at home they were beaten with the great whips of their chiefs, abroad despised by the Chinese and the lamas and insulted by the Tibetan herdsmen of whom they begged their daily pittance; but, like roaming wolves, they enjoyed liberty in the steppes and mountains, the carelessness and serenity of healthy animals; and their life was sweet to them.

The narrowness of the valley of the Za Chu compels the traveller frequently to cross from one bank to the other; and already the river was difficult to cross. At nine o'clock in the morning, that is to say almost at neap tide, it measured 95 feet in width, 3 feet in average depth and flowed at the rate of 4 feet to the second. We had to take the packages that would not resist the water from the yaks, which stood too low on their legs, and strap them one by one to the saddles of the horses, which made us lose an hour at each of the last two crossings.

On the 16th of April, we were approaching Tachi Gompa, when two armed men rode up to us and told us that the noble lamas wished to see us take another road. Dutreuil de Rhins replied by producing his Chinese passport, whereupon the two abashed horsemen went to the right about. Soon we pitched our camp, at an altitude of 14,450 feet, on the bank of the Za Chu, on a platform over a mile long by not much more than 300 yards wide. Although we were close to the monastery, we could not see it, as it was hidden by a jut of the mountain. The two horsemen returned, this time on foot, to tell us that, as we carried an authorisation from Peking, we were free to go where we pleased, but that my lords the lamas intended to hold no communication with my lords the foreigners.

In order to try to bring the lamas to a better frame of mind, to explain the necessities of our situation to them and to assure them of our friendly intentions, we sent our interpreter to them with a few presents for the decoration of their chapel. On reaching the gate of the convent, the interpreter found no one to speak to; he had to perform his message after the manner of a herald of old, by proclaiming the object of his mission in a loud and audible voice. The lamas occupied in singing their office sang more lustily, so as not to hear ; and the interpreter returned with labour lost.

Dutreuil de Rhins and I went to see the abode of these difficult monks. Its appearance was as picturesque as could be wished. Between two approaching projections which compress the bed of the river, the mountain stands a little way back, without, however, leaving any flat surface: very steep at the summit, it descends to the water's edge with an irregular slope, broken at intervals. On the other bank rises a high wall of rocks. In this nest, the convent of Tachi, whose white houses, scattered over the mountain-side according to the disposition of the ground, stand out brightly against the brick-red of the rocks, lies hidden from the eyes of the world. The every-day road respects its solitude; only two very rude paths bring it into communication with the herd of vulgar men, who, all unworthy of attention or esteem, supply the monastery with butter, flour, meat, money and with its very monks. Every year, it is the object of a pilgrimage for the people of the surrounding districts, who gather from several dozens of leagues in every direction to offer the lamas their respects and their alms, to attend to their spiritual and temporal affairs, to their pleasures and their salvation. For it is not only a pilgrimage, but a fair as well.

We had arrived just at the time of this gathering. All round the convent, the sides of the mountain were strewn with white or blue tents for the rich and elegant and with common black yak-skin tents for the poor. The highlanders had brought the skins of yaks, sheep, wild horses, bears, wolves, foxes and lynxes, besides rhubarb, wool and antelope-horns ; the people from the towns and the valleys offered woollen stuffs from Lhasa and Jyerkundo, musk, tsamba, salt, a few arms and copper vases from Dergyeh. A Hindu, who partook quite as much of the vagabond as of the merchant, was selling saffron and a few valueless trinkets, such as coral beads and artificial pearls. In the court-yard of the monastery, beside the chapel, two or three Chinese merchants had installed themselves. Two pigs sprawled outside their door, grunting and squealing when the customers knocked up against them in passing. Inside were piles of cottons and of bricks of tea, bags of flour, a few rolls of silk, boots, porcelain cups, tobacco and a confused heap of rusty iron-ware, gun-barrels, hatchets, stew-pots. The faces of the Chinamen, for all their gravity and composure, betrayed a certain constraint, a mixture of contempt for this crowd of an inferior race which surrounded them and of anxiety at feeling themselves alone and defenceless in the midst of these barbarians, a sudden whim on whose part would be enough to change their momentary kindliness into violent enmity. However, the crowd which thronged in fairly large numbers into the narrow valley seemed gay and good-humoured. All wore their holiday clothes : dresses of blue or red woollen stuff, sometimes, for the women, striped with different colours or trimmed with hems in gaudy tints. The young men, who had washed their faces and combed their hair for the occasion, looked proud and pretentious, with a silver ring in their left ear and a sword adorned with big coral beads passed through their belt, and joked and flirted with the young women, whose hair, plaited into numberless little tresses, was laden with silver coins, pearls and turquoises, while their fresh red faces, rid of the ordinary coating of black, bore no mark of moral shyness. Here, in the midst of a group, stood two men haggling over a piece of business, obstinately bargaining and discussing : they took each other's right hands, hidden in their long sleeves, to indicate by a pressure of the fingers the

9

price which they offered ; they exchanged remarks with the bystanders, who endeavoured to make them come to an agreement. There, gamblers were seated, wrapped up in their game, now calm and silent, now stamping and shouting. Further on, some idlers stood round two poor little beggars, who, with their faces covered with hideous and grotesque masks, sang and danced frenziedly like people possessed. And, everywhere, pots of chang were drunk and numberless cups of tea.

From time to time, the great round head of a lama passed by, with a severe and inquisitorial eye. We ourselves moved about freely among the crowd, which made way before us out of distrust rather than respect. Nevertheless, their looks showed no ill-will, but rather curiosity and, in many cases, a frank astonishment, which never seemed to wear away. And yet the Tibetans whom we had met until then on the roads or seen in their tents had very soon become accustomed to the strangeness of our appearance. I have often observed that isolated individuals are much less surprised at the sight of a stranger and less struck by his singularity than are the same individuals when united in a crowd. In fact, when, among two or three men, there is one who is different from the others, they will more easily admit the lawfulness of this difference and will feel less entitled to dispute his right not to be like the others ; but, when the same man shows himself in the midst of several hundreds of people all alike among themselves and differing from him alone, his oddity will obviously appear opposed to common sense, absurd and inadmissible.

Unfortunately, we had other things to do than quietly to look on at what was happening : we had to procure provisions ; and, although everything that we wanted was there, it was impossible for us to obtain a single thing. The people avoided speaking to us and, when they had no choice, told us that the lamas had forbidden the sale of anything to the foreigners. We tried to come to terms, to treat with them, but in vain. The Chinese merchants themselves, who were more particularly obliged by our passport to assist us, coldly and politely avoided our entreaties. To infringe the orders of the lamas would have injured their trade; however, wishing to run with the hare and hunt with the hounds, they sent to our camp, with compliments and fine words, a small bag of rice, a piece of butter and a brick of tea. The butter was rancid and the tea musty, but the intention was the thing and we were grateful to them for it.

As it was now impossible to carry out Dutreuil de Rhins' original plan, we decided to make for Jyerkundo, a commercial centre of some importance and the residence of two interpreters of the Imperial Legate of Sining, who act as consular agents. We were assured that we should there be able to procure all that we needed. Now Jyerkundo is only fifteen days' march from Tachi Gompa and we had supplies left for a month. We were therefore able, instead of confining ourselves to following the road, to make important reconnoitring excursions to right and left in the basin of the Upper Mekong, so that the ill-will of the lamas, far from diminishing the scientific interest of our exploration, increased it and seemed to offer no inconvenience save that of prolonging our journey. We little thought that this was to lead us to the disaster of Tumbumdo.

Dutreuil de Rhins at first thought of going down the Za Chu. But the river, which is deep and contained between perpendicular rocks, leaves no practicable passage on its banks; and it is also impossible to follow it along the ridge of the mountains, which are too irregular and intersected by too precipitous a series of ravines. There is no way of going down the Za Chu, below Tachi Gompa, except in the winter, on the ice. Dutreuil de Rhins therefore resolved to take the road to Jyerkundo which leaves the valley of the river to cross its great affluent, the Purdong Chu, and runs to the source of the Zeh Chu, one of the principal tributaries of the Za Chu. By ascending the first of these two rivers to its origin, we would have completely solved the problem of the sources of the Mekong and fixed the northern boundary of its basin.

On the 23rd and 24th of April, we marched through a country of deep ravines and grassy hills, of which the ground had recently thawed and made a puddle of water at each step that we took. A chief lama of the Zachukkapa, coming from Lhasa, joined us and travelled a few leagues with us. He was more amiable than his fellow-countrymen whom we had seen at the foot of the Sok Gema La. He had that great ease of manner and that rather haughty courtesy which characterises the grandee in Tibet as elsewhere. He blamed the conduct of his colleagues at Tachi and begged us to give him the pleasure of our company as far as Zachukka. Our duty as explorers obliged us to decline this polite offer, by accepting which we would no doubt have averted a great misfortune, but swerved from our scientific task.

After climbing the Purdong Chalma La, at a height of 16,700 feet, we descended abruptly to the bank of the river, at 2,000 feet lower, by a steep slope, covered with stones, mud and melting snow. The Purdong Chu is an encased torrent, not wide, but deep, with troubled and tumultuous waters. It can be forded only in the morning, when it measures 53 feet across, 2½ feet deep and flows at the rate of 5 feet a second; at 6 o'clock in the evening, the average depth is increased by 18 inches, the width by 6 or 7 feet and the speed by over 3 feet, so that it sends down 1,890 cubic feet per second instead of 630. Leaving the bulk of the caravan and lightly equipped, we explored the upper basin of the river for five days, from the 26th to the

30th of April. The valleys are tightly compressed between high, steep and sometimes perpendicular mountains, whose bare, rocky summits seem to have been carved by some fanciful sculptor, so strange and complicated are their shapes. They are peopled with large bears, which the spring was beginning to bring out of their caves. We penetrated to the sources themselves, in the solitude of the eternal snows, at the foot of an insurmountable barrier.

Resuming our journey on the 2nd of May, we entered, the next morning, a gloomy and desolate gorge, through which we splashed pitifully until we reached the summit of the Zeh La, one of the highest passes of Eastern Tibet (17,120 feet). This is the source of the Zeh Chu. We descended into the valley by an almost perpendicular slope of 160 feet, upon which was heaped an enormous mass of snow. The astonished yaks hesitated for a moment; then, taking a sudden resolution, they flung themselves down like an avalanche, disappearing in the thickness of the snow, grunting and breathing loudly. We pitched the tent a little lower, on a spongy soil, which, after a few minutes' trampling, was changed into a swamp. We woke the next morning trembling with cold and with stiff legs. We hastened to descend the valley, which soon became less wild and less cold and which remained strikingly picturesque, with the red hue of the ground enlivened by the green of the grass on the less steep slopes and with its great masses of bare, vertical rocks, looking like mighty strongholds of 1,600 feet high and more. The necessity for taking observations and then the bad weather, the fog and the snow, kept us for some days in our camp of the 5th of May. We consoled ourselves for our inactivity by hunting wild geese, which abound in these parts.

On the 10th of May, we halted at the spot where the road leaves the valley of the Zeh Chu to make for the basin of the Yangtzekiang and for Jyerkundo. Since leaving the Zeh La, we were on the territory of the Raki Tibetans, who had shown themselves as unamiable as the Gejis and who had likewise refused to supply us with a guide. We had with us only one of those young *clerici vagantes* of whom I have already spoken. He was accompanying us for the sake of having the entrails of a sheep which the Moslems refused to touch, but he knew the country very little and his usefulness was on a level with his wages. Some Tibetans whose tents stood near ours came to see us. Dutreuil de Rhins made himself very pleasant, indulged all their childish curiosity, gave them a few trinkets which seemed to please them, flattered them with good words and chaffed them with merry jests to encourage them to show confidence. It was in vain. To all our requests for information they replied in a manner which was both circumspect and evasive; they shuffled, contradicted themselves, ate their words and, if we pressed them too hard, took refuge in an apparent stupidity, suddenly pretending to be unable to understand us and ignorant of the most elementary things.

"The chief of the Rakis is a great chief," we said.

"Oh, a great chief! He has many yaks and sheep, oh, ever so many!"

And their features combined with their accents to express ecstatic admiration.

"And does he live far from here?"

"Over there!"

And a vague movement of the head seemed to point to the east.

"How many days' march is it with yaks?"

"Oh, it's far, very far. It would take five or six days."

"If we could see him, we should give him some handsome presents and you would have your share of them, if you would take us there."

"We do not know the way; and then we have something to do here and we are obliged to go on to Jyerkundo."

"What is the name of the place where your chief lives?"

They hesitated, exchanged glances and ended by saying:

"Pam Jong."

"But you have just told us that your chief is five days' march from here and, from what you and others before you have told us, it is twelve days from here to Pam Jong."

"Just so. Twelve days going slowly and five days going fast, with a good horse."

"A moment ago, you showed us the east as the direction in which your chief lives, whereas Pam Jong is on the south. Besides, Pam Jong is the residence not of your special chief, but of the Nanchen Gyapo, who is the King of the Dungpa and the Gejis as well as of the Rakis."

"The foreign lord knows everything. The Nanchen Gyapo is the chief of the Rakis."

It was impossible to get anything out of them or to convince them of their inconsistencies. They opened wide, stupid eyes at every word of our interpreter and declared that he spoke the Lhasa dialect, which they did not understand. Dutreuil de Rhins broke off the conversation and sent for tea. He asked them if they liked sugar and, on their replying in the affirmative, gave them some lumps. But they had never seen white sugar and its colour frightened them. He ate a lump himself to reassure them; they persisted in refusing it: they had too much distrust of everything that came from Europe, too great a prejudice against the powerful witchcraft and subtle poisons of the foreigners, enemies of Buddha and tools of the evil one. This distrust and prejudice are, in a certain measure, natural among half-savage herdsmen, isolated in their remote retreats; but they are also carefully fostered and increased by the lamas, who are jealous of holding undivided sway over the minds of the people who feed them. The lamas, in fact, teach that we are the soldiers of the Spirit of Evil, who are to invade the whole earth, glorifying falsehood and sin, until the day when Buddha himself, alive in the person of the Dalai Lama, shall arise, gird on his sword and put his foot in the stirrup for the destruction of his enemies and the triumph of his religion. Although a certain number of the less narrow-minded lamas do not indulge in this trash, the anxious and intolerant ignorance of the remainder has only to spread the legends in order to bring about the most grievous consequences. Had they been left to themselves, these wild highlanders would have been more tractable, for they are not bad at bottom; but, when the fear of the despotic and mischief-making authorities is added to their own natural distrust, they become impossible to handle. Dutreuil de Rhins told me that he had found it easier to get on with the savages of Africa, who are given to sudden and capricious fits of violence, but who are less obstinate in their suspicions and less resolute in their ill-will.

We dispensed with the aid of our neighbours to go and explore the course of the Zeh Chu below where we were. After five hours' march, we were stopped by enormous perpendicular rocks, through which the river forces a narrow passage and flows swift and deep and encumbered with great blocks of stone. There was absolutely no means of scaling the mountain. Dutreuil de Rhins, in order to see if it was possible to follow the bed of the river itself, bravely urged his mount into the roaring water. The horse, which suddenly plunged in up to the neck and struck its nostrils against a rock, was nearly carried away with its rider. Fortunately, we escaped with the fright and we rode a long way into the mountains in order to try to circumvent the obstacle. We camped at the top of a pass, at exactly the height of Mont Blanc, on the way to Chamdo, and the wind overthrew our encampment. The next day, we succeeded in reaching the Zeh Chu again through the deep gorge of a torrent. There, an extraordinary spectacle awaited us. Above and below us ran the river, squeezed between two walls of rocks several hundred feet high and apparently quite vertical. It looked as though the mountain had been sawn open. We were obliged to throw our heads right back to see a thin strip of sky, on which the rocky ridges outlined their grey lace-work. This is continued for I know not how many miles with windings in every direction. There is not the smallest ledge on the walls to afford a foothold. We were obliged to turn back. On the brink of the torrent and close to the confluence, we saw, for the first time since leaving Cherchen, some real small trees, willows six or seven feet high. This was the lowest point that we had observed for a long time: 13,670 feet.

On the 14th of May, we returned to join the bulk of our caravan. It was cold and snow was falling thickly. Dutreuil de Rhins, wanting a cup of tea, went to a tent on the roadside to ask for fire. Just as the Russian, Razoumoff, was about to raise the door-curtain, a Tibetan rushed at us, flinging stones at us and shouting to us not to go in. As other men were approaching, threatening us and uttering cries which we did not understand, Dutreuil de Rhins, to intimidate them, ordered Razoumoff to fire a blank cartridge into the air. The Tibetans kept back and Razoumoff entered the tent and came out at once with some live embers which he had taken from the hearth. He told us that there was no one in the tent except a little bleating lamb and a sick man lying on the ground, groaning and giving out a fetid smell. We now knew why the Tibetans had tried to keep us away ; for it is one of their customs never to enter a tent which contains a sick man whose condition is beyond hope. Any violation of this rule never fails to bring great misfortunes and they are always careful to shut up with the dying man a young lamb, to which they ascribe the power of warding off bad luck. However, we withdrew to a couple of hundred paces and quietly made our tea and dried our feet at the fire, while the Tibetans watched us from a distance.

After rejoining our caravan, we resumed our journey to Jyerkundo. Going through very large and almost level valleys and over low hills, we passed by the Poroka La to the basin of the Yangtzekiang, or Blue River, which the Tibetans call the Do Chu and the Chinese the Tungtingho. The comparatively numerous inhabitants of these valleys are rich in herds. They employ these in order to carry on a lucrative trade with passing caravans by exchanging fresh yaks for tired and worn-out yaks at the rate of one to two or three, according to their condition. When the tired beasts have browsed placidly for a few weeks and recovered a fairly good appearance, they are passed on again at the same price to other caravans. At our request, they brought us five beasts, three of which appeared to have been recently acquired and were in a very bad state. Their owners, nevertheless, praised them to the skies, asking their pick of three of ours for each of them, and explained to us that they were making a very bad bargain, for our animals were sure to die within twenty-four hours. Upon our refusal, they went off and then came back, lit a fire, produced a stew-pan, tea and tsamba and, while lunching to protect themselves against the pricks of the stomach, reopened the negotiations. Hours elapsed, during which they displayed all the resources of their artful and crafty minds in order to induce us to buy chalk for cheese. They gave way regretfully and then ate their words, pretending to misunderstand our proposals and to confuse the yaks one with the other. At last, having exhausted their provision of tea, of tsamba, of craft and of patience, they were contented to take a small profit instead of a large one. We left our worst four beasts with them in exchange for their best two. The knaves, pretending to be hustled in the hurry of departure, tried to take away the good yaks and to leave us the bad ones; but they reckoned without their host and gained nothing by their trick but shame.

On the 21st of May, we made the ascent of the Serkiem La, behind which lies Jyerkundo. It is a mountain consisting of terraces rising one above the other. When the panting, perspiring traveller has climbed a very steep slope and rejoices at having finished his labours for the day, he perceives that he has another similar slope above his head. He moderates his joy, takes fresh courage and resumes the ascent. We camped on the fifth floor. We had just settled down, when we saw two Chinamen pass on foot carrying a few pieces of clothing on their backs. They were two merchants who had had their animals stolen by the Tibetans during the night and who were returning to Jyerkundo in this sorry state to lodge a complaint with the agent of the Imperial Legate. They cherished no illusions as to the platonic character of this step ; but they had to go back, in any case, to procure fresh beasts.

The next day, after climbing the sixth and last storey, we were descending by a winding path like a balcony contrived in the perpendicular side of the mountain and hung over a deep precipice, when suddenly, at a bend in the way, we saw before us, planted on the top of a rock, the square buildings of a monastery, with its red, blue and yellow-striped temple, and, lower down, clinging to the slope of the mountain, the white houses of a little Tibetan village. This was Jyerkundo. The bottom of the valley is at an altitude of only 12,460 feet: in a few hours we had gone down 3,600 feet.

Meanwhile, we had sent our interpreter on ahead to present our passport to the Chinese agent and to beg him to have a house placed at our disposal during the time which we would need to recruit our caravan. It was raining, a phenomenon which we had not observed for a whole year, and the worn felt of our tent was no longer water-tight. The road had led us to the bank of a modest river which flows to the foot of the village and beyond. Over it was built—an unwonted luxury—a shelving bridge, fitted with hand-rails, a sort of porch and a staircase that led up to it. It looked very picturesque; but the horses energetically refused to pass over this unknown machine and dashed into the water, which, for that matter, led to no inconvenience. Our interpreter was waiting for us on the other side, having accomplished his mission. The results were not brilliant. On his arrival, the inhabitants had thrown stones at him and replied to his questions by an obstinate silence or derisive laughter; and it was not without much beating about the bush that he at last succeeded in finding the abode of the *tungchen* Pu Lao Yeh. The latter received him politely and agreed to procure us a house; but the superior of the monastery interfered, forbade the population, upon pain of a fine and bastinado, to let us a house, to sell us anything whatsoever or even to speak to us and exacted that we should vacate the place within twenty-four hours. After fixing our camp at two hundred paces from the village, we set out forthwith to ask the tungchen for explanations. We found him waiting for us in his doorway, which was reached by three uneven and unhewn stone steps. Beyond stretched a narrow passage in which played a little monkey from the forests of Nyarong; on the right stood the wall of the next house and on the left a small barn, serving as a stable, with barely room for two horses. At the end of the passage, a staircase made of rough, knotty wood led to a sort of antechamber on the first floor, with doors opening upon one or two rooms and a larger one leading to the private chapel. We climbed up a stairway on the right consisting of a few steps ending in a very narrow and very dark apartment; turned to the right, feeling our way along the walls as we went; and, going down two steps, with our backs bent so as not to knock our heads against the door-frame, entered a damp room, badly lit by a small window with paper panes looking on the passage. A heavy smell of must, of fusty air and of rancid butter came from it. The floor was of beaten earth and uncarpeted. The furniture consisted of two or three chests and stools. At the back, according to the Chinese custom, stood a wide stone platform, covered with felt, with, in the middle, a low tea-table. This was the reception-room of the representative of His High Excellency the Imperial Legate.

Our host was very simply but tolerably cleanly clad in the Chinese fashion; only, his *makoatso* was of Tibetan red wool. In his hand, he held a string of Buddhist beads, which was intended, as was a little sacred statue conspicuously placed on a bracket, to give the people a lofty idea of his piety and to ingratiate himself with them. Later, it became clear to us that religion did not fill a great place in his heart and served him only as a political mask. His tall stature and large nose distinguished him from the every-day Chinese type. His gait was slow, as were his speech, his measured gestures and movements, his vague and somewhat dull glance; his thin lips hardly opened when he spoke. His person and his physiognomy gave the impression of a reflective, prudent, weak man, crafty by necessity rather than by character, who felt ill at ease in a part that laid upon him greater responsibilities than he had the personal authority to face, of a man who must suffer because his honorary and pecuniary position was not commensurate with the difficulty and delicacy of the task that devolved upon him. He told us how happy he was to receive guests so highly and strongly recommended by the imperial government. The mere sight of us would have sufficed to inspire him with the keenest sympathy for us and this feeling was still further increased by the fact that he knew the bonds of close friendship that united our two great countries, France and China (as a matter of fact, he knew nothing about them and said this at all hazards in order to curry favour with us). Moreover, he had already learnt to value the Europeans in the person of Mr. Rockhill, of whom he plumed himself upon being the intimate friend, for he had had the pleasure of travelling for several days in his company. He placed himself entirely at our disposal and assured us that we could rely upon his complete devotion. If it depended only on himself, all our desires would be immediately satisfied; but, to his great regret, he was but one man in the midst of ignorant and obstinate barbarians, who distrust the Europeans because they do not know them. The lama, their chief, was a greatly venerated and all-powerful personage, over whom he had no authority. It did not, alas, behove a modest tungchen to revoke orders which a chief lama had given!

Dutreuil de Rhins replied curtly that he was going to stay a fortnight, that he meant to have provisions and animals and that, if the chief lama had anything to say, he would go and pull his ears for him. Fright suddenly enlivened the Chinaman's ordinarily impassive face:

"No scenes, I entreat you, no scenes! You could not wish to place me, your friend, in a position of such cruel embarrassment. Reflect that I could not answer for what might happen. Really, I am not the master here; I cannot give a single order. The chief lama does as he pleases. He does not even receive me and does not condescend to come to see me.* How then could I interfere with him? When Mr. Rockhill came, they tried to harm him and he was obliged to go away secretly under cover of the night. Still, if you will be reasonable, there will be a way of coming to an understanding. There are some Chinese merchants here who are subject to my authority. They shall sell you flour, rice, tea, the material for a tent. A certain number of the natives owe me taxes and forced labour: I will call upon them to supply me with beasts and barley, which I will pass on to you. As you are here by command of the Emperor, on imperial territory, no one can object to your stay, provided you do not live in a house. On this last point we shall obtain no concession. I would with all my heart give up my own dwelling to you, were that possible; but I am only a tenant and, if I entertained you here, I should get the landlord into trouble."

Pu Lao Yeh thought himself a sly politician to lower himself in order to lower our pretensions, to take credit to himself for good-will, good offices, devotion towards us, while throwing the responsibility for all the difficulties on the native leaders. It was the same artifice as on the Nam Cho and, here and there, the thread with which the trick was patched up was visible to the naked eye. We talked of the general situation of the country. Pu Lao

* This was a lie. The chief lama, or rather the *shadso* of Jyerkundo comes to see the tungchen whenever there is any business to be discussed.

Yeh thought this a good opportunity to retrieve himself in our eyes. He explained to us that the Tibetans of this district were very turbulent and divided into a large number of small cantons of which the chiefs were independent of one another and none too obedient to the Nanchen Gyapo, their nominal prince. Thefts of cattle, raids, armed attacks were constantly and repeatedly taking place. He was incessantly obliged to interfere in order to allay quarrels, settle differences, prevent conflicts. Although this was an arduous task, the more so as he had no soldiers at his disposal, he performed it fairly successfully, thanks to the authority which he derived from his capacity as representative of the Imperial Legate, whose name was everywhere feared and respected; thanks also to the personal influence which he himself had been able to acquire with the native chiefs, who were very powerful personages in the eyes of the Tibetans, although very insignificant in those of the Chinese. They were grateful to him for the generally successful efforts which he made to preserve peace and recognised so thoroughly the useful part which he played that they had sent a petition to the Imperial Legate, begging him not to recall Pu Lao Yeh and promising to increase his salary. The worthy man spoke with conviction and with a self-complacent leisureliness, forgetting that he was contradicting himself. His vanity compromised his diplomacy. In fact, he now overpraised himself as greatly as he had slandered himself before. We soon had a first proof of this. One of our yaks was stolen during the night and the enquiry opened at our request by the tungchen was without result.

Pu Lao Yeh had a colleague of inferior rank to himself and of an entirely different character, called Li Lao Yeh. He was short, he had a small face hideously pitted with the small-pox, a small, flat nose, small, narrow and very bright eyes. His movements were brisk, his gait decided, his expression gay, his voice hoarse and loud. Pu was the diplomatist, Li the soldier. He was often with a sword in his belt and a horse between his legs. Whenever there was a bad business anywhere, at Pam Jong, in Zachukka, on the Nyam Cho, among the Gejis or elsewhere, he set off to reconcile the different interests, to calm the excited passions, to instil sense into the stupid and heart into the wise, negotiating, promising, threatening, always ready to draw his sword if need be. Prudent, nevertheless, he knew that soft words are better than hard blows. He came up to us with outstretched hands, pressed ours vigorously and cordially, made us sit down on a plain bench in an absolutely bare room and gave us buttered tea and indifferently savoury pipes:

"I have not much to offer you," he said, "but what I have I offer with all my heart. Here, you see, we are not in China; Tibet is a savage country, where ceremony is almost impossible. However, since you started on your travels you must have known worse times: it is not always pleasant, eh?" And, noisily laughing his hoarse laugh, showing his yellow teeth and slapping his thigh, "I know all about it," he continued, "I, who am always travelling over hill and dale. One has rough times in these horrible mountains and among this race of knaves, all obstinate as mules. I admire you for venturing to come from so far and for resisting so many difficulties. Look here! You are brave men and, if I go to Sining soon, I should like to go with you; I should feel safer."

To-day, this sentence has a sad and ironical sound.

Meanwhile, thanks to our two tungchens, we actively pushed on our preparations. We changed our gold at the rate of one pound of gold to fifteen of silver, a very bad exchange in itself, but excellent considering the country which we were in ; we chose fresh yaks ; our men repaired the pack-saddles ; tailors sewed up the new tent ; our barley was grilled in huge pots and the grilled grains were ground to make tsamba ; we got together white flour, rice, butter and tea. As for the sheep, we could not find as many as we wanted and they cost very dear, averaging four rupees apiece. Pu Lao Yeh advised us to procure them at Labung Gompa, where one of his friends was the superior. There was good pasture-land in the neighbourhood and sheep cost only from two and a-half to three rupees. We wanted but little more : a few tools, some brandy in case of sickness. I went to see the Chinese merchants who lived right in the middle of Jyerkundo and availed myself of the opportunity to see the place. Between our tent and the main village stood a few lonely houses, inhabited by poor creatures, wretchedly ill-clad and following some despised trade, such as that of the blacksmith. Their children brought us dried cow and horse-dung for fuel, in return for a slight payment. Two of them one day proposed that we should buy their squalid little persons for a few rupees :

" It would please mamma," they said.

A little path leads up from the river and is used by women who walk laboriously with their backs bent under a heavy barrel full of water : the bottom of the barrel rests on the small of the back and the top is fastened with ropes or straps which the woman holds in her hand. At the edge of the river, some men had fitted up a shooting-range, having us in view, perhaps. They were fairly good marksmen, so long as they had a rest for their guns and leisure for taking aim, and I noticed that their muskets did not carry straight beyond 130 to 160 yards. The entrance to the village is adorned with a very modest chorten and mani. Next comes a lane a little over 200 yards long and forming two very pronounced bends. It is so narrow that two horses are not always able to pass through it abreast and is lined with sullen walls pierced here and there with little embrasures which seem to distrust the passer-by. In all, Jyerkundo may perhaps contain eighty houses, sheltering five hundred inhabitants, including fifteen Mongols and twenty or thirty Chinese. The remainder of the canton numbers possibly as many more inhabitants, housed in some hundred tents and making a sum total of one thousand laymen. The monastery, which we were not allowed to approach, is famed for its wealth and contains at least three hundred lamas in permanent residence. The superior is a very great religious person, for he has several other convents under his authority, with about three thousand monks.

In the middle of the village, the little street widens out to form a tiny square, in which a few morose old men, in the company of some lean, snappish, mangy dogs, sit warming their aches in the sun and catching their fleas. The house occupied by the Chinese merchants stands in this square. I found five or six of them in a large, smoky room, seated on chests and stools and pulling at their hubble-bubbles. They were from Chensi and represented houses at Tasienlu. They exchange cottons, flour, tea, vinegar, brandy, tobacco, porcelain, copper and hardware for furs, yak and sheep-skins, musk, gold-dust, stag-horns, rhubarb and wool. They were fairly satisfied with their little trade:

"We sell all this very cheaply and it is worth less still," they said, showing me their wares, a collection of the very worst articles produced by the Middle Kingdom, "but it is good enough for these penniless barbarians. They have never seen anything better and they are quite contented. There are no Yangjens* here to disgust them with it. As we are alone, without

* Europeans.

competitors, we buy and sell pretty well at our own prices. Certainly, the Tibetans are greedy and bargain shamelessly; but at bottom they know nothing of trade. We profit by this and, although we are sometimes beaten, robbed and held to ransom by these rogues, we always come off to the good."

Their language was not quite so explicit as the above, but amounted to it; and it was fine to see the proud disdain with which they spoke of those coarse Tibetans, of that tribe which was there for them to exploit and fleece to their hearts' content.

While completing our preparations, we took care to collect information respecting the numerous roads which, starting from Mongolia, from Sining, from Lhabrang Gompa, from Songpanting, from Tasienlu, from Chamdo and Batang, from Lhasa, all meet at Jyerkundo and give a real strategic and commercial importance to this place of inconsiderable size. We ascertained that there were four roads leading to Sining for us to choose from. One goes through Tun, in Tsaidam Mongolia; the second passes between the great lakes of Kyaring Cho and Ngoring Cho; a third goes north-east, in a straight line, to the east of those lakes; and the fourth and last crosses the Yellow River three times, at Archung, the residence of the King of the Goloks,* Rircha Gompa and Kueiti. The first is, at the same time, the longest and the easiest: it is the only one followed by the Chinese officials and the merchants, the only one that is safe; but it had already been explored by several travellers, including, among others, Przevalsky and Mr. Rockhill. Although we had covered more than two hundred leagues since leaving Nagchukka, through unexplored country, rugged mountains and a still more rugged population, and although these travels, added to the long and irksome marches patiently pursued

* Golok means bad head; *cf.* Bashi-Bazouks.

during the past three years, might perhaps have entitled us to avoid new labours, new fatigues and new dangers, nevertheless Dutreuil de Rhins, whose ardour for knowledge made him indifferent to every difficulty and every danger, resolutely struck the too well-known Tsaidam road from his programme. He rejected the fourth road for opposite reasons. It has never been studied and is only partly marked on the maps, but Dutreuil de Rhins was uncertain whether the Ma Chu was everywhere fordable at this season, while he was sure that the Goloks would not allow us to pass without plundering us, even if they did not massacre us.

There remained the second and third roads. The former, which coincided for the greater part of the way with the direct road from Lhasa to Sining, brought us as near as possible to our original plan and allowed us to verify the supposition which makes the course of the Ma Chu pass through Lakes Kyaring and Ngoring. The other had the two-fold advantage of shortness and newness, for it was marked on none of the maps and was mentioned only in the vaguest manner in the Chinese geography. Moreover, nothing prevented us, if we thought fit, from pushing on to the lakes on our way. No doubt, this road went very close to the country of the Goloks, whose hordes often crossed it; but the other road was almost as dangerous. Besides, an explorer who has no faith in his star and dare not defy fate would do better to stay at home in his dressing-gown, with his feet on the fender. In a word, Dutreuil de Rhins decided in favour of the shortest road, which is sometimes followed by the special couriers of the Chinese administration, who, with two horses, cover the distance of over 500 miles between Jyerkundo and Sining in eighteen days.

CHAPTER IV

FROM JYERKUNDO TO SINING—DEATH OF DUTREUIL DE RHINS

The village of Tumbumdo—Our caravan is attacked and pillaged by Tibetans and Dutreuil de Rhins killed—A useless combat—The convent of Labug takes our part against the people of Tumbumdo —Intervention of the Chinese agent—I leave for Sining; a deserted and unexplored country; the Golok bandits; the Upper Yellow River—Our provisions fail—The Koko Nor; Tongkor—Sining; the Imperial Legate; our baggage is restored to us—The monastery of Skubum.

On the 1st of June 1894, we set out at the first gleam of dawn, happy to leave this inhospitable place, to know that the caravan which we were now leading would be our last and to feel the object so long dreamt-of and longed-for almost within reach of our hands. Pu Lao Yeh went with us for a very short way and took leave of us with his excuses at not being able to go further, as he was detained by a very urgent piece of business. None of his servants was free and the little monk who had come with us as far as Jyerkundo had deserted at the sight of the reception which his great brother had given us. We were therefore without a guide, a matter which gave Dutreuil de Rhins hardly any concern. This time he was wrong. The tracks of the road were lost in grassy bogs and he missed his way and went up a valley instead of crossing it. Being thus obliged to make a considerable circuit, he was unable to camp that same day at Tumbumdo and had to halt half-way. One of the ancients might have believed that a hostile god was contriving everything to lead him to the spot and time at which his evil destiny awaited him.

On the next day, our new caravan was greatly tried by the difficulty of the road, which climbed or descended steep slopes and passed through rocky ground and bogs in turns. Several of our yaks fell by the road. After seven hours' march, we were approaching Tumbumdo when rain began to fall, lightly at first and then extremely heavily. Our clothes were soon soaked through and Dutreuil de Rhins, who complained of acute pains in the shoulders, hurried on to find shelter in the village. On our arrival, we found all the doors closed and no one outside. In answer to our summons, two men appeared and told us that there was no room in the houses. As the valley was very narrow and the few places where the incline was not too steep seemed to be covered with crops, we asked them to show us a place where we could pitch our tent. They answered with careless insolence :

"Go down the valley; you'll find a place there."

We saw a walled enclosure surrounding a rather large space of empty ground with an unoccupied shed. It was a cattle-enclosure which was not being used at the time, as the herds had been sent to the pastures for the summer.

"Let us camp in that yard which you are not using," said Dutreuil de Rhins. "We will pay you."

"The owner is away," replied the owner himself, "and has taken the key with him."

"Nonsense!" retorted Dutreuil de Rhins, bluntly, losing patience. "I can't remain in the rain like this. Open that gate at once."

The man went away grumbling and called his daughter, who came with the key and took off the padlock. There was nothing inside except a little fuel:

"Leave that there," I said to the owner, "we shall want it. Here! Here are two rupees and, before we go, we will pay you for the use of the enclosure."

"Ah, you are people who know how to talk! If you want anything, just come and tell us: we will supply you."

And, in fact, a real zeal to serve us followed upon the ill-will shown at the start. They brought us water, straw, a lump of butter. A boy of about sixteen appointed himself our scullion and devoted himself fervently to his chance employment. The rain stopped and a few people came to see us. Dutreuil de Rhins produced the Tibetan letter which Pu Lao Yeh had given him and asked if anyone knew how to read. The young scullion offered his services and read the document to those standing around. It was a summarised translation of our Chinese passport, with a special and urgent recommendation, in the name of His Excellency the Imperial Legate, that they should not steal our horses, nor our yaks, nor anything that was ours.

"*Di tébo ré* (Very good, excellent as the thumb compared with the fingers)," said the Tibetans, raising their thumbs in the air to mark the liveliness of their approval.

All this smacked a little of hypocrisy and it would have been prudent not to linger. That same day, a *dorgha* came from Jyerkundo on behalf of Pu Lao Yeh. A dorgha is the name in Tibet, as in Turkestan and Mongolia, of a man who combines the duties of a policeman and a courier and who, in a general way, is the errand-porter and factotum of an official of any kind. This one, who was called Tiso, wore his hair shaved, for he was a Golok by birth. This ex-brigand and son of a brigand had settled down, had married a Taorongpa wife and, changing his trade with his country, had become a policeman in the Chinese service; but he was careful to keep his shaven head, a sign of kinship with the Ma Chu bandits which might be valuable on occasion. He squinted in a burlesque fashion, grinned and laughed incessantly, always wore a hurried and excited air, spoke quickly, fluently and noisily, was fond of giving advice when he was not asked for it and boasted readily. He told us that he had been charged by Pu Lao Yeh to assist us in making our purchases at Labug Gompa; that he had much influence in the country; that he was a particular friend of the chief lama's; that he felt a great sympathy for us; that he would serve us zealously and hoped that we should reward him with our customary generosity; that, if we started on the next day, he would have the pleasure of going with us; that for the moment he was very busy and begged for permission to leave us until the morrow. And he went off.

On the following day, having risen before daybreak, I was giving instructions to prepare for our departure, when Dutreuil de Rhins came out and, seeing the sky covered with black and lowering clouds, gave the order to remain. He told Razoumoff to occupy his day in making the men practise their shooting, which had been neglected during the journey. I myself made an excursion up the torrent on whose right bank Tumbumdo stands. This is the Deng Chu, a little affluent of the big river, the Do Chu, a glimpse of whose valley was seen from our encampment. I passed a village whose inhabitants kept fiercely aloof. The few people whom I was able to accost answered my questions in a curt, dry and evasive manner. When I returned, I had a vague and confused feeling that things might go badly. Just then, I saw Razoumoff, knowing that Dutreuil de Rhins could not see him, indulge in one of his ordinary eccentricities. He was showing off before some Tibetans, ostentatiously directing our men's drill and grotesquely mimicking their awkward movements. I put an end to this scene, which had the two-fold drawback of making the Tibetans think that perhaps our intentions were not strictly peaceful and of showing them that our men did not know how to handle their weapons.

The sky seemed to brighten a little and Dutreuil de Rhins spoke of breaking up camp in the afternoon. But he changed his mind:

"Bah!" he said. "Why risk wetting everything and spoiling everything for the sake of going three or four miles? It's not worth while."

For that matter, the rain soon began to come down and flooded us in our tent. However, Dutreuil de Rhins fixed the start for three o'clock on the next morning, whatever the weather might be.

We had just fallen asleep, when they came to tell us that two horses had disappeared. Shortly after nightfall, a heavy shower had driven our sentry to take shelter for a few minutes in the shed and, when he came out to go his rounds, the two animals were missing. I was able by the light of a lantern to follow tracks of horse-shoes, accompanied by the tracks of Tibetan boots, until where they were lost in the stones on the ground. The first tracks were those of our horses, for the Tibetan horses are never shod; and the others were certainly those of a native, for none of our men wore those boots. Besides, the tracks were all equally fresh and, as those of the Tibetans were always evenly beside those of our beasts, it was evident that the latter had been led away by the former. The theft was therefore duly established and there was no doubt but that it had been committed by a man acquainted with our habits who had taken his measures in consequence, possibly by the over-zealous scullion. Nevertheless, at peep of day, we sent two armed men on horseback, one of whom knew the language of the country, in search of the missing horses, knowing that they would be found if, against all probability, they had escaped of themselves, in spite of the care that had been taken overnight to fasten them. But, after many hours, the two men returned without having seen anything.

The natives, meanwhile, instead of coming to our camp as on the previous day, kept aloof and sneaked off with cunning speed so soon as they saw us go towards them. Those who allowed themselves to be taken by surprise were indifferent to the glamour of rupees and to soft words alike and, in a tone that seemed to reproach us with their theft, declared that they had no chief or that they did not know his house. This display of ill-will and insincerity confirmed Dutreuil de Rhins in his conviction that the villagers were the culprits and in his determination not to yield. He had good reasons for this. When he left Jyerkundo, he had no more horses than were absolutely indispensable and he had no money left with which to buy others. On the other hand, he feared that, if he did not insist upon obtaining justice, he would encourage the Tibetans to commit fresh thefts and would run the risk of losing all his animals. He consulted me and consulted Mohammed Isa, the interpreter, and we were all of the same opinion. An expedient must be found which would induce the population to emerge from their silence and the invisible authorities to show themselves and interfere. Dutreuil de Rhins thought that the best thing would be to seize two horses belonging to the Tibetans, not, as Mohammed Isa suggested, by way of restitution, but as a pledge, while declaring that we would restore them so soon as we should have come to an understanding with the authorities, whether these undertook to hunt for and recover our animals or took measures to prevent any similar act in the future. On the whole, however irritated he might be, his intentions were exceedingly moderate and he was so far from expecting a serious fight that he did not even order the few rounds of ammunition to be taken from the chests containing them.

The orders given in consequence were executed at daybreak the next morning, while we were preparing to start. Did the Tibetans grasp the meaning of our declaration? I cannot say; but the promptness with which they seized upon this opportunity to attack us seemed to me to show that they were waiting for it and that they had only been looking for a pretext, good or bad. A clamour arose, grew ever louder and soon filled the whole village. A formidable cry of "*Ki ho ho!*" rang through the valley and we saw a few men run in the direction of the monastery, which was hidden from us by a projecting portion of the mountain. The shadso, that is to say the lama charged with the temporal administration of the convent, is at the same time, as I learnt later, the chief of the whole canton of Tumbumdo, which numbers seven villages. Hardly had these men returned, when, as we were beginning to leave the enclosure, I heard a musket-shot and the sharp whizz of a bullet. It was a quarter-past four in the morning. Meanwhile, we formed our march according to our usual order: Dutreuil de Rhins in front, armed with his Winchester rifle; I bringing up the rear, armed only with my compass. The village is situated on an eminence in the angle formed by the confluence of the Deng Chu with the torrent which we had come down on our way from Jyerkundo. The road retreats a little, describing a small curve in order to cross this torrent and to pass along the side of the mountain on the right bank of the Deng Chu. The houses are similar to all those in Tibet, with thick walls, narrow embrasures and flat roofs with parapets.

At four paces from the enclosure which we had just left stood a regular donjon, square, very high and pierced with loop-holes, through which issued the barrels of fire-arms. The shots, rare at first, became more and more numerous. We abstained from replying, thinking that it was merely a threatening demonstration. Dutreuil de Rhins, who had taken up a post of observation behind one of those little stone walls, called *pagra*, which

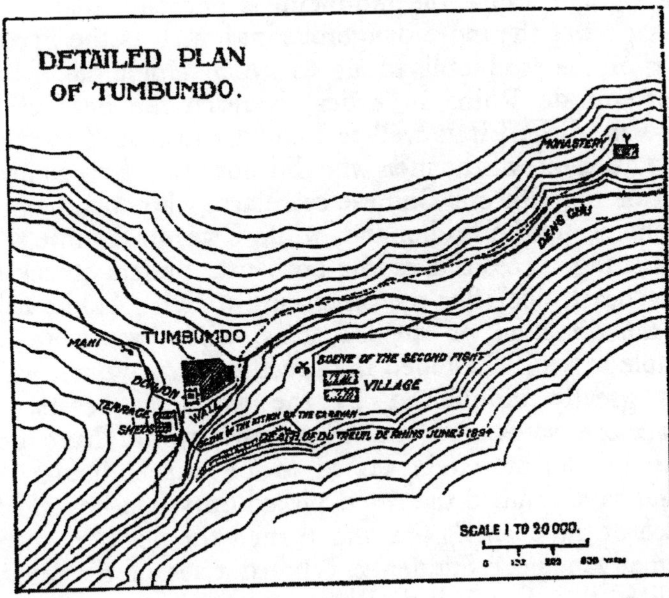

run through the Tibetan valleys in every direction, said, as I joined him :

"Those fellows don't shoot badly ; a bullet has just grazed my coat. The devil! One can't see as much as the tip of the nose of one of those blackguards!"

"We're in a bad position," I replied. "We shall all be killed, if we don't hurry and get to a more favourable place."

He made no reply, but he stood up and we crossed the torrent together. The firing of the Tibetans became very brisk and was regularly kept up and, several of our animals having been struck, we began to fire back, but sparingly, for we had only seventy-two rounds in all. We were then following the mountain-side on the right bank, exactly opposite the houses and within range of the Tibetan muskets, without being able to move off to the right, because the mountain is perpendicular. The passage was the more dangerous inasmuch as the narrowness of the road obliged us to go in single file. I left Dutreuil de Rhins in order to reach the head of the caravan, to lead it as well as I could and myself to take a rifle from one of the men who did not know how to use it. I came up with our Chinese secretary, who was dragging his horse by the bridle, and, while I was unfastening the rifle slung across the saddle-bow, two bullets struck the poor beast, one after the other, and it fell. While firing in the direction of the Tibetans, whom we were still unable to see, I hastened the speed of the caravan, which was greatly diminished by the wounded beasts. A few more steps and the worst part would have been passed; the mountain ceased to be perpendicular, we could have climbed the slope, placed ourselves beyond the reach of the enemy's fire and turned the position to our own advantage. Suddenly, I heard cries of distress; I realised that Dutreuil de Rhins was wounded. Turning round, I saw him at thirty paces from me, still on his feet and leaning on his rifle. I rushed to him and he fell swooning in my arms. He had had the fatal idea of stopping for a few moments to fire, instead of continuing his march; and this was doubly dangerous, for he was wearing his coat that day with the fur outside and made a good mark and, also, the Tibetans, who are very unskilful when shooting at the moving mark, are very straight shots at any fixed object. I laid the unhappy man on a piece of felt in a spot where the road widens slightly and behind a little wall a foot high, so that he was sheltered from the bullets. I sent Mohammed Isa to the Chinese agent of Jyerkundo, with instructions to bring him at once, and I released the horses which we had seized, hoping that the Tibetans would give us at least a moment's breathing-space, which I meant to employ to prepare a litter and carry off the wounded man as quickly as possible. The sight of the wound left me no hope; the bullet had penetrated far into the belly, a little below the left groin.

"Do not touch me," he murmured, "I am in too great pain. Make terms with the Tibetans and take back the caravan to the place we came from."

And he asked for a glass of water.

In obedience to his order, I sent the cook, who spoke the Tibetan language, to parley with the natives. I had no great confidence in the success of this negotiation, although the firing had ceased for the moment; but, in addition to the fact that Dutreuil de Rhins' instructions were formal, there was nothing better to do in the state in which he was. Meanwhile, I had a litter prepared with a camp-bed and I began to dress the wound in accordance with the medical instructions which I carried on me. The wounded man spoke a few more indistinct words as though dreaming:

"Bandits! . . . Labour lost. . . . Fine weather for starting! . . ."

As a matter of fact, the sky was clear and blue. Then the unhappy man, who was ready for the last start, threw up blood and fainted. His head and hands were colder than the stones of the road.

They had at last brought the camp-bed, but there were no sticks to carry it. They went to fetch some, while the other men, at about a hundred and fifty paces from me, close to a little hamlet whose inhabitants, fortunately, had taken no part in the combat, were struggling to collect the scattered yaks and to reload the fallen packages. The confusion, the lack of coolness in our men, the absence of their leaders delayed this business unduly. I was still alone with Dutreuil de Rhins, who did not regain consciousness and was growing colder and colder, when I saw, in the bottom of the valley, three Tibetans run along with bent backs, crouch behind a wall one hundred yards in front of me and fire at me over it. Their bullets flattened themselves on the metal-work of the medicine-chest against which I was leaning and I had not a single cartridge with which to reply. At the same time, my emissary returned at a run :

"They won't let us stay," he cried, "we must go at once!"

And he went out of his way to avoid me, fearing, no doubt, that I should stop him; but I did not think of trying to do so, the poor lad was so frightened and was running so fast. He had just seen death face to face and the sight had thrown his heart into his legs. I gave him my orders for the caravan, that they should at once bring me the shafts for the litter, that they should start the convoy with all speed and that the armed men should join me. To execute this commission would have taken two minutes. Unfortunately, he did not hurry to convey my orders. I saw him talking with a Tibetan of the neighbouring hamlet, who waved his hat and made great movements with his arms as though to interpose his mediation with the aggressors; and, meanwhile, no one came to my assistance and the firing was breaking out at several points at once. The enemies came nearer and increased in numbers. I shouted: no reply. I ran myself to fetch the man and the things that I needed to carry the wounded man.

"Be off quick," said the Tibetan with the hat, "and they will cease firing."

Thinking it dangerous to go down the road to the bottom of the valley, I gave orders to march at mid-slope, above the hamlet that had kept neutral; but the inhabitants categorically objected to this and I did not think it wise to add to the number of our enemies. While Razoumoff was taking the forty rounds of ammunition* from the cases in which they were packed, I tried to go back to Dutreuil de Rhins. It was too late: the Tibetans, ever more numerous, for they were constantly coming up from the other villages, had advanced and taken up their position so as to prevent me from retracing my steps. As always happens in such a case, I bitterly regretted not having followed my first idea, which was to make off at once, notwithstanding even the wishes of my chief, forgetting the reasons which had made me reject this idea and which, had I to do so over again, would still have obliged me to act as I did. At this moment, I was in a painful dilemma: was I to leave our chief to his now inevitable fate, but to save that by which he set store above all else, I mean the scientific results of his mission, the cause and fruit of long labours and long sufferings, or was I to sacrifice everything to an honourable, but useless attempt to snatch from the enemy's hand a man whose life had perhaps already left his body? I did not hesitate, however. I kept five armed men with me and, although their awkwardness, combined with the insignificant quantity of ammunition in our possession, forbade all hope of achieving a result of any kind, we opened fire on the Tibetans. The latter, cleverly hidden behind walls that served them at the same time as a rampart and a rest for their muskets, shot at us from three sides at a time. Our

* There were also a few rounds, fifty perhaps, for Dutreuil de Rhins' Winchester; but we were unable to find them.

animals fell one after the other, the bullets rained around us, flinging up fragments of stones in our faces or tearing our clothes. By singular good fortune, only two of our men were hit, one in the shoulder, the other in the hand. Then, when our supply of ammunition was exhausted, a troop of the enemy came to fire at us almost point-blank from behind.

"Stop firing," they cried, "and we will leave you alone."

Razoumoff, whose rifle was still loaded, took aim at the most prominent among them. But, in spite of my rage and of the pleasure which it would have given me to see one of those brigands bite the dust, I stopped Razoumoff, saying:

"If you kill him, Dutreuil de Rhins will pay for it."

It was then about three hours since the first shot had been fired. And the Tibetans rushed upon us, waving their swords, charging with their lances and uttering savage yells. My terrified men fled, excepting the interpreter, whom I held back by the tail of his coat. I tried to reason with the barbarians and to remind them of their promise; but they drove us along by main force, striking us with the flats of their swords and the shafts of their lances and shouting:

"*Song, song!* (Go, go!)"

A lama on horseback, in full dress, apparently a stranger to the canton, came riding by. He wore an air of solemn good-nature. I begged him to interfere and he replied, with hesitating gravity:

"No one shall be hurt."

And he did, in fact, make some timid efforts to allay the wrath that had been stirred up. It was in vain. My interpreter, whom I had had the greatest difficulty in holding back until then, took to flight and I had to yield to force. I retired slowly, with the lances in my back, amid the furious shouting of the Tibetans, who were exasperated by my slowness. When they were not pushing me with the shafts of their lances, they fired at me at ten paces, deafening my ears with the noise of the reports and the whistling of the bullets. I was now convinced that my last hour had come and that they were sparing me for a moment only to make me taste the relish of death the better. However, I walked with a calmness which, although artificial and studied at first, gradually became natural and easy to me. Suddenly, I heard a shout of "*Ching, ching!* (Stop, stop!)" I turned round and saw two muskets pointed at me and fired at the same moment. I stood firm and they flung themselves upon me, rifled my pockets, robbed me of my watch, the only object of any value that I then had, and began their former game once more.

Shortly after, still driven on by the yelling crowd of Tibetans, I came up with one of our men, who had sat down behind a projecting rock. He was wounded in the hand and the sight of his own blood had deprived him even of the courage to run away. When he saw the Tibetans, he began to tremble and cry and hurriedly got rid of a carving-knife which he was carrying in his belt. Taking him by the arm, I shook him violently:

"This is not the time to cry," I said and made him take back his knife.

The Tibetans seemed curiously astonished at this scene; their shouts and threats ceased. I thought that I might profit by this and, laying my hand familiarly on the shoulder of the boldest:

"Let us go that way," I said, pointing to the top of the valley.

Taken aback for a moment, he soon recovered his assurance and, whirling his sword, he let fly with all his might at my head. Fortunately, I was able to ward off the blow with my left arm. At the same time, the others once more began to shout, to strike me, to push me, to fire off their muskets and again forced me to go down along the torrent. As I passed at the foot of a big village, perched on the side of the mountain, the inhabitants, from their roofs, flung huge lumps of stone at me, which might well have done for me. Then the convent trumpet sounded, the firing ceased, my escort stopped and the children came and threw stones at me with their slings. I had reached the boundary of the canton of Tumbumdo, on the banks of the Do Chu.

A great silence reigned. My power of will, until then violently strained, so as not to show weakness in the eyes of the enemy, now relaxed for a moment. The murmur of the deep waters of the stream seemed to call to me and to claim that dreary life which had remained faithful to me despite myself. Of what use was that life to me? Had I not lost all that made it precious to me? Was I not alone, stripped of every resource, surrounded by inexorable enemies, without anyone whom I could trust? And, if men's hatred spared me, had I not vast deserts to pass through, where cold, hunger and the wolves awaited me? And, yet, had I gone through so much to abandon all in the despair of the moment? Was there nothing more to be attempted and must I cast off my burden because it seemed to me too heavy? What had all this hard journey been but one long lesson in patience? Had I not there learnt that there are no clouds so thick but the sun dispels them, no night so dark but retires before the dawn? Come, then! Let us take up our burden again: a day will come when our shoulders shall be relieved! Besides, if the Tibetans had not killed me when this would have been so easy, was it not a sign that they were not implacable, that there would be a means of saving what was not already irreparably lost? As though to force myself to hope and to show my scorn for hostile fortune, I took my compass from my pocket and began to take my bearings as I went up the narrow valley, deeply set between high mountains with rounded tops. I was resolved to look for the dorgha whom we had seen two days before and who could, perhaps, help me. I had taken a few steps when I met a man on horseback who greeted me with a kindly air. This simple greeting gave me more pleasure than I can tell. It was like that vague quiver in the air which is the forerunner of the awaited dawn.

After walking less than two miles, I found four of my men, who, no longer hearing the sound of firing, had sat down by the roadside, hoping that I would come that way, if I were still alive. It was exactly half-past nine and it was more than two hours since I had left the battle-field at about four miles' distance. I passed quickly in front of several villages and, a couple of leagues further, I came to the hut of the ferry-man, for the Do Chu, which is eight or nine yards deep and 130 to 160 yards wide, is not fordable. It is crossed by means of little boats, each of which is made of two undressed yak-hides sewn together. The ferry-man told us that Tiso, the dorgha, was on the other side of the river; and, when we asked him to take us across, he began by saying that he would want much money for that, in this way expressing his opinion, which, for that matter, was very well founded, that people whose appearance was so little in their favour could not be rich enough to pay him for his trouble.

"You have received orders concerning us," I said. "Our caravan has remained behind because the beasts are tired. I have gone on ahead myself to have the flour which we need got ready at Labug Gompa. When the caravan comes, you will be paid."

The good man looked at me from head to foot with a suspicious eye:

"So you," he said, in a voice that betrayed his surprise and his doubts, "are the man about whom Pu Lao Yeh sent me his instructions?"

"Just so, but hurry!" I replied, adding a few imaginary details to reassure him completely.

Few things in my life have been so painful to me as this little comedy, which was, unhappily, indispensable. At last, the ferryman made up his mind, fetched two of his boats, which were drying under a shed, and carried us to the opposite bank.

Hardly had I set foot on land, when I met the man whom I was in search of. I told him our terrible adventure. He showed some compassion, much alarm and more embarrassment:

"However," he said, "all is not lost. The shadso of Labug Gompa, which is near here, is a great friend of Pu Lao Yeh's and you can rely on him. I will go to see him presently and we will discuss what measures to take. Meanwhile, come to my house, where you will find food and shelter, and I will at once send a messenger to Tumbumdo. He will arrive there to-night and will perhaps get something out of those people."

I accordingly spent the night at Tiso's house, which was in a village at two leagues from the Do Chu, within the jurisdiction of Labug Gompa.

On the next morning, the 6th of June, I received a visit from a tall, thin old man, with long grey hair and regular features of the Tibetan type. He was the diplomatic agent of the shadso of Labug, who hardly ever leaves his convent himself and who, above all, may not compromise himself by seeing non-Buddhist strangers. He was accompanied by a lama and by servants bringing meat, tsamba, tea and butter. This old Nestor, whose grave, gentle expression and simple, easy ways prejudiced me in his favour, made me a regular speech, long and elegant and full of dignity and cordiality. He told me that his chief had sent him to bid me welcome and to assure me of his sympathy and concern in the great misfortune that had befallen me. The shadso had been to Peking and had heard speak of France as a great and noble country ; he would see to it that her representatives were well treated on the territory under his jurisdiction and would do what he could to prevail on the people of Tumbumdo to restore the baggage and animals of our mission, to respect the life of Dutreuil de Rhins, or, if he were already dead, at least to give up his mortal remains. In the meantime, he would take care to provide for my wants and begged me to stay quietly in the house where I was, for fear of complicating what was already a very difficult matter. Having finished his speech, the old man set out at once, with the dorgha, for Tumbumdo.

They returned in the afternoon, in the company of the tungchen Li Lao Yeh, who, at Mohammed Isa's entreaties, had gone to Tumbumdo on the evening of the 5th of June. He had been very badly received by the population, who had threatened him with death and obstinately refused to listen to reason. He had seen our Chinese secretary, whom he had left at the village with Mohammed Isa ; but he had heard nothing of Dutreuil de Rhins or myself. Only, it was rumoured that I was seriously wounded and, as he found no trace of me when going up the Do Chu, he had already given me up for lost, when he met the men sent from Labug Gompa, who reassured him as to my fate, whereupon he hurried to come to see me. He averred that he and Pu Lao Yeh would make every effort to obtain satisfaction, that they would convoke the general assembly of the twenty-five Taorongpa chiefs and persuade them to intervene with the people of Tumbumdo to force them to give way ; he exhorted me to have patience and eagerly invited me not to go out nor to take any personal steps, which would be dangerous to myself and prejudicial to the interests which I wished to defend, or, at the very least, useless.

On the 7th, they brought me provisions from the gompa, but no news. About mid-day, as, in the sadness and impatience induced by my forced inactivity, I was pacing up and down the terrace of the house, which overlooked the valley, and examining the too-restricted horizon, I suddenly perceived something red moving on the bank of the river. That something could be only a man's clothing and the red was too bright for it to belong to a native. I sent to see and they brought me Parpai and Tokhta Akhun. These two men had displayed a certain firmness in the combat of Tumbumdo. Parpai had bravely fixed his bayonet at the end of his rifle and had stuck to his post so long as the ammunition lasted and the number of our aggressors did not outflank us. Tokhta Akhun had even distinguished himself by going under the noses of the Tibetans to fetch a rifle which had been abandoned by its owner; but he was stopped by a group of the enemy and prevented from rejoining us. Both of them, instead of going down the road, had lost themselves in the mountains, where they met each other and chance had led them to the valley of the La Chu. Their situation was a critical one: they had no supplies except two pounds of tsamba, they had lost the hope of ever finding me, they did not know the roads and they knew that long days' marching through hostile or desert country separated them from the nearest places where they might obtain some help. However, seeing that the sun had reached its highest point, they had sat down beside the clear stream with real eastern apathy, had taken out their bag of flour and set about lunching. In reply to my questions, they said that they had observed absolutely nothing: as regards Dutreuil de Rhins, they had neither seen nor heard anything and they did not know what had become of the man who was still missing, ex-captain Ahmed.

The next day was the first day of the fair at Labug Gompa: the valley was alive with numerous gay wayfarers in their holiday clothes; but none of them was of any use to me. On the 9th, tired of champing the bit, I resolved to make an attempt to go in search of news and, if possible, to return to Tumbumdo. This step was an unreasonable one, but I felt that I must ascertain for myself whether it were impossible and try to find out what they were keeping from me. The boatman on the Do Chu refused to ferry us across and, on the other side, the road was guarded by armed horsemen, so that we had to go back to our lodging, or rather our prison. On the 10th, by means of promises which happier circumstances enabled me to keep, I persuaded a young Tibetan who came to see us from time to time to go to Tumbumdo and try to discover what was happening. He returned at five o'clock in the evening and told me that Li Lao Yeh had been obliged to leave Jyerkundo to settle a conflict that had broken out between the people of Surmang and those of Lhasa and that two of our men were kept prisoners at Tumbumdo; but he had seen or heard nothing on the subject of Dutreuil de Rhins. On the next morning, the Do Chu ferryman charitably came to warn me that fighting men had been posted on the banks of the stream to assassinate me if I appeared; but, about mid-day, I received better news: my host, the dorgha, who had gone, on the 7th, to the convent at Labug with a message from me to the shadso, at last returned, explaining that his delay, which was a long one, seeing that we were not two miles from the monastery, was due to the fact that he had gone to meet a powerful lama of the neighbouring district of Zachukka, who had now arrived at Labug Gompa.

This lama, whose name was Yapsang Tenam, was the chief of the convent of Tubchi and, as he was a native of the country around the Koko Nor, he was commonly called "the Chinese." The dorgha represented him to me as being a dreaded justiciary, endowed with a great spirit of enterprise and having a large number of valiant men-at-arms under his command; he told me, moreover, that this lama had appeared to him to be favourably disposed towards the cause of our mission. I therefore sent him back to this singular monk, captain of mercenaries and justiciary, to beg him to interfere and to explain to him that I would recognise his services in a more substantial manner than by mere thanks. I could not have a better go-between in this negotiation than the dorgha Tiso; for not only had he shown great readiness to serve us and had his loyalty been guaranteed by all those who had interested themselves in us before or after our misfortune, but also the fact that he was a Golok allowed him better than any other to influence the Zachukkapa, who were kinsmen and friends of the Goloks and who shared with them many characteristics that distinguish them from the other Tibetans. Yapsang Tenam forthwith dispatched a haughty and threatening letter to the chief of the Tumbumdo convent, swearing that, if justice were not promptly done, he would cross the river at the head of his men-at-arms. At the same time, he let me know that he could not interfere more actively at the moment, because the omens were not favourable and the moon was unpromising. I then sent the dorgha to Jyerkundo, to see Pu Lao Yeh and tell him how astonished I was not to have heard from him for so long; that I did not doubt but that he had busied himself in this grave matter with the zeal which both his duty and his own interest prescribed; that, nevertheless, it was strange that he should delay in having Dutreuil de

Rhins conveyed to me, a concession which it ought not to have been difficult for him to obtain from the people of Tumbumdo, since a refusal on their part would serve them not at all and would only aggravate their crime and the punishment that awaited them; that, if he were unable to obtain the restitution of the baggage and animals of the mission, he ought at least to insist upon the immediate restitution of the papers and instruments, as well as the release of those of our men who were still detained at Tumbumdo: this was of urgent importance to us, whereas the people of Tumbumdo could not derive any benefit from keeping either the one or the other.

Tiso set out in the morning and, that same evening, two dorghas arrived from Pu Lao Yeh, accompanied by our Chinese secretary, Mohammed Isa and Ahmed. I had no great praise to bestow upon any one of these three men. Mohammed Isa had displayed a ridiculous fear at the beginning of the fight: true, he had acquitted himself very well of the mission upon which I had sent him to the tungchen of Jyerkundo, but he had done wrong in not returning to me at once. He made the excuse that he had been forcibly detained at Tumbumdo, in which case it was very strange that they should have left him his rifle, his cartridges, his revolver, his sword-bayonet and his horse and that they should have allowed him, on his own confession, to return on the third day to Jyerkundo, where he remained for twice twenty-four hours without letting me hear from him. The probability is that, despairing of my luck, he intended to abandon me, but that the tungchen refused to look upon the matter in his light and forced him to rejoin me. The Chinese secretary had disappeared so soon as Dutreuil de Rhins was wounded and had left me alone at the very moment when he would have been particularly useful to me in helping to attend to our leader and perhaps in carrying him away, while the other men were engaged in collecting the scattered caravan. He hid himself somewhere or other and, when the fighting was over, showed himself to the Tibetans, who, of course, respected his Chinese nationality and even showed him hospitality. As for the former captain of Yakub Beg, he had prudently concealed himself in the midst of the yaks, which had served him as a rampart, and, when the Tibetans carried off the animals, they carried off the captain at the same time, without, however, doing him the least harm.

Mohammed Isa told me that, when I was driven out, the Tibetans at once hired two wretched vagrants to take up Dutreuil de Rhins, bind his hands and feet and fling him into the waters of the Do Chu. He added that, at that moment, he still gave some signs of life; but this last detail was not confirmed by the dorghas of Pu Lao Yeh, whose information was official and whose evidence agreed in all other respects with that of Mohammed Isa. Although I did, at first, accept the version of out interpreter, I am inclined to think, on reflection, that it should be received with caution, for not only was Mohammed Isa always greatly given to exaggeration, but it is not likely that Dutreuil de Rhins, who was already cold when I was obliged to leave him, can have survived for several hours more. The accounts which were then given me by our secretary, our interpreter and the dorghas corroborated what I had already heard elsewhere and proved evidently that the aggressors had acted only upon the instructions received from their chief, the superior of the convent, who commanded them to kill the Europeans and to spare the others and who then, when Dutreuil de Rhins had fallen, ordered them to seize upon him, the baggage and the animals, but to kill no one so soon as we were disabled and disarmed. This quite explained the Tibetans' conduct, which at first seemed very strange to me. Dutreuil de Rhins was considered and treated as alone responsible for an act which was a mere attempt at pressure to obtain the justice denied us, but which it had pleased our aggressors to qualify as an act of brigandage in order to palliate their own.

In certain conventicles that had taken place since among the Tibetans, there had, according to Mohammed Isa's account, which the others neither denied nor confirmed, been a strongly-urged question of preventing me from reaching China and of doing away with me as an inconvenient witness. It would have been simpler for our enemies to do away with me when they showed me the polite attention of accompanying me for more than an hour to the river; but they had not thought of everything and it now occurred to them that my complaints were very annoying and that my depositions at Sining would be unfavourable to them, whereas those of our servants, who were almost all Chinamen and people of low condition, could easily be influenced in such a way as to throw the fault upon the Europeans. However, I troubled but little about what I heard in this connection, for it could be only a rumour spread with a view to intimidating me and I was firmly resolved not to yield by a line's breadth to any pressure of this kind. Lastly, I was told that all that could be found of our baggage had been collected at the instance of the Chinese agents and placed under seal by the authorities of Tumbumdo, who, however, persisted in refusing to restore any part of it. The negotiations, moreover, had become more difficult because Pu Lao Yeh was alone at Jyerkundo: his colleague, Li, had had to go to the Tao La to settle the difference to which I have referred above, a difference caused by the Tibetans, subject to Lhasa, who had gone in search of salt in the direction of Surmang and who laid claim to the right to revive an old custom by which the population, who were once themselves subject to Lhasa, were obliged to furnish a thousand yaks for the carriage of the salt from their territory to that of the Debajong. All this I learnt on the 12th of June. I at once made the Chinese secretary write to the tungchen all that I had instructed the dorgha Tiso, in the morning, to tell him in connection with the baggage and papers and I also directed him to order a search to be made for the body of Dutreuil de Rhins, so that we might give it a befitting burial. Alas, it was a very useless recommendation : the river had long since carried off the sad remains in its deep waters, confined between perpendicular banks, and he who had been snatched from the honour due to him in life was to be deprived also of honour in death.

The night that followed was the most anxious and the longest of all. I tried in vain to sleep : the rain, which had not ceased pouring in torrents during the day, now soaked through the ceiling of the narrow and damp lodging that served as my bed-chamber. Wrapped in a dirty blanket, worn and full of holes, which I owed to the charity of my hosts, I was soon wet through and lay shivering on my straw mattress, which swarmed with vermin. I moved it to each corner of my cell in succession, but to no purpose, for the rain entered everywhere. I cursed with all my heart the lama who, on the preceding day, clad in the sacred emblems of his office, had gone to pray on the river's bank and to fling pellets of flour and butter into the water, in order, by this propitiatory sacrifice, to prevail upon the genius of the waves to send down the rain which was wanted for the barley-crops. I remained thus almost all the night, sitting with my blanket over my head, thinking of those terrible things which had happened beyond recall, of that shipwreck in sight of port, of that death on the eve of happy days. A brutal certainty had suddenly destroyed the vague hope which I had insisted on preserving against all likelihood. The loss of a chief whose noble and courtly soul had not belied its kindness to me during the whole course of three and a half years of life shared in common and had changed the bonds of discipline, which united me to him, into the sweeter and surer links of friendship; my sorrowful powerlessness to help and relieve him in his distress ; the bitterness of the defeat inflicted by barbarians devoid of all generosity; the fruits of long labours, which had ripened only by dint of care and pain, spoiled by an hour's storm ; the absolute destitution which condemned me to rely upon the charity of strangers, wavering between their prejudices and their humanity, between the fear of the present and the fear of the future; the sense of my solitude, of my subjection, of the inanity of my efforts deprived of any point of support: all these miseries, added and multiplied together, gave me the impression that I was sinking into a dark and silent depth from which there is no returning. Two things, however, strengthened me and inspired me with the energy to fight against despair: on the one hand, the consciousness that, in these painful circumstances, I had done nothing which I did not consider useful to the interests of our chief and of our mission, nothing that was inconsistent with our dignity as men and Europeans, and that I had abandoned nothing to the fear of approaching peril, but only to material necessity ; and, on the other hand, the feeling that there still lay upon me great duties which, whatever measure of success I might achieve, demanded all my zeal and all my strength.

Nothing happened during the next two days and I did my best not to give way to the evil suggestions of impatience, which, in Asia, is the most serious and the most dangerous of faults. On the 15th, the dorgha Tiso returned with the tungchen's reply. The tungchen regretted that he had not yet been able to do anything because, in the assembly of the twenty-five Taorongpa chiefs which he had summoned, the majority were against us and some of them used violent and threatening language; he asked me nevertheless to have confidence in him, assuring me that he would do all that he could to appease their minds and to satisfy my demands; he hoped to come to see me to put before me the results of his efforts and to procure for me the means of reaching Sining; in the meantime, he was writing to the shadso of Labug to supply me with the money and the provisions necessary for my support and that of my men.

What Pu Lao Yeh told me of the hostility shown by the majority of the assembly did not astonish me, for not only is the canton of Tumbumdo one of the most important in the district, but, above all, its monastery belongs to the rule of Saskya, as does the Jyerkundo monastery, on which it depends* and of which the chief lama is the most influential and powerful individual in the country. The latter, therefore, from a spirit of comradeship, supported his colleague and subordinate with all the weight of his high authority and carried with him all the convents of the Saskyapa, which seems to predominate in this part of Tibet. On the other hand, the monastery of Labug, which belonged to the reformed order of the Gelupa, of whom the Dalai Lama is the chief, had taken our part, because it

* To employ a comparison which the reader will easily understand, let us say that the convent at Tumbumdo is the residence of an abbot, that at Jyerkundo of a provincial and that the general of the order resides at Saskya Gompa. In the same way, the superior of Labug is a provincial of the Gelupa order and it might well be that the lama of Tubchi was a mere abbot who was more powerful temporally than his hierarchical superior, the provincial of Labug.

did not consider itself bound to make common cause *per fas et nefas* with the monks of another rule and because the Gelupa, without being less fanatical than the other lamas (the reader will remember the reception which we met with at Tachi Gompa), are more devoted to the Chinese government, which gives them its special protection.

Here is a fact which will throw more light than any other upon the real sentiments of the lamas of the reformed rule. A very numerous caravan, sent to Tasienlu by the Panchen Rinpocheh, the second in dignity of the Gelupa lamas, had come to Jyerkundo about the beginning of the month. It was led by a religious of high rank whom we had often seen on our road and who had treated us with politeness, but reserve. Shortly after the disaster to our mission, he sent me a message to express his regrets at the misfortune of which we had been the victims and to assure me that, if a similar thing had happened to us within the jurisdiction of Lhasa, we should only have had ourselves to blame, but that, in a country where we had the right to travel by virtue of a passport from the Emperor, the case was different and that he, for his part, disapproved in the highest degree of the action of the people of Tumbumdo. It will be seen that his reservation as regarded the Lhasa jurisdiction was a pretty strong one and that his friendliness towards us depended solely upon the orders of the Chinese government.

On the 16th, the shadso of Labug sent me a little money and some provisions and informed me that he had had a conference with the lama of Tubchi touching the best way of assisting me and of making the people of Tumbumdo disgorge and that they would act with energy so soon as the circumstances and the almanac should be propitious.

On the same day, I tried to distract my thoughts by going to see an old *spiyu*, or fastness, whose ruins rose picturesquely on a tall rock on the other side of the valley, some 400 yards from where we were. It was difficult of approach because of the steepness of the slope and, when I had reached the top, I saw that the peak on which the castle was built was separated from the mountains on the left bank of the La Chu by a very deep and unsurmountable precipice, so that it was isolated on every side. It was a very strong position in the absence of cannon; and the very thick pieces of wall, ten yards high, which remained and a few cells, overlooking the valley through narrow embrasures, that still stood intact would have afforded a solid defence in case of need. When I returned from this excursion, I was given to understand, with much circumlocution, that I was not to go out, or they would be responsible for nothing.

Confined to my gaol, I can think of nothing better to pass the time than to describe it in detail, as the negotiations are stopped for the moment. Imagine a square court-yard of about 30 feet, surrounded by a plain wall on one side and by galleries or sheds on the three others. Under two of those sheds are a dung-heap and Dutreuil de Rhins' white horse, which was given him by the imperial vice-legate and brought back by Mohammed Isa. The third shed serves us as a drawing-room, dining-room and kitchen. It is furnished with two stones, which do duty for a stove, a stew-pan and a wooden dish. In a corner is a little dark hole with a litter in it: this is my bed-room; in the opposite corner, a staircase leads down to the street and up to the terrace that runs above the galleries. The front looks over the narrow little rough and winding street of the village, which leans against the mountain; on the left, a yard similar to the first shelters, at night, a she-goat and its kid ; the back gives a view of the valley, which is four hundred yards wide, stony, almost barren, between fairly high and gloomy mountains, enlivened, however, by a few poor barley-fields and the clear and pretty current of the La Chu ; the terrace to the right rests upon the main building, the walls of which are constructed of flat, unhewn stones. The first floor consists of a barn full of straw which opens on to the terrace ; above it are the rooms of our host's family. Their large window is fitted with shutters of wood painted red and sometimes shows the little old wrinkled head of the grandmamma, a very good person for a daughter and sister of brigands. As for her daughter-in-law, who is one of the beauties of the country, I should be pleased to introduce her to you, but she left the house, with her children, a few days before our arrival. The entrance to the apartments of the master of the house is on the street and is reached by a wooden ladder, which leads to a square hall, around which the different rooms are distributed. The reception-room is very small and is furnished with a platform covered with a piece of felt and a tea-table ; the walls are adorned with somewhat clumsy, faded and peeling pictures representing flowers, animals, human figures.

But let us return to the court-yard : it was a reduction of the "Court of Miracles," peopled as it was by half a score of beggars in rags and tatters, the staff of a mission of the French government, employing its enforced leisure as best it might. Razoumoff chattered incessantly ; Parpai mended his clothes ; Tokhta rubbed his bad leg ; the cook, whose work had never been intricate, had a holiday, for, by the munificence of the lamas, we had some solid quarters of beef which had been preserved since the last autumn and which was eaten raw, in thongs, in the Tibetan manner : he employed this holiday in hunting his parasites ; the Chinese secretary, an eminently serious man who had never burst into song in his life, now, seated on the edge of the terrace, warbled a tune that would have served to bury the devil to ; Mohammed Isa sat squatting in a corner, trembling with fear and dressed in a filthy, worn-out coat of black cloth, under pretence of mourning, but I soon discovered that it was rather from a fear of showing his European clothes and I peremptorily made him doff his disguise and bring out his English coatee adorned with brass buttons, like those worn by the soldiers in India : nevertheless, he was perhaps right not to dare to display those buttons, for they are usually seen on sturdier breasts.

The days came, the days went, slow and dreary, void of occupation, filled with preoccupation. But there is nothing so sad but has its comical side. The interlude was supplied by our friend the shadso of Labug : one day, he sent his lay and clerical delegates to tell us that in the treasure of the convent there was a European machine which they did not know the use of, but which they supposed to be intended for a mincing-machine ; it was out of order and the shadso sent word to me that, if I would repair it, I should have a great claim on his gratitude. I replied that I had an ingenious and skilful Russian artisan in my service, who would perhaps be able to do what was necessary. They brought us the mysterious machine, which proved to be a sewing-machine that had come from Russia. In addition, as he did not doubt but that we were prepared also to mend anything that Europeans know how to manufacture, the shadso sent us several objects, instruments or arms out of use: an American revolver and cuckoo-clock, a Russian fowling-piece, an English telescope, a French watch, two Swiss musical-boxes. Our court-yard was thus transformed into a workshop and a European museum, which attracted all the people of the village, men, women and children. The sewing-machine puzzled the idlers, the musical-boxes amused them, the telescope, with which they saw nothing, but by means of which they were persuaded that European eyes pierced through the thickest mountains, filled them with superstitious respect; as for the cuckoo-clock, no sooner was it in going order than it became a popular favourite. It achieved the greater success inasmuch as the hands completed the circuit of the face in fifteen minutes, which enabled the cuckoo to give a larger number of performances, to the great joy of the spectators. It was curious to see these Tibetans, but lately so hostile and infuriated, now so respectful, merry, good-humoured, smiling amicably to the unhappy foreigners who had just been fighting against their brothers. I reflected in how small a measure the ill-will which we had since long encountered among these people was due to their natural wickedness, but much rather to the policy of their lords and masters, a policy of fear and sectarian tyranny, which keeps up in every class of society a spirit of mutual spying and of universal distrust, destructive of all pity and justice.

From the 16th to the 20th of June, matters made no perceptible progress, notwithstanding some conversations which I had with delegates from the convent of Labug, from Pu Lao Yeh and from Yapsang Tenam. However, I prevailed upon them to procure me the barley which I considered necessary for my journey to Sining and I had it made into tsamba. I debated for a moment with myself whether I should go secretly with my horse and my interpreter to the nearest Chinese post of Kanzeh, which was half-way to Tasienlu and about as far as the distance from Milan to Strasburg. By travelling double stages, I could reach it in eight or nine days, half the time, or a little more, needed for the whole journey to Sining. But this post consisted only of a very insufficient force of twenty soldiers, commanded by a mere lieutenant, who took his orders from the Viceroy of Sechuen and had no authority in the Jyerkundo country, which was under the Imperial Legate of Sining; also, I had no passport for Sechuen. It was a desperate expedient which my situation, uncertain though it were, did not seem to me to justify: it was better to wait. At last, on the 20th of June, Yapsang Tenam came and camped with some armed men on the banks of the Do Chu and laid definitely before me the conditions upon which he was prepared to intervene. These were, first, a reward in money for himself; secondly, an undertaking given in my own name, in the name of the family of Dutreuil de Rhins and in the name of our government to forego any further claims if he succeeded in restoring the baggage which I had lost and in punishing the offenders. His object was to avoid any intervention on the part of the Chinese, whom the Tibetans prefer to know to be at a distance than to see close at hand. I replied that, as for the money, I would gladly give him the sum demanded on my arrival at Sining (we had not in our boxes enough money having local currency); that I would pay half of that sum if all the papers, documents, instruments and collections were restored to us and the other half if he brought me the body of Dutreuil de Rhins; that, if he succeeded in these two matters and furnished me with the means to reach Sining, I declared myself personally satisfied, but that I could not answer for it that our government, even in the supposition that all our baggage and our money were restored to us, would refrain from claiming any further reparation or damages; that, in the matter of the punishment of the offenders, it must take the regular course; that an act of violence must not be atoned for by another act of violence; that, if the offenders were sentenced on the spot after a regular trial, I was not in a position to guarantee that there would be no appeal to Sining or Peking; lastly, I recommended him to use prudence and not to forget that it was a question less of waging war than of saving manuscripts which a spark was enough to destroy, but which nothing could replace. Although my language was not entirely to Yapsang Tenam's liking, he did not throw up the game: he parleyed with the people of Tumbumdo and then, seeing that they were obstinate and that they resisted more strenuously than he had expected, he sent, on the 23rd, to his own district for reinforcements, which were to be ready in three days.

Meanwhile, the tungchen did not come, in spite of his promise, and the superior of Labug Gompa sent to me to express his astonishment, adding that, if he did not come soon, the convent would procure me the provisions and animals which I needed for my journey to Sining. On the 25th, I at last saw Pu Lao Yeh, who seemed struck with consternation. He bore witness to being painfully affected by the calamity that had overcome us and by the pitiable condition to which we were reduced and showed his regret that the body of Dutreuil de Rhins had not been found and that there was now no hope of ever finding it. He added that the negotiations with the people of Tumbumdo were no further advanced and that, as ill-luck would have it, two facts kept alive their obstinacy and that of their partisans. In the first place, in the fight which had followed on the fall of Dutreuil de Rhins, a Tibetan had been killed by one of our bullets, which had passed through his chest from front to back. I replied that, if that were so, the Tibetans had only themselves to blame; that, at that moment, we were more than ever on the lawful defensive; that our enemies, after wounding, or rather killing our leader, after recovering possession of their animals, after giving us to hope that they would cease hostilities, had suddenly renewed their attack with a perfidy that doubled the gravity of their crime; and that, moreover, if we had killed one of their men, there was no doubt but that the Tibetans would not have failed to take an easy revenge when I fell into their hands.

"They did not know of it then," said Pu Lao Yeh. "Also, if they did not kill you, it was not that they did not intend to do so, but they pretend that you threw a spell over them and that the spirits protected you. In any case, I assure you that I have myself seen the dead man. Certainly, no one can blame you for it, seeing that you were obliged to defend yourselves, and I only mention the fact to explain to you the persistent ill-will of the people of Tumbumdo. In the second place, the Rakis accuse your leader of having, in your absence, ordered or allowed one of their men to be shot dead: here is the petition which I have received on the subject."

So saying, he showed me, with an embarrassed air, a piece of paper half the size of a man's hand, containing two lines of writing, without seal or signature. I replied that this story was a contemptible and ridiculous trick, an odious machination invented by our enemies to make some sort of excuse for their conduct by charging their victim with an imaginary crime and that any difficulties which we had had on the way with ill-disposed inhabitants had never degenerated into an affray, thanks to the spirit of wisdom and moderation which our leader had never failed to show. And I mentioned the incident of the 14th of May,* which, distorted in the main and in detail with more audacity than skill, had possibly served as a groundwork for the fabrication of the charge with which they were trying to sully the memory of Dutreuil de Rhins. This incident was, in reality, so devoid of importance that, during the two days which we spent near the spot where it happened, we never heard speak of it

* See p. 137.

and that, during the whole of our stay at Jyerkundo, no one said a word to us about it. It was not until several days after the fight at Tumbumdo that the Tibetans had thought of employing it to lend colour to the calumnies with which they were seeking to palliate their crime. There could be no greater proof of the knavery of the accusers than the care which they had taken to remove my evidence by pretending that the act with which they were reproaching Dutreuil de Rhins had been committed in my absence, whereas it so happened that, during all the time that we were on Raki territory, I had never left my leader's side. Lastly, in spite of the indignation deserved by the ignominious methods to which the Tibetans resorted in their defence, I was not without deriving a certain satisfaction from them, since they proved that our enemies were conscious of the iniquity of their conduct at Tumbumdo and that it was impossible for them to lay the blame upon us.

Pu Lao Yeh did not wait for me to develop the whole of my argument before he assured me that he had never believed that story and that he recognised in this calumny one of the ordinary methods of procedure of the natives. He next told me that I must stay another fortnight. I observed to him that he had already kept me waiting five or six days longer than was arranged and this to no good purpose and I asked him what he proposed to do in that fortnight and if he could promise to come to a result of some kind within that time. He replied that his authority was too uncertain for him to give me any positive assurance; that I must even not cherish too great a hope of obtaining the result by which I set the greatest store, for he had been told that all the papers were burnt; but that I knew that he was not a rich man and it would take him quite a fortnight to get together what I needed for my journey. At the same time, he took from his breast a set of twenty rupees strung together, saying that this was an ornament of his wife's which she had consented to give up to him for me and that it was all that he had been able to find, because his colleague's wife was very miserly and had refused to hand over her jewels. The poor man was at great pains to play his comedy of zeal and devotion. There was no denying that he had the good intention to serve me, but he puffed it to excess and affected this great spirit of sacrifice only because he wished to force as great a one upon me. I told him that I could not accept the money which he offered me ; that I had only to say a word to the lama of Labug to have everything that I required ready for me by the next day ; and that I did not mean to remain much longer.

Pu Lao Yeh had his own reasons for wishing to prolong my stay. He dreaded the intervention of the Imperial Legate as much as did the Tibetans, although for other reasons: the Tibetans feared any Chinese meddling in their affairs, because it would be more or less prejudicial to their independence ; Pu Lao Yeh feared that he would be made to bear the responsibility for the difficulties from which he had not succeeded in saving his government: that was why he was trying to settle things as best he could before the Imperial Legate was told of them and, if he were forced to admit the impossibility of this, he wished at least to be the first to inform Sining of the events that had taken place, so as to present them in the most favourable light to himself. As for me, I did not care whether I found a well or ill-informed hearer at Sining ; besides, I considered that the failure of Pu Lao Yeh and his friends to obtain satisfaction arose either from radical impotency or from defective zeal and that, in either case, it was my business to betake myself, with the least possible delay, to the only authority capable of removing that impotency or reviving that zeal. I was kept back only by the hope that Yapsang Tenam's efforts might be more effective than those of Pu Lao Yeh. I had heard that the latter did not look favourably upon the lama's attempt. I taxed him with this and told him how wrong he was, since he and the lama both had the same object in view, adding that, if their combined influence and forces succeeded in making the people of Tumbumdo yield, the authorities at Sining would thank him and he would reap both honour and profit. He protested that he had done nothing to impede Yapsang Tenam's action, that he had long had excellent relations with him, and he promised me to act in concert with him as to the best measures to be taken to achieve the desired result and even, as he was in the minority among the Taorongpa, to instigate a collective intervention of all the Zachukkapa chiefs. I replied that, in that case, I would wait patiently.

The tungchen thereupon left me and went to the convent of Labug. He soon returned with horses and provisions and told me that we must not reckon on the intervention of the Zachukkapa chiefs, that the lama of Labug was formally opposed to it and that I must leave at once. I retorted curtly that I should leave when I pleased. The delegates of the shadso then spoke and assured me that their superior was inspired by my own interests and those of the cause which I was upholding as well as by those of the country as a whole; that he had been in favour of Yapsang Tenam's intervention so long as he thought that demonstrations and threats would be sufficient, but that he disapproved and would do all in his power to prevent a recourse to arms which would provoke a general war, the issue of which would be in doubt owing to the strength of the people of Tumbumdo and their partisans; that, on the other hand, my departure for Sining would probably make the people of Tumbumdo more tractable, because it would spare their susceptibilities and allow them to appear to be yielding to the Chinese government and not to a foreigner and adversary and also because they would become more frightened if the intervention of the Imperial Legate appeared to them to be more imminent.

This was very well argued and these reflexions were the more calculated to convince me inasmuch as I had already made them myself and as they came from a man to whom I owed everything and without whom I could do nothing. It would, no doubt, have been very picturesque to fling that *condottiere* of a Yapsang Tenam with his band of moss-troopers against Tumbumdo, to make twenty or thirty native chiefs take up arms for or against me, to cause a fine breaking of lances and a fine plunder; but that was not what we had come to Tibet for: we had come to work; and, given the impossibility of doing anything for Dutreuil de Rhins, of even showing him the last duties, I considered myself fortunate in having been able to gather round me all the men of the mission, without exception, and my only object now was to recover the scientific documents. Now there was always the danger that an armed attack would prompt the Tibetans to burn these, if they had not already done so. By vexing the only friends of whom I felt certain, I risked the chance of setting them against me, of depriving myself of all support and of rushing into a new disaster without even having right on my side. Nevertheless, I wished to know Yapsang Tenam's opinion: that was why I put off my departure; but I waited in vain for him to send a messenger to confer with me and I could dispatch no one to him because Tiso had been sent on another mission by the tungchen.

On the evening of the 27th, being still without news, I decided to start the next day. As I wished to arrive first and as soon as possible at Sining and as I wished also, out of respect for the memory of my unfortunate chief, to carry out the programme of our mission to the end as he himself had settled it at Jyerkundo, I was resolved, in spite of the danger, to follow the direct and unexplored road which skirts the country of the Goloks. But I did not care for the brigands to be told beforehand of my passing and I therefore continued to declare to all-comers that I should not start before the 30th and that I should go through Tsaidam. Only, I sent for Pu Lao Yeh and the shadso's delegates and confided my plan to them. They dissuaded me eagerly and told me that they would not answer for my safety except on the Tsaidam road and that they could not procure me a guide for the other. I replied that my resolution was immovable, that I had no time to lose and that I should quite well find my way alone. At last, they determined to acquiesce in my plan, which, however, was executable, they assured me, only if the secret were not rumoured forth too early and if I marched very quickly. I charged them to follow up the question of the restoration of the mission documents by every means, even by payment; I especially urged them not to allow themselves to be turned from their efforts because they were told that the papers had been burnt; and I made them understand that, if this rumour were true, the action of the Chinese government would be twice as vigorous and the punishment twice as severe. I recommended them also to resume their search for the body of Dutreuil de Rhins and, if they found it, to send it to Sining, I undertaking to pay for their outlay and trouble. They swore that they would do all that they could and the best guarantee of their sincerity was their desire by a tangible result to prove the truth of their zeal and the usefulness of their services to the Imperial Legate, who would soon be informed of the business and would ask them for an account of their action.

The shadso sent me a letter for his brother, a lama in residence at Tongkor Gompa, and a guide, an old, but still active man, who had formerly been a merchant, who had often made the journey to Sining by the different roads and who, having one day fallen into the hands of the Goloks, had been pillaged, ruined and reduced to turning monk. That night, I once more saw Tiso, my host : Yapsang Tenam had asked him to tell me that he saw no objection to my departure ; that, on the contrary, matters would probably take a better turn because of it and that he would continue to deal with the people of Tumbumdo in accordance with my last instructions.

Although the interference of this lama did not have all the success that I hoped for, it did, at least, thanks to the anxiety which it caused, make my friends the tungchen and the shadso display more liberality and a greater eagerness to contribute towards the expenses of my journey. I handed Tiso, as a reward for his excellent services, a certain quantity of gold which I had found sewn up in the clothes of one of my men and, while the village was still sleeping and a little quivering of the air accompanied the first pale rays of the dawn, I left this sad, though hospitable place, where I had passed twenty-three days of anguish and mortal weariness. Notwithstanding the thought of the sufferings and dangers that awaited me on this new journey undertaken with the slightest possible resources across an unknown, mountainous and desert country, infested with bands of brigands and as wide as that which stretches between Lyons and Florence ; notwithstanding my grief at recognising my helplessness and at being obliged to leave everything behind me, buried in a disaster from which perhaps nothing would ever again emerge, I felt a genuine relief from the necessity that drove me from these parts, to which such cruel and gloomy memories were attached.

We went first towards the north, in order to avoid the more populous parts of the turbulent region of Zachukka and to give the impression that we were making for the Tsaidam road. Shortly after our departure, while we were crossing the high hills on the right bank of the La Chu, we suddenly saw, at some distance, coming in an opposite direction, a troop of thirty or forty mounted men armed with muskets and extraordinarily long lances. On seeing us, they stopped and we ourselves halted, wondering what could be the meaning of this challenge and whether the road was already going to be barred to us. However, I ordered the march to be resumed; the Tibetans, closing up their ranks, did the same and passed close to us without saying anything. It was the head of the canton of Chinto and his escort; when he learnt who we were, he sent two men on horseback to the village to forbid the inhabitants to admit us to their houses or to supply us with any goods. When we passed through this village, which squats humbly and slily in a slightly wider portion of a narrow valley, there was not a soul outside.

A little further, we came to where four valleys meet, between two monasteries which, instead of settling themselves comfortably in the plain by the waterside, have taken refuge in the barren ruggedness of the mountains: on the right, a Saskyapa convent scatters its many-coloured buildings along the side of the red hill; on the left, a reformed and more modest convent perches its white walls on a projecting rock. Next, going up the Chareh Chu, we passed before a village and, a little further, before a long array of tents drawn up in line at the bottom of a valley, pressed one against the other and surrounded by a wall of stones, high as a man and pierced with loop-holes. We felt ourselves to be in a curiously ticklish country, plundering or plundered as the occasion demanded, at the gate of the Goloks, those mountain pirates, and of their advance-guard, the Zachukkapa. We camped, at nightfall, in a deserted corner and, the next day, a first pass took us into the territory of the short-haired Zachukkapa and a second led us from the basin of the Do Chu to that of the Za Chu, which is sometimes called the Za Chu Golok to distinguish it from the Za Chu Mekong. The gorges of the basin of the Do Chu, its narrow, deep and gloomy valleys, with their swift and roaring torrents, and its steep, grassy, rounded hills were succeeded by the wide, clear and sad valleys, the slow and silent rivers, the flat and bare hills of the basin of the Za Chu. On both sides of the road stood snow mountains, of which those on the left form the sources of the river. The country, more barren and doubtless higher, became gradually less populous ; the houses were replaced by tents, which themselves disappeared on the 30th of June, when we had the pleasure of seeing the last of them. After crossing the Za Chu, which was fifty yards wide and half a yard deep, we went up the valley of its affluent, the Cha Chu, the volume of which is very similar. Our delight at finding ourselves alone, without alarming neighbours and masters of all we surveyed, was spoilt by a very bad storm, which dashed handfuls of hail in our faces. When the wind dropped, the hail gave way to rain and the rain to snow. We had to lie down in the mud and the little calico tent which had been given us prevented us, it is true, from seeing the clouds, but not from receiving their water. A few men pretended to be ill, being of opinion that I was going too fast. Indeed, we had far to go every day and little to eat. For all our food, we had barley-meal mixed with about a tenth part of sand and gravel to make up the weight, unstalked tea and rancid butter; we had also taken two sheep with us, but, as they delayed our march, we killed them and carried only the best pieces. This was little for ten men, for fifteen or, perhaps, twenty days: the more reason to hurry on. I said that all laggards would be abandoned without pity and forbade every man to turn his head to see if anyone was left behind. My threat took effect; the idlest found their legs again and forgot their aches and pains.

On the 1st of July, at the foot of some snow-topped mountains, we came to the source of the Cha Chu and, in order to cross the not very high Pachong Pass, we splashed through deep, slippery mud strewn with a host of great stones. The northern slope was covered with snow, sometimes to a height of several feet. As the darkness of the night was invading the cold and desolate valleys and rugged mountains that surrounded us, we camped, again in the rain and snow, on the bank of a torrent that ran into the Ma Chu. The next day, still in bad weather and in the teeth of the wind, we finished the crossing of the chain that separates the basin of the Za Chu from that of the Ma Chu, or Hoangho, and went down the valley of the Kala Chu, which runs into Lake Kala Nam Cho and runs out of it again under the name of Kiang Chu. This valley, which is two miles wide, rich in water and grass and peopled with wild yaks, is a sacred valley. It is overlooked by the white summit of the Kula Dagseh, the throne of a revered spirit, a *sidag*, to whom every traveller must do homage, if he would avoid misfortune. On the slope of the hills is a little wall of dried ox-dung against which, in legendary antiquity, stood the tent of a nymph, or *spamo*, the sovereign of these parts and a great huntress; and the traveller who passes before this relic of her wandering palace never fails to bow and to mutter a few deprecatory words.

On the 3rd of July, the fine weather fortunately returned and we crossed the great valley of the Kiang Chu, the river of the wild horses. The valley is seven miles wide at this spot and stretches for a distance of fifty miles from the mountains that rise to the south of the Ngoring Cho to the valley of the Ma Chu itself, drowned in the mist of the distant horizon. The ground is now grass-grown and marshy, for want of a slope to drain the water, and now pebbly and barren. We halted to take a cup of tea on the bank of the sluggish and muddy river, not far from the road which the Goloks take when they go for salt to the Kyaring Cho. Our guide told us how, many years before, he was surprised by the brigands with his caravan of forty-two men, as he was descending the pass which leads from the Ngoring Cho to the Kiang Chu, and how the brigands, discharging their fire-arms and uttering savage yells to terrify the peaceful merchants, had flung themselves upon them with couched lances, carried off the beasts of burden, robbed the men of their trinkets and exchanged their old clothes against the newer ones of their victims. My interpreter, who had long been anxiously examining the horizon, suddenly cried :

"There are the Goloks !" and pointed to a great dark, moving mass, strewn with gleaming points, far across the plain.

It was a huge herd of wild yaks, whose horns, shining in the sun, looked in the distance like the lances of a squadron. We laughed heartily at the coward and finished the stage gaily, although the danger was more than imaginary ; but we had so little to lose that, had the robbers come, themselves would have been robbed.

On the 4th of July, we came to the brink of a little lake hidden in a fold of the mountains on the right bank of the Ma Chu and stopped for a few moments, beguiled by the charm of the landscape, so rare in this centre of

Asia. The easy slope of the hills was thick with long, close, supple grass, such as we had never seen, and, in this narrow frame of verdure, the lake smiled sweetly under the pure sky. There was no other sound and no other movement than a light buzz of insects in the air, a light antelope's flight at the bottom of a gorge, the light quivering of the ripples shimmering on the surface of the water. We would gladly have lingered in this peaceful, warm and luminous retreat, which lightened some of the burden with which our hearts were weighted. But we had to go on, for the road was long and time precious. We crossed the Ma Chu, which, at this spot, is a slender river, fifty yards wide and not much more than two feet deep. It flows through one of those valleys which are exactly characteristic of this region, many miles wide, flat, stretching out as far as the eye can reach, resembling the alleys of a classical park immensely magnified, even as the mountains which hem them in on either side remind one, with their flat, monotonous and unending lines, of some classical building whose proportions have been enlarged by extending it indefinitely. We have here an architecture of straight, horizontal lines which takes the place of the Gothic architecture, with its broken, perpendicular lines, of the basins of the Za Chu Mekong and the Do Chu. Allowing for the differences caused by the decrease in height (13,000 as against 16,000 to 17,000 feet) and by the greater display of the mountains, one is struck by the resemblance between the appearance of this country and that of the Ustun Tagh, even as the Pachong La had seemed to me an exact counterpart of the Karakoram. At more than eight leagues to our left, at the end of the valley, rose a great chain of snowy mountains in front of which runs the famous road from Lhasa to Sining which we had intended to take when leaving Nagchu. It passes between the two lakes,

Kyaring and Ngoring, and is, therefore, constantly traversed by bands of the Goloks, on their way to fetch salt, which abounds in those lakes and in which they carry on a lucrative trade, for they make sure of a monopoly in it through the terror with which they inspire their neighbours.

Beyond the valley of the Ma Chu, we climbed a mass of mountains, which is wide, but not very high, by a series of passes called the Maladun, that is to say the Seven Passes of the Ma Chu, although I counted only three. On leaving this mass, we dropped into the valley of Dug Jong, similar to the last, except that it is almost without water and barren. It also opens on the Golok country, which, in the distance and almost endlessly, displays its lofty mountains, whose whiteness seems to evaporate into the sky. The brilliancy of the sun in the spacious horizon was very painful to the sight. Our guide suffered from it to such an extent that he was unable to see the road and that I had to correct his mistakes and myself to direct the march across the Dugri Mountains by the compass and the appearance of the ground. In this way, we arrived exactly at the fork formed by our road with that of Lhasa, south of the Stongri Cho and north of the Stonga Alacha mountains, which must be numbered among the strangest in the world, uncommonly rugged and abrupt, slashed and jagged and bristling with rocky white crests. After passing the southern extremity of the Stongri Cho, the road crosses a valley, still very wide, but more broken up than the others, which reveals, on the left, a close chaos of ugly mountains, bare, grey and dismal, which suggest the sands of Gobi and separate us from the Mongol country, and, on the right, much further away than it seems, a prodigious and resplendent mass of snow and ice, which strikes any man, however accustomed to mountains, with admiration and astonishment.

Since leaving the great peak of the Akka Tagh, we had seen none that presented so marvellous an effect. It was the Amyeh Machen, the sacred mountain of the Goloks, before which they pray, striking the earth with their foreheads, while its redoubtable divinity, who is not assimilated by Buddhism, protects their independence, makes their herds increase and prosper and blesses their marauding raids.

We had at last succeeded in crossing without let or hindrance the regions generally frequented by the Goloks. On the 7th of July, we found a camp of Panak Tibetans, numbering some ten heads, on the shore of the Peritun Cho. These Tibetans, who watch their herds on horseback, in the Mongolian manner, have a rather bad reputation as thieves, but they are not so quarrelsome as the Goloks and do not, like these, travel in large bands. They were not greatly to be feared, therefore, and we had only to look after our goods to protect them. We would have been glad to renew our stock of provisions, which was coming to an end; but they would have none of our rupees, declaring that they accepted only Chinese money. Beyond the Peritun Cho, the country was once more inhabited, which seemed to confirm our guide's statement that these Panaks had come so far only to escape taxation.

The appearance of the country had now decidedly changed and recalled the Altyn Tagh, with the narrow gorges of the Chemorong Chu and Angarong Chu and the deep gash of the Yamatu, similar to that of the rivers of Kashgar. When we had passed this last river, we did twelve miles without finding a drop of water, going first through pretty, verdant valleys, studded with tiny flowers and scented with fragrant herbs, and next through a wide, flat valley which stretched between dusty hills and which might have been compared pretty correctly with the Sanju valley, if it had had trees and crops. In the evening, we at last came to the bank of a very modest river, the Cheche Chu, where we drank our last cup of tea and ate our last pellet of tsamba. This was on the 9th of July. Notwithstanding the uncommon swiftness of our march, it was less than I had reckoned upon, as I had expected to reach Tongkor Gompa on the 10th, whereas, now, the greatest effort could not bring me there before the 12th. I resolved to make for the nearest habitations as quickly as possible and, as there was none on the direct road, I resigned myself to lengthening the journey by half a day and turned straight towards the Koko Nor.

Having taken our last meal, we pursued our way until nine o'clock in the evening and camped in the middle of a large steppe, having marched for fifteen hours that day. Before five o'clock the next morning, we had done half a league across the same steppe, which measures over twenty-five miles in width and stretches as far as the hills which edge the Koko Nor on the south. This dull waste, with its sandy clay soil, at one time offers level ground, covered with gravel and tall grass, and at another is intersected by ravines with perpendicular sides or else bristles with earthy, white paps, sometimes with downs. We could have believed ourselves back in Kashgar. In the middle lies a small lake, the Konga Nor, with marshy banks, infested with mosquitoes, and a little further to the north runs a slimy river, the Obeh Chu, a smaller reproduction of the Cherchen Daria. We lost two horses in the crossing and the men, wearied by the unusual effort of the previous day, by hunger, by a violent north wind, which raised clouds of dust, arrived exhausted at the foot of the hills. We began to climb them slowly by a stony ravine, but we still failed to see the longed-for smoke, to hear dogs barking or herds lowing. To complete our wretchedness, there was no water anywhere: we explored every corner of the mountain, but everything was hideously barren and dry.

At last, we discovered in the hollow of a rock a small store of the precious fluid, just sufficient to fill all our cups. We lay down here. The next morning, a slender stream of water was trickling between the stones of the ravine.

We resumed our march and, as we went on, the water became more plentiful, the hills greener; and soon we saw, hanging on the mountain-sides, black tents similar to those of Central Tibet, but much larger, without being any higher, and measuring as much as 50 feet by 30. They were occupied by Panak Tibetans, who revived us with cups of excellent buttered tea and agreed to accept three rupees for a sheep; they took good care, however, to break one of the rupees to make sure of the quality of the metal. At a short distance further, I met a little Chinese merchant, whom I asked if he had any provisions to sell. He said yes, that he would let me have all that I wanted and that I could pay him at Sining, where he would be in a fortnight. One hour later, he brought me all that I had asked him for, apologising for not being able to do more. I never saw him again nor was I able to learn who he was or what had become of him.

These mountains to the south of the Koko Nor are comparatively very populous and the pastures, which grow richer and richer as one approaches the lake, feed great herds of excellent horses of Mongolian breed and of fine red cows like those of Europe. On leaving the hills, one emerges on a grassy plain, sloping gently towards the immense lake, which is overtowered, far away in the north, by snow mountains. This lake, which the Mongols, with their usual poverty of imagination, have called simply the Blue Lake, is not by a long measure so picturesque as the Nam Cho or a large number of other Tibetan lakes, for it is not so well framed and decorated with mountains; the scenery is empty and spacious; but, on the other hand, it is infinitely less wild and rugged, infinitely more friendly towards man, who, under the genial warmth of the sun, feels much more at his ease here. In the middle of the water stands a little barren rock, used as a dwelling-place by four or five solitary lamas, who never go on land and who receive their provisions in the winter only when the lake is frozen; for there are no boats on the Koko Nor. This eyot is sanctified by legend, according to which it was brought by a divine bird to close the orifice through which the water, coming from the place where Lhasa now stands, poured and transformed the meadow into a lake.

Along the Koko Nor, the traveller comes across numerous tents, some of which are of felt and round, like those of the Mongols: they are never pitched on the plain, but take shelter at the foot of the mountain and hide away in the dales, so that they rarely catch the eye of the wayfarer. On the 12th, we joined the Tsaidam road again and, on the 13th, we once more came upon the old Lhasa road. On the same day, we arrived at the gorge of Tongkor Gompa, which is very deep, steep and rocky. At the bottom, by the water's brink, grew a cluster of shrubby trees, the first that we had seen for eleven months, that is to say since leaving Cherchen. This was to us an undeniable emblem of civilisation. On the slope of the rocks stood the monastery buildings, built in the Chinese style, one of which served the Labug convent as a hostelry, a warehouse for goods and a residence for its representative, who was an own brother of the shadso. The little brother was not worthy of the big one: he was short and fat, with an apoplectic face and unruly movements. He had drunk a good drop of brandy that morning and received us with enthusiasm and with tears in his eyes. The next day, having recovered his composure, he was more reserved, but nevertheless lent me some fresh horses and some money. We descended swiftly to Tongkor by a carriage-road, feeling, in spite of the terrible memories that kept on coming to the surface, the immense relief of thinking that an enthralling, ungrateful, interminable task was ended at last. From every side, the waters of the rivers and brooks ran softly murmuring; the abrupt sides of the mountains were divided into fields of crops of different colours; the valleys were strewn with villages with white houses surrounded by green trees; a large number of Chinese came and went, busy, active and calm, looking so refined and graceful by comparison with those rude and rough Tibetans; and the carriage-wheels grated, the horses neighed, the dogs barked, the cocks crowed. Life and plenty had followed upon scarcity and death.

At mid-day, the walls of Tongkor came in sight, marking their geometrical square and their regular battlements among the confused and disordered lines of the mountains. Père Huc gives us an animated and picturesque description of this town which leaves the impression of something singularly fierce and gloomy. The reality, on the contrary, gave me an impression of brightness and gaiety: this was because Père Huc came out of the light, whereas I came out of the shadow, and, as the Persian poet says, "To the houris of paradise, purgatory is a hell; but ask the damned in hell: purgatory is a paradise!" Those truculent Tibetans, whom the good father depicts for us in the streets and inns of Tongkor with their swords stuck in their belts, their shaggy hair, their repulsive dirtiness, their proud gait, their abrupt gestures, their loud voices and their fierce glances, are, in fact, quiet people enough, even somewhat timid, because they feel that they are among strangers, a little awkward in their

Sunday clothes; people who have washed, combed, decked themselves out to make themselves presentable in a polished town, who make it their business to appear elegant and well-mannered, as is seemly in the noble neighbourhood of a sub-prefect of the august Emperor; and if, sometimes, they shout and make a noise, this does not mean that they wish anybody mortal harm, but that they are amusing themselves, that they are gay and merry and that they want everybody to know it. Père Huc compared them with the Chinese; I compared them with themselves and I was pleased with them for their efforts to clean and polish themselves. For that matter, the Tibetans are far from being in a majority at Tongkor, which is, above all, a town of Dungans and Chinese and, although these Chinese inhabitants are not the flower of China, they were a change after the Tibetans. I saw the sub-prefect and the colonel, who, knowing nothing as yet, were greatly astonished and touched at the piteous state in which I was and at the catastrophe of which we had been the victims; they showed me a very genuine sympathy and did me every service that lay in their power, during the few hours that I spent in their town.

On the next day, the 15th of July, at five o'clock in the evening, I passed through the west gate of the town of Sining, which at first appeared to me a very imposing, bustling, noisy, populous city, and I was a little deafened by the tumult that reigned in its narrow streets. The inns were full of people and I had to instal myself provisionally in a miserable tavern, than which I had seen none worse in the whole course of my journey. I at once sent my card to the Imperial Legate *(Kincha)*, Koei Choen. My arrival and the sad news which I brought made a great sensation in the Yamen: a number of functionaries and officers, with the prefect at their head, came to call on me that same evening and, seeing my lodging, at once had the best inn in the town evacuated and placed it at my disposal. On the 16th, I had an interview with the Imperial Legate, who received me with great honour. His face betrayed the profound agitation into which he was thrown by the tragic and unexpected nature of the affair in question, the grave responsibility which it caused him to incur, the vexation which it promised him. He was quite overcome, he kept his eyes lowered or raised them only with an effort, he spoke in a low, very gentle and uncertain voice. After expressing to me, with emotion, his sorrowful concern in my great misfortune and his intense regret that the event had not permitted him to receive Dutreuil de Rhins with the honours that were due to him after so long and arduous a journey, he decided to go in person to Lanchow in order to telegraph to the government in Peking, to arrange with the Viceroy as to the best steps to be taken and to obtain from him the necessary resources and soldiers for an armed expedition to Tumbumdo. Alone, indeed, he was able to do nothing, for he had hardly any money and disposed of no troops except a few Mongols encamped in their own country and armed with bows and arrows.

In the meantime, I made him at once send two of his interpreters to Jyerkundo to recall the two interpreters on service, Pu and Li; to carry a mandarin's button, with the official thanks of the Imperial Legate, to the superior of the convent of Labug, in recognition of the assistance which he had given me; to order the body of Dutreuil de Rhins, if it could be found, to be conveyed to Sining; and to call upon the people of Tumbumdo to restore the lost baggage and, especially, the papers. I hoped that the Tibetans, on receiving the direct and express orders of the Imperial Legate, knowing that he was determined to act and to treat them with rigour and thinking that perhaps they would escape more lightly by making an easy concession, would no longer persist in their refusal. I was right; but, as the interpreters took the high-road through Tsaidam and, in spite of the orders of the Imperial Legate and the pecuniary encouragement which I gave them, travelled by short stages, I did not hear of the partial success of their mission until I reached Peking. In addition to this, the Imperial Legate advanced me, even before I asked for it and not only promptly, but abundantly, all the money that I needed, so that I sent back my guide to Labug, in the company of a caravan which was going there, with letters for the lama and the tungchen, money to refund their outlay and various presents.

Meanwhile, I had explored every corner of the town of Sining, which is small enough, in spite of the number and importance of the dignitaries whom it shelters. Its walls, which are higher than those of Khotan and which look dignified with the dark colour which the years have given them, form a quadrilateral of four thousand by two thousand feet, containing a population of about fifteen thousand inhabitants. In this figure I include the garrison, which consists of three thousand soldiers on paper, although the effective force does not exceed fifteen hundred men, the pay of the other fifteen hundred going to swell the salary of the very amiable general of division, the commandant of the place. Without the walls lies a considerable suburb, peopled almost exclusively by Moslems, to the number of nearly ten thousand. These are distinguished at first sight from the rest of the population by their little caps, which are polygonal, instead of being round; by their generally taller stature; by their very prominent features, their firmer and manlier gait, their brisker movements, their bold glance and an air of turbulence and bravado that betrays their impatience of the yoke. They take little trouble to conceal their contempt for the Chinese infidels or their sympathy for the Europeans. On the second day after my arrival, some of their notables and mollahs came to offer me their condolence and I had always every reason to be satisfied with them and with their correligionists in the other parts of China.

The little streets of the town are generally calm and lonely, frequented by rare pedestrians picking their way through the mud, the filth and the dogs and lined by low, bare walls, with hardly any windows to them, for the Chinese lodgings are lighted most often from the inner court-yards. Only in one or two streets which have shops drawn up on either side is there an animated crowd, a crowd in which an occasional wild and discordant note is struck by a thick-set, stupid-looking Mongol, with a face shining with grease, or a more slender, but still very clumsy Tibetan. The great number of saddlers, felt-makers and sellers of hides, skins and furs indicate the neighbourhood of a nation of horsemen, herdsmen and hunters; but, close at hand, in the carpenters' shops, those great displays of substantial coffins, giving out a good smell of dry wood and presenting their inviting and comfortable interiors to the public, recall old China, sedentary and slumbering in the coffin of her traditions.

I will speak here neither of the trade of Sining town nor of its monuments. I shall have occasion to return to the former in the second part of this work and, as for the monuments, it is unnecessary to enlarge upon them, for all the buildings in China are but repetitions one of the other and are more remarkable and more imposing for the vast extent of their inner courts, which follow one another in long rows, than for the effect of the architecture, which is heavy and as it were crushed under the excessive development of the roofs. The insignificance and ugliness of the human constructions are atoned for, in a certain measure, by the beauty of the site. The valley in whose bottom the town stands opens, in its bright and happy grace, like a basket of verdure and fruit, between high hills whose natural ruggedness is modified by a few crops and a few trees scattered over their sides. They are not so near as to interfere with the free effusion of the light nor so far that one is unable from any part of the valley to distinguish the details of their structure. What remains of their barrenness, the steep red rocks that everywhere pierce through the thin vegetal layer, reminds the traveller of the proximity of Tibet; but he feels very far removed from that country of poverty when he sees at the foot of the rocks and thrown into relief by them that flourishing champaign covered with kitchen-gardens, with wheat, barley and millet. Although the fertility of the soil is not very great in itself, he is nevertheless driven to admire it, when he reflects that he is at a height of 7,400 feet, that is to say far above the extreme point reached by the coarsest crops in our own alpine regions.

Here and there the picturesqueness of the hill-slopes is increased by the varnished roof of a Buddhist temple and one might think that the religion of Sakya Muni reigns over men's souls, even as his temples command the valley; but, on climbing the path that leads to the sanctuary, one discovers that it is abandoned, almost without worship or worshippers. A custodian alone keeps watch over the chapel which contains the gods of bronze or of striped and gilded wood: in the middle sits Buddha, grave and calm, with his long mustaches drooping after the fashion of a Chinese mandarin, himself bearing the stamp of a dull serenity, as though he felt, from the destitution to which mankind has condemned him, that the end of time is at hand; on either side stand the spirits whose mission it is to destroy the infidels: they are gigantic and grotesque, armed from head to foot; they roll furious eyes and show fierce teeth: vain grimaces which there is none here to see or fear. Around the chapel are disposed clean and well-paved courts, well-constructed buildings, bathed in the warm light of the sun, cooled by a vivifying breeze, and, from the outer galleries, the view embraces the whole landscape, in its severe frame of mountains, and looks down upon the valley, upon the watered-silk ribbons of the rivers and brooks, upon the check mantle of the fields dotted with houses and with clusters of white flowers, upon the grey walls of the town, which, from this height, resembles a town of dwarfs. This charming abode ought to be peopled with monks, but the hostility of the Confucian administration and the steady indifference of the populace tend to keep it empty: in the air, which ought to drone with pious orisons, the only sound was that of a profane lute, twanged by a Chinese, the one inhabitant of the place besides the watchman. He was a consumptive patient, who had been recommended by the doctors to breathe the pure air of the hills and who had come to spend the fine season in this deserted convent. At the moment of my visit, he had taken shelter from the heat of the day in a charming, verdant summer-house, beside a pond of clear water, and, to hasten the flight of time, was accompanying on his instrument the shrill and quavering song of one of his friends, who had come up to enquire after him. The Buddhist monasteries of China are not only country refuges for the use of convalescents: they serve also as pleasure-resorts for the townsmen, who often send one of their cooks to prepare a good dinner for a troop of merry table-companions in one of these charming retreats so well-suited to promote gay conversation and a good digestion.*

Very different from this is the famous monastery of Skubum, a really Tibetan monastery, dependent administratively upon the Imperial Legate. It is the most celebrated of the convents of Kansu and the most important after that of Lhabrang. It is separated from Sining by an easy road of seventeen miles, following a little tributary of the river, which leads first to a small, bustling village, full of shops and inns, of merchants and pilgrims, purveyors and clients of the monastery. I there met a lama doctor whom I had already seen at Tongkor, an old man with a lively and prepossessing air, a voluble talker and a curious type of adventurer. A native of Ladak, he had left that country many years since, to escape creditors who put forth exorbitant pretensions to be paid. He had shaved his head, placed the threatened remnants of his fortune in a bag, girded up his loins and, saddling a stout hack, had set out with a light heart for Lhasa, where he arrived as a devout pilgrim as well as an unscrupulous debtor. Received as a monk and furnished with the Dalai Lama's blessing, he studied medicine at the same time as theology, visited the principal sanctuaries of Tibet, travelled through Nepal, Kashmir and a portion of India, made a long stay in Turkestan and in Mongolia, where he followed the trade of a horse-dealer, pushed on his peregrinations as far as China and Eastern Tibet and then, beginning to feel the weight of age, settled down at Tongkor. I do

* There exists a fallacy, difficult to uproot, that China belongs to the Buddhist religion. As a matter of fact, there is a fairly large number of Buddhist monks in China; but there is no Buddhist population. The case is the same with the majority of the nations which the fancy of the statisticians includes among the votaries of Buddha. In point of really Buddhist nations, I know only the Mongols and the Tibetans, or less than six millions of people (*Cf.* my "Scientific Mission in Upper Asia," Vol. I., pp. 378-380).

not mean to say that he kept the house, for he was still very active. To-day, he was at Tongkor; to-morrow, he was seen at Sining; and, soon, at Skubum or Lhabrang, on the banks of the Koko Nor or at the gates of the Great Wall, with the Salar Moslems or the Tsaidam Mongols. He travelled by hill and dale, in the stone cities or the woollen tents, atoning for his lapses from his monastic vows by frequent devotions at the most reverenced sanctuaries, gathering simples, selling prayers and incantations, prescriptions and remedies, spices and tea, stuffs and horses and, in general, all that was to be sold at a profit. He knew how to read and write his mother-tongue, was fairly well-versed in Tibetan literature, spoke the Turkic and Mongolian languages decently, jabbered Hindustani and murdered Chinese. Ever ready to serve me, he cured me of a painful cramp in the stomach by means of a certain black powder of his compounding, gave me many particulars about the countries which he had visited and tried to sell me a one-eyed horse with a cracked saddle. The variety of the nations which he had seen and the manners which he had observed had singularly enlarged his ideas and his theology smacked of heresy. He expressed to me his opinion, based upon a great abundance of arguments, that the three religions—the Buddhist, the Christian and the Moslem—were, at bottom, only one and the same religion, laying down the same rules of morality, and that Sakya Muni, Jesus and Mohammed were prophets inspired by one and the same divinity, who bears different names—Sangyé, God the Father or Allah—a divinity one in its essence, but infinitely varied in its attributes, a principle from which everthing emanates and to which everything must return:

"In short," said he, "the difference between the three doctrines lies in this, that the Buddhists look upon the divinity as immanent in all nature, which is only a perceptible and hence illusory manifestation of the supreme Intelligence, whereas the Christians and the Moslems, with their narrow and precise minds, consider God as a Being distinct from all the others and outside nature, although He is infinite. Now this is a contradiction, for, if God be distinct from other beings and outside nature, He is necessarily limited by them and it. In the same way, the Christians and Moslems think that God wished for the creation of the world and that this creation pleased Him, that He is offended by bad actions and gladdened by good ones, that He desires the conversion of sinners ; and yet they add that He is perfect. These, again, are two contradictory propositions, for a desire is an aspiration after that which is wanting ; now, if God be perfect and absolute, He can want for nothing : therefore He can desire nothing nor feel either joy or sorrow."

And the worthy man wiped his forehead with his wide red sleeve ; for he spoke with heat.

The monastery, which is in a lateral ravine, is not visible from the village. You have to go round a projection of the mountain before you can catch a vague glimpse, through the trees, on the slope of the hills, which are hollowed out like a cradle, of a few pieces of wall, rising in storeys one above the other, and the gilt roof of the great temple. This wild and towering site was chosen expressly, according to the Buddhic custom, to show how greatly superior to the worldly life, which seethes in the plains, is the religious life, which blows on the uplands, in a purer air, untrodden by the crowd, where man is freer, more the master of his soul and his destiny, delivered from the slavery of earthly relations, interests and passions and by so much the nearer to the divinity as he is further from the vulgar herd, its ignorance and its blindness and more wrapped up in silence and calm, which are the forerunners of eternal peace. When you have passed through the entrance-gate, you see a large number of different, scattered buildings, large and small, chapels or dwellings of lamas, so that this monastery resembles a village. Three thousand five hundred monks live here, each in his own room or house and each on his own money; for the community supplies its members with only a piece of woollen stuff and a certain quantity of barley per year and with three measures per day of buttered tea, which is prepared in colossal cauldrons on huge cooking-ranges.

Among the visitors, some of whom receive the hospitality of the convent in return for their pious donations, the Chinese are remarkable by their scarcity; on the other hand, people come from every corner of Tibet and Mongolia, even from British Tibet and Russian Mongolia. They all seemed very devout and very much occupied in prostrating themselves and burning lamps before the sacred images or in turning round the sacred edifices. I saw, however, a Mongolian lama who was abominably drunk and who was still holding in his hand one of those little tin cups which serve to measure brandy. The figures which he described as he walked scandalised some and roused laughter in others. He greeted me in Russian as he passed and I was not vey proud that the first words that I had heard for a long time in a European language should come from such a mouth. But for how much did this imperfect fact count beside all the perfections acquired and heaped up in this great prayer-factory? On every side, banderoles covered with religious inscriptions streamed in the wind, rows of cylinders, large as barrels and full of mystical invocations and sacred formulas, turned on an axis, driven by hand, uttering numberless orisons. It is a pity that steam-engines have not made their way so far: by their means, a much greater output could be secured and perhaps it would become possible to counteract the terrifying sum-total of imperfections, which increases day by day and which, for some years, has been visibly dragging poor humanity into a circle of ever more deplorable ills.

In one of the principal temples, glittering with a multitude of lighted lamps, perfumed with the smoke from the censers, several hundreds of monks were assembled, chanting the divine office in a double choir and presided over by a mitred and crosiered chief lama. In the last row and alone in the middle aisle was an old monk, kneeling on the bare flags, with bent head, motionless: feeling his approaching end, he had resolved to give up his personal property and to divide it between the coffers of the convent and his poor colleagues, in order to spend the rest of his days in meditation and privations and, having nothing more in this world, to hoard up an inexhaustible treasure for the next. A large court beside the chapel was filled with children, with novices learning their lessons aloud under the direction of professors. When school was over, the noisy and restless band filled all the space around, crowded about me to look at me and prevented me from passing; but a disciplinary prefect came up with a great whip at the end of his bare arm and all the little friarlings flew off hurriedly and laughing.

At last, we came to the marvel which has made Skubum famous throughout the world. In the small court-yard of a chapel stood a few shrubs* of which the bark and even the leaves were studded with Tibetan characters. According to the legend spread in Europe by Père Huc and widely diffused among the

---

* The lamas have it that these shrubs are sandal-trees, shrubs held sacred by the Buddhists. The tallest is just about ten feet high; the leaves are lanceolate and not very sharp-pointed. There are no shrubs like them in the country.

Buddhists of Asia, these letters were formed spontaneously by some unknown mysterious influence. At first sight, I thought that they had been artificially carved by means of a knife, although the incisions were neither very clear nor very fine; but the two lamas who accompanied me said that it would be considered a sacrilege to apply the steel to these revered trees, for they grow upon the exact spot where the great reformer Tsongkapa was born and it was the very blood which escaped from his mother's womb that fertilised the soil and gave birth to the first of these trees, from which the others sprang. For this reason, childless women come to this place to pray and lick the ground at the root of the tree that stands in the centre of the court: it is an infallible remedy for barrenness. The lamas went on to say that, in order the better to assert the miraculous origin and virtue of these plants, the monks had, with their finger-nails, traced religious characters on the trunks and leaves. I told them what I had heard said of these characters, that they were the result of a miracle and appeared upon the new leaves without any human intervention. They told me that this was a fable, born in the imagination of clumsy people given to exaggeration and to attributing a marvellous character to everything at random.

"However," they said, "the legend is based upon fact: the first shrub that grew on this spot, immediately after the birth of Tsongkapa, did bear letters proclaiming the divine mission of the child. This shrub, which is much smaller than those which you see here, is preserved to-day inside the temple with the gold roof and none is allowed to see it except the loftiest incarnations of Buddha. It is related that letters appeared upon its new leaves in divine circumstances, but the impiousness of the age has withdrawn the favour of heaven from us and the sacred tree is dumb."

This golden-roofed temple, so jealously closed, stands in the centre of the monastery and contains one half of the body of Tsongkapa's father, whence the name of Skubum, which means mausoleum. This was the only portion of the convent which the lamas were able, by dint of entreaties, to save from pillage and ruin at the time of the Moslem revolt of 1862. All the other edifices are, therefore, of recent date and, at the time of my visit, the monks were still engaged in building. Among the masons and carpenters, I observed a large number of Moslems, men of acknowledged skill, who were only too pleased to earn money in the service of the idolators and who considered themselves free to destroy what they had done so soon as the occasion offered.

I here end my narrative, sparing the reader the story of the 1,532 miles which I had still to travel on horseback in order to reach Peking, where I arrived on the 16th of December 1894. Nor will I enlarge upon the negotiations which, thanks to the good offices of the Viceroy of Kansu and of the Imperial Legate of Sining, backed up by the firm and persistent action of M. Gérard, at that time French Minister in Peking, ended by bringing about the restoration of the documents of the mission and, later, in consequence of a Chinese military expedition, the punishment of four of the Tibetans who were most deeply compromised in the crime of Tumbumdo. The head of one of them was set up on the gate of Sining. Unfortunately, it was impossible to touch the superior of the convent of Tumbumdo, whom I have always regarded as the real culprit.

PART THE SECOND

A GENERAL VIEW OF TIBET AND ITS INHABITANTS

CHAPTER I

A DESCRIPTION OF THE COUNTRY AS A WHOLE

The region of the lakes—The region of the rivers.

TIBET occupies the most enormous and the highest mass of mountains in the world. Bounded roughly by the Dapsang peak on the west, the towns of Skardo and Simla, the chain of the Himalayas, Likiang, Tasienlu, Sungpan, the monasteries of Lhabrang and Skubum, the Koko Nor, the Kyaring Cho and the Bayen Kara, Akka Tagh and Ustun Tagh Mountains, it affects the shape of an immense shoe, or, geometrically speaking, of a trapezium with elliptical sides. It measures 1,600 miles in its greatest length between Skardo and Sungpan, 250 miles in its shortest width from the Karakoram Pass to the banks of the Sutlej and 800 in its greatest width between the Koko Nor and the southern bend of the Takiang or Blue River. Its total superficial area is considerably more than a million square miles, covered by a series of snowy mountain-chains, which are gathered up on the meridian of the Karakoram into a narrow sheaf, spread out towards the east in the shape of a fan, turning north and south, and then close up again, turning in the opposite direction. Physically, Tibet is divided into two parts, the lake region and the river region, which surrounds the former on three sides in a semi-circle. The lake region, which extends between Lake Pangong, the sources of the Indus, the Dam Larkang La, the sources of the Salwen and the Blue River and, lastly, those of the rivers of Turkestan, takes the form of an axe, having a width of 200 miles at the handle-end, on the side of Lake Pangong, 450 at the other extremity and a length of 700 miles, and covers a surface equal to that of France. As this part of Tibet is the furthest from the sea, atmospheric precipitations are rarer here than elsewhere, the climate is exceedingly dry and the rivers are unable to acquire enough power to overcome obstacles and to force a way to the sea. The mountain-chains are widely spread, rounded, ill-jointed and separated by almost level valleys,* similar to the Pamirs, at a considerable absolute altitude, but fairly lower than that of the summits. There is no sufficiently determined general slope to enable the waters to collect into rivers; the streams and torrents run into numberless lakes, scattered in every direction like the fragments of a broken mirror. The draining of the waters receives so little assistance that the ground, except on the declivities, is entirely soaked in water, which is frozen and solid during eight months of the year and muddy and shifting in the heart of summer, exactly as in the Siberian tundra.

No other country in the world has a like mean altitude with a similar surface. This mean altitude is over 16,500 feet, the valleys being at 14,500 to 17,400 feet, the peaks at 20,000 to 24,600, the passes at 16,400 to 19,000. The northern part of this region is the highest: the valleys there are never lower than 15,800 feet; and the temperature is very severe, rising with difficulty, in summer, to 15 or 16 degrees at one o'clock in the afternoon and falling to zero or lower at night: in winter, a sharp cold rages of 40 degrees or more. Vegetation is almost non-existent and such grass

* These are the valleys called *tang* in Tibetan, as opposed to *rong*, an embanked valley or gorge.

as grows is never green. The Tibetan herdsmen do not come to pitch their tents there. To the west of the 80th degree of longitude, they go as far as a little to the north of the 34th parallel, but to the east they venture only a little beyond the 33rd in the warm season and remain below the 32nd in winter.

That portion of the lacustrine reign which extends in an elliptical segment between Lake Pangong and the Nam Cho, along the itinerary of Nain Singh, being more to the south and a little less high (15,000 feet on an average) is more habitable and even contains a few poor market-towns built of stone, such as Rudok, Ombo and Senja Jong. It is almost quite unsuited to cultivation, there are no trees in it and, at best, a few pastures of short, hard grass in the midst of absolutely barren wastes. The waters are more abundant and seem to wish to unite into rivers, without, however succeeding. This is a transition zone. Further south, after crossing the southern chain of the Nam Cho, the transformation is complete. There, in the same way as in the west and east, the so to speak shapeless mountainous mass which, like a donjon, commands the centre of the Asiatic continent, becomes articulated, diversified, fashioned. The climate is less dry, provides more moisture and assists the erosive work of the waters, which have hollowed out deep valleys and found a course towards the sea. Thus great rivers have taken birth : the Indus, the Sampo or Brahmaputra, the Salwen, the Takiang, the Mekong, the Hoangho. Near the sources, the appearance of the country changes but little : we have still the same wide valleys, very high and inhospitable to life. At the sources of the Blue River, the country is uninhabited and the Tibetans do not take their herds beyond a broken line drawn from the extreme north-west of the Koko Nor and passing through the Stongri Cho, the Ngoring Cho, the source of the Mekong and the

Tang La Pass. Between the Tibetans and the Mongols lie desert marches which grow narrower as we go further east, that is to say as the ground becomes lower, so that, on the northern banks of the Koko Nor, the two peoples touch and intermingle. In Eastern Tibet, the vegetation, very scarce and poor, begins to appear at a line drawn from Dam (14,400 feet) to Labug Gompa (12,400 feet); then, a little more to the south still, the mountain-slopes become clad with mean and thinly-scattered timber: juniper-trees, tamarisks, willows, pines and firs, cedars, elms. The more we go towards the east, the closer the mountain-chains come together, narrowing the valleys, the ground of which falls lower and lower without any notable decrease in the height of the summits, so that the country bristles with very tall mountains, steep, rocky, difficult to climb, which leave between them only a series of very restricted spaces for pasture and agriculture. Nevertheless, as we go lower, we see the crops improve, the forests thicken, the villages become more numerous until, at last, when we leave the Tibetan prison-house, at the border of the Chinese country, the valleys do not go above 8,200 feet, are fertile, produce wheat, vegetables, fruits, even grapes, pomegranates, rice in the more southern, such as Batang, and important towns arise—Batang, Darchado, Sungpang, Tongkor—where the two ethnical elements, the Chinese and the Tibetan, clash and mingle together. On the west, towards Ladak, we see the same contraction of the mountain folds, the same deep and narrow valleys, separated by enormous rocky walls; only, the altitude remains higher, the vegetation is thinner and there are no trees. The southern zone of Tibet, formed of the basin of the Sampo-Brahmaputra, is the most favoured by nature. The valleys are generally a little wider and their greater proximity to the equator permits rice, apricots and jujubes to be grown at an altitude of 11,500 feet. It is here that the most important towns in the country are built: Shigatse, Lhasa, Gyangtse.

Tibet is a hard and miserly land which only grudgingly yields a little bread to the men who inhabit it. The wildest cantons of Switzerland are as pleasure parks beside it. In whatever part of it one may be, one is surrounded by heights which the snow never leaves, lashed by violent and piercing winds, exposed to arctic colds. The appearance of the scenery is austere, monotonous, overwhelming, thanks to the hugeness of the proportions, and seldom enlivened by the least touch of fugitive grace. Life there would be almost insupportable if the sky and the water were not clear. Such a country as this could even less easily than Turkestan be the cradle of a brilliant civilisation; it was destined only to serve as a refuge for some race wanting in ordinary intelligence; and, in fact, the Tibetan people have never achieved more than an indifferent culture, a pale reflection of the civilisations of China and Hindustan. The Tibetan writers themselves have had the rare modesty to recognise the inferiority of their country by calling it *Kob yul*, the barbarian land.

CHAPTER II

THE INHABITANTS: THEIR PHYSICAL AND MORAL TYPES

Statistics; ethnical name of the Tibetans—Physical characteristics—Moral characteristics.

THE immense territory which I have described is very sparsely inhabited. There would not appear to be in all more than three millions of Tibetans, subjects of the Emperors of China and India respectively,* but all, in spite of the distance that separates them, present a remarkable unity of manners and language. They all give themselves the generic name of Bodpa. The inhabitants of the kingdom of Lhasa and those of Ladak look upon themselves as the purest portion of the Bod race and distinguish their congeners of the north and north-east by special names. The nomads who frequent the pastures of the high table-lands between Lake Pangong and the Nâm Cho are called Changpa (Byangpa), that is to say the Northerns. The nomadic or sedentary Tibetans who live beyond the Nam Cho and to the north of Chamdo, from the district of Nagchu Jong† to the Koko Nor and to Tasienlu, are designated by the word Horpa, which probably has the general

* I do not include in this figure that part of the population of Nepal, Bhutan and Burmah which is connected with the Tibetan race. Mr. Rockhill's conclusions on the statistics of the Tibetan population agree with mine. I am certain that all the other estimates are exaggerated.

† The people of Nagchukka are already Horpa, while those on the banks of the Nam Cho are still Changpa.

sense of barbarian. The Mongols are often so called in the books, whereas in modern usage they are more often given the more precise name of Sokpo. In Western Tibet, where the Mongols are very little known, the word Horpa is applied solely to the Moslem Turkomans of Kashgar. The herdsmen of the steppes in both the west and the east are called Dogpa (Hbrogpa), in opposition to the sedentary husbandmen. None of these names has any ethnical meaning and all the Bodpa, from the Koko Nor to Baltistan, look upon one another as brothers.

They all have a certain family likeness, but they are a heterogeneous family, whose members recognise one another only because they do not resemble the neighbouring families and not because they resemble one another mutually. When you see a Tibetan, you at once decide, judging by his manners and his dress, that he is not a Chinese, nor a Mongol, nor a Turkoman, nor an Indo-European, but you would do wrong to conclude that all the Tibetans are cut after the same pattern, for, should a neighbour come into sight, you will see that he differs almost as greatly from his fellow-countryman as no matter which Chinese, Mongol or Hindu. If you take a group of fifty Tibetans, you may be able to pick out among them three or four different types, which have little in common with one another. Only, the same types are found pretty well everywhere, because among all the ethnical groups that have contributed to form the Tibetan people there have, for thousands of years past, been intimate, frequent and uninterrupted relations which have completely mixed up the ethnical frontiers while unifying the language.* It therefore becomes

* Whatever the dialectical differences may be, they are less great than formerly existed in France on a much smaller surface, nor do they prevent the Tibetans of the most distant districts from understanding one another.

impossible to evolve a general type from amid this confusion. As to describing with exactness and classifying the three or four irreducible types to which all the individual types may be carried back, this is an enterprise that could be attempted only by a specialist who had first studied the question very minutely on the spot. Here, however, are some of the characteristics that are most often seen : a high, narrow and sometimes receding forehead ; large ears standing out from the head ; a nose sometimes wide and flat, but oftenest prominent, not unfrequently aquiline, but almost always with wide nostrils ; eyes less prominent and not so almond-shaped as in the Mongols : in certain individuals, even, the almond-shape is hardly noticeable ; large, prominent cheek-bones ; a long, bony face, sometimes square, hardly ever round as in the Mongols; a wide split mouth ; strong teeth, very often irregular and rotten ; lips thick in some, but thin in the majority; hands and feet large and clumsy ; thick, hard hair, with a more or less pronounced tendency to wave ; beard rare, with a few exceptions : I have seen Eastern Tibetans bearded like patriarchs, but, as a rule, it is their custom to remove the hair from their faces with tweezers. The stature of the Tibetans is above the middle height and is taller in the north-east of Tibet, where it averages 5 feet 5 inches, than in the west, where the mean height is two inches less. Their bones are large, their muscles undeveloped, hard and firm ; stoutness is extremely rare, even in the women. I met no fat people, except among the monks ; and even then I saw none that could be described as obese. The skull is visibly brachycephalic, but less so than among the Mongols. The colour of the eyes is light brown or hazel, of the hair always black, of the skin indeterminable, because of the dirt with which all alike are covered ; nevertheless, I had the good fortune to see a few Tibetans who had just washed themselves: they appeared to me to be bronzed like Italians, with a slightly reddish foundation. The collection of legends of Padma Sambhava speaks of Tibet as the land of the red-faces, *dongmar bod yul*. There is no room for establishing any characteristic distinction between the Tibetans of Lhasa and Tachilhunpo, of whom I saw a fairly large number, and the nomads of the north and north-east, except that the latter naturally have a rougher bearing. On the other hand, the Panaks of the shores of the Koko Nor must be set apart; they are much nearer the Mongols than the other Tibetans and, in particular, their eyes are more almond-shaped, their noses less prominent and their figures more thick-set.

The Tibetans have much more suppleness, agility and grace in their walk than the inhabitants of Chinese Turkestan; they move very fast, excepting the grandees, with comparatively short, quick steps, wriggling their hips as they go. I have pointed out elsewhere how easily they accommodate themselves to the excessive altitude of their country, which is no inconvenience to them. Thanks to this power of accommodation, they are able, without too much difficulty, to endure long marches and to indulge in rapid journeys of which few Europeans would be capable in such mountains as these. Nevertheless, I did not find that the Tibetans were better able to resist fatigue or to endure suffering than we are: rather is the contrary true, for, though their bodies are less delicate, they have not so powerful a moral energy.

It is, perhaps, a rather deceptive undertaking to try to draw a moral portrait of the Tibetan. The few characteristics which are common to all the inhabitants of Tibet and to them alone in no way help to compose the Tibetan soul, but are simply superadded, resulting as they do from historical antecedents and social and political conditions. In general, it may be said that the Tibetan possesses gentleness not devoid of hypocrisy; he is weak, timid, obsequious and distrustful, like all weak people. This is a consequence of the clerical government that is laid upon him, a tyrannical, sectarian, suspicious government, trembling lest it should see its authority escape it, mindful to keep every one in a state of servile dependence and making a system of mutual spying and informing the basis of the social edifice. Fear hovers over the whole of Tibet: the government fears its subjects and the subjects their government; each man dreads his neighbour, his enemy and his friend; the private individual is afraid of the arbitrary power of the official and the lama; and these both tremble before their superiors, who, in their turn, stand in constant alarm of the secret intrigues which they discover or imagine among their inferiors. Fear usually leads to cruelty and this explains the frequency of murders and especially of cases of poisoning, as well as the barbarity of the punishments to which the Tibetans condemn their criminals; for their hearts are not naturally hard and closed to pity. It goes without saying that the Tibetans show even greater distrust with regard to strangers than to their fellow-countrymen and that is why it is so difficult to extract the least information from them. But it is so greatly a matter of policy that the Ponbo Tibetans, who detest the Buddhists, open out quite readily to Europeans, in whom they see a possible support against their orthodox enemies. In the same way, the Tibetans of the east, who are divided into independent and mutually hostile tribes, exposed to the raids of their neighbours and always upon the alert against attack, are much more disputatious and quarrelsome than their congeners in the west and south and yield with less constraint to the violent impulses of instinct.

There is no traveller but has observed the heedlessness of the Tibetan. He does not love long reflection: "Sufficient for the day is the evil thereof" is his maxim; and, when occasion offers, he amuses himself, sings, dances and has good cheer without troubling about the morrow. And what is there of which he should take heed? The social organisation is such that he can scarcely hope to rise above his condition and that, wherever fate has caused him to be born, he is almost sure of his daily pittance, with which he is contented because he knows that he can obtain no better. Anxious characters occur only in societies as complex and as unstable as ours, where there is a superabundance of population, where nearly every man, instead of finding a place kept for him in the sun at his birth, is obliged to make one for himself by his own efforts, at the cost of much time and trouble, where it is impossible to procure contentment cheaply, where men's ambitions are unloosed by the capacity which all possess or believe themselves to possess for climbing to the topmost summits.

It is well to be on one's guard, in a certain measure, against the accusations of lubricity made against the Tibetans by the missionaries, who are always curiously inept when speaking of this sort of matter, and by the Chinese, who are always full of national pride and smug respectability. I do not believe that the Tibetans are, at bottom, worse in this respect than the majority of men. To tell the truth, notwithstanding the recommendations of the Buddhist religion, they attach but a very slight importance to what others regard as very immoral. Their example serves excellently well to prove the vanity of the theory according to which the inhabitants of cold countries have naturally better morals than those of hot countries. In any case, the Tibetan, who is coarser and less restrained by prejudice than the Chinaman, indulges his libertinism with less refinement and less viciousness. He is also less proud and less of a scoffer ; he is not prone to insolence and depreciation and is given rather to displaying frank admiration. He has a simple gaiety, an ingenuous good-humour, that causes him to be amused by the least thing, like the big baby that he is. Of very indifferent culture, both in the towns and the steppes, he has a less prudent and less industrious mind than the Turkoman of Khotan or Kashgar ; and yet education is a little more wide-spread in Tibet than in Turkestan. But this education is limited to the first elements of reading and writing and to prayers and the catechism ; and this necessarily rude religious instruction has but increased the profoundly superstitious character of these minds as yet dark and crammed with childish fears and credulousness. However, the Tibetan is the intellectual superior of the Mongol, less heavy and less stupid ; he does not lack vivacity or goodwill ; and, with good management, there is someting to be made of him.

CHAPTER III

HISTORICAL SKETCH

Origins of the Tibetan people—The chief tribes in the sixth century A.D., according to the Chinese writers—The first Tibetan kingdom between the seventh and the ninth centuries—Struggles between the civil power and the religious power.

We have no precise and certain information as to the origin of the Tibetan race. The Tibetans declare that they are descended from an ape-god and a female demon *(shrinmo)*: in the same way, the Turkomans contend that their first ancestor was a wolf. The Chinese state that the Tibetans are the descendants of the Sanmiao tribes, which Chun, the mythical emperor who lived in the twenty-third century B.C., sent to the neighbourhood of the Koko Nor. This would prove that, in the opinion of the Chinese, the Tibetans originally occupied the fertile valleys of China, whence they were driven by the conquering people of the Hundred Families, and that the settlement of the Tibetans in their present country dates back to prehistoric ages.

It is very probable that the Tibetans belong to the same stock as the different Turco-Mongol nations. Not only is there a considerable resemblance between the physical types of all of them, but their respective manners and beliefs present striking analogies. No doubt, the processes of civilisation being much the same in all races, we must not, in order to prove their ethnical relationship, rely too much upon the identity of certain customs between two nations nor even upon the similarity of the general principles which serve as a basis for their respective social systems. Otherwise, it would be very easy to demonstrate that the Chinese have the same origin as the Greeks. But, in the case of the Tibetans, we observe between their oldest usages and those of the Turkomans and Mongols resemblances so close, following one another sometimes so exactly down to the smallest detail, that it is impossible not to see more in this than a chance coincidence. The difference in language is a difficulty: we know that the Tibetans speak an idiom which is partly monosyllabic like Chinese, partly agglutinative like Mongolian, and which already possesses rudiments of declension and conjugation which permit it to have a syntax more nearly allied to the Turkic than to the Chinese syntax; moreover, its vocabulary is quite special. It is certain that, if the hypothesis of the common origin of the Tibetans and Mongols be correct, the former have undergone remarkable modifications in the course of the ages, as their physical type proves. It is very possible that, coming from Mongolia, they found another race settled before them in the land of the sources of the great rivers and that they mixed with this race and, in a certain measure, borrowed its language and its corporal structure. Perhaps a few remnants of this primitive race still survive among the wild hordes of Sechuen, Yunnan or the Himalayas.

The Tibetan legends of the Book of Kings teach us nothing as to the origins: they are only inventions, laboriously arranged by pedantic scribes, which remind one greatly of the traditions of primitive China, distorted with a puerile rationalism by later historians. This is the same system that consists in attributing to a series of very wise kings the discovery and application of the arts necessary to life and the establishment of the institutions that are the ground-work of society. The first of these kings, Nyati Tsanpo, is said to have come from India; he entered Tibet from Bhotan and crossed Mount Yarlhachampo to go to Lhasa. This is a legend which was evidently fabricated by the Buddhist monks accustomed to attribute everything to India and which must be rejected at once. Nevertheless, it is not impossible that the monks, in saying this, were unconsciously uttering a truth and that a part of the Tibetan people did, at an extremely distant period, issue from the plain of the Ganges. The oldest certain mention made of the Tibetans in history is to be found in the annals of the Hans, which speak of them under the general name of Kiang and relate that, in 770 B.C., they were at war with the Chinese.* As early as the commencement of the Christian era, traders crossed Tibet to go from Palibothra Regia (Patna) to the capital of China, passing through Nepal and Lhasa. Pliny the Elder calls Tibet the land of the Attacori, a name which we find again in Ptolemy under the form of Ottorokorrha, a town situated near the Sampo and corresponding very probably with Lhasa. The Alexandrian geographer already knows the real name of the Tibetans, *οἱ βαῦται*; but for him the Bauti are only one of the hordes inhabiting the country lying between the Himalayas (Emodes) and the Nan Chan (Kacian Mountains) and he places them north of Lhasa. However, it seems that this was the chief of the tribes of Tibet, since it gave its name to the River Bautisos, an ideal generalisation of all the streams which derive their source between Nepal and Tsaidam and which, for Ptolemy, all join the Hoangho.

In the fourth century of our era, the Tibetans assisted in bringing about the downfall of the Tsin

* We must not attach much importance to this date of 770, as Chinese history acquires no certainty until the second half of the third century B.C.

dynasty: they then numbered one hundred and fifty tribes, sub-divided into a swarm of little clans, established on the left of the River Min and of the Takiang. Their most important chief resided to the east of the river of Lhasa (Loso), probably on the site of the present town. The annals of the Soei and the Tangut give us the principal tribes in the sixth century and supply indications of sufficient precision to enable us to place them on the map. They are, beginning at the north-east:

1. The Tukuhun, so called after the name of a Turko-Mongol chief who came from Liaotung to settle in their country in 312. They occupied the region lying between Sining and the Yellow River, the neighbourhood of the Koko Nor and Tsaidam. They are the ancestors of the Panaks and the Gomis. Their capital was situated at 15 or 50 lis to the west of the Koko Nor. In the fifth and sixth centuries, their dominion extended as far as Cherchen. The women of the country of the Tukuhun, like the Tibetan women of our own day, parted their hair into a number of little plaits and adorned it with beads and shells. The bulk of the population certainly remained Tibetan, but the Turko-Mongolian element introduced by the invaders was far from unimportant, numbering no fewer than 1,100 families, according to the annals of the Soei;

2. The Tanghiang,* to the south of the above and to the east of the River Tao and of Sungpanting, occupied the mountainous district of the Upper Yellow River and the Za Chu. They were a people of horsemen, warlike and given to pillage, having no houses, but only yak-skin tents. We recognise in them the ancestors of the Goloks, the Zachukkapa and the people of Ngamodo. It was from one of their tribes, probably

* The term Tangut comes from the name of this horde. It is the Mongol plural of Tang.

that of the Topa, that the celebrated Sihia dynasty took its origin;

3. Various tribes, such as the Chunsang, Misang and others, to the south of the Tanghiang and doubtless corresponding with the people of Dergyeh and the five Horpa clans;

4. Nukno, that is to say the kingdom of women, or, more correctly, Nuwangkno, the country governed by a queen. This country, situated to the east, or rather to the south-east of the Tanghiang and to the north-east of Yachow, is the modern Toskyab and Somo. Mr. Rockhill notes that, when he passed through the Horpa, Somo was governed by a woman. We must be suspicious of information given by the Chinese authors, who are apt to exaggerate customs differing from their own and who imagine that, if women do not occupy in a particular society a place as low as that which they fill in Chinese society, they become sovereign mistresses through this very fact. Note that, in Nukno, all the officials who are not employed in the interior of the palace, the military officers and the priests are men;

5. The Tangchang, to the west of Sechuen (Tasienlu);

6. The Tengchi, beside the above (Litang or Batang);

7. The Pelan, to the west of the Tanghiang, occupied the country of the Nyamcho, of the Taorongpa and, generally, the territory of the Nanchen Gyapo. Their name is found under the form of Paliana in Ptolemy, who places them at Long. 162° 25′, Lat. 41° between Tsaidam and Lhasa;

8. The Tomis, to the west of the above, occupied the present territory of the Hortsi Gyapeko in the basin of the Sog Chu;

9. The Tufan, to the south of the above and east of Nepal, occupied the Lhasa country and the whole

province of Bu: they were the most powerful tribe in Tibet from the fourth century onwards;*

10. The Silis, to the south-west of the above, a tribe of 50,000 families dwelling in towns and villages. Their country was South Chang and more especially the neighbourhood of Tachilhunpo;

11. The Changkiepo, nomadic highlanders, numbering about 2,000 tents to the south-west of the Silis, that is to say on the confines of Nepal, in the neighbourhood of Nilam;

12 and 13. The Yangtung, divided into Little and Great, were nomads who grazed their herds west of the Tufan, north of Nepal, south of Khotan, that is to say in West Chang and in Eastern Ngaris, or, roughly, between Long. 77° and 83°. The Little Yangtung lived in Ngaris and the Great in Chang;

14. The Great Poliu or Polu, to the west of the Yangtung. These are the people of Ladak;

15. The Little Poliu, to the west of the above, occupied what is now Baltistan. They were at the outlet of the road to Kashgar through the Pamirs.†

The annals of the Soei and the Tangut depict to us these Tibetans of yore as very similar to those whom we see to-day, with their dirty faces, their tangled hair, their long skin robes, their yak-hair tents in the north and their flat-roofed houses in the south. Even as to-day, they made barley-beer and kneaded pellets of tsamba into a buttered drink; they had a taste for brigandage and never went out without their bows and their swords; their manners were very free and the punishments which they inflicted upon criminals very

* They had absorbed, among other nations, the Supi, who probably inhabited Nagchukka and Namru.

† Klaproth: *Historical Pictures of Asia*—Bushell: *The Early History of Tibet*—W. Rockhill: *The Land of the Lamas—Tibet: a Geographical, Historical and Ethnographical Sketch derived from Chinese Sources*—Bitchourine: *A History of Tibet and the Koko Nor* (in Russian).

ferocious. Their women wore their hair divided into a mass of little plaits* and coated their faces with a black glaze. The crops were scarce and comprised little besides barley, buckwheat and pease. The father passed his authority as head of the family on to the son when the latter was grown up. Their religion was the same as that of the ancient Chinese and the ancient Turkomans, consisting in ancestor-worship and a coarse naturalism: we shall see presently that this religion has survived almost in its entirety among the people. The priest-wizards, similar to the Turkic *kams*, wielded a great influence over the superstitious minds of the ancient Tibetans; by means of sacrifices and prayers they gave a religious sanction to the oaths of political fidelity which the chiefs took to the prince every year and, with greater solemnity, every three years; and it is related that, at the great triennial celebration, human beings were sacrificed. For the rest, the civilisation of these Tibetans was very rudimentary; they did not know how to write and, to convey orders or establish contracts, they used notched wooden pins, like the old Turkomans and like the Tibetan or other hordes who live in the south-eastern corner of Tibet to this day.

About the year 630 A.D., the Tibetan Prince Srongtsangampo (the very mighty and very wise [?] Srong)† collected a large number of Tibetan tribes into a confederation and founded a great State, with Lhasa for its capital. This new kingdom took the name which it has since kept, Tufa in Chinese, or rather, according to the old pronunciation, Tupat. *Pat* is a transliteration of

---

* At least, among the Tanghiang Tibetans of the north-east.

† Srong is often pronounced Rong, wherefore the Chinese writers have transcribed this name as Lung. The meaning of Gampo or Sgampo is very doubtful (*Cf.* Jæschke's *Dictionary*, p. 114). This sovereign is more shortly called Srongtsanpo.

the word *Bod*,* which the Tibetans use to denote their country and their race; *tu* represents the Tibetan *mt'o* (pronounced *t'o*), or high. The Arabs have turned it into Tibbet,† which is pronounced very nearly as if composed of the two English words "tub, but," and Marco Polo wrote Tebet, which afterwards became Tibet or Thibet.‡ A few rays of civilisation began to illumine the country. Srongtsanpo sent a missionary to India, who brought back a writing and translated two or three Buddhist treatises; he gave some encouragement to the religion of Sakya Muni and built several temples: the lamas rewarded him later by raising him to the dignity of an incarnation of Avalokiteshvara. However, Buddhism spread very little in Tibet in this reign. It was not until after the arrival, in the middle of the eighth century, of Master Padma Sambhava, the tamer of demons, that the monasteries were founded and a regular clergy created. The influence of Chinese civilisation at once made itself felt with much greater strength than that

---

* Generally pronounced Bod as written.

† They ought to have transliterated it with a *T'* and not with a *T*; but we know that it was their custom to Arabicise foreign words by substituting the simple *t* for the aspirate *t'*. As for the reduplication of the *b*, this is a later corruption, which probably owes its origin to the effort that was made to pronounce the particular sound of the vowel *u*.

‡ *Cf.* M. L. Feer's pamphlet, *Etymology of the word Tibet*. I think that I am right in writing Tibet without the *h*, because, first, the letters *Th* represent to me not a *t* aspirate, but the English sound of *th*, which cannot be figured in any other manner; secondly, it is absolutely useless to encumber the spelling of names so current in every-day use as that of Tibet with superfluous letters which are not pronounced and cannot be pronounced; thirdly, if it be thought necessary to represent the Tibetan aspiration, then there is all the greater reason for changing the vowels *i* and *e*, which make the original word quite unrecognisable; fourthly, the oldest texts of Marco Polo give Tebet oftener than Thebet; fifthly and lastly, it is possible that the first syllable, instead of being a transcription of *mt'o*, is that of *stod*, which has the same meaning and almost the same sound, but without the aspiration.

of the Buddhist religion. Srongtsanpo recognised the suzerainty of the Emperor of China, married a princess of the imperial family, doffed his hides of beasts in favour of silk garments in the Chinese fashion, surrounded himself with Chinese *literati* who conducted his official correspondence, sent the children of the Tibetan nobility to study the classical literature of China and had workmen brought from Singan to make paper and ink. At the same time that they were putting themselves to school in China, the Tibetans acquired a material power which they were never to know again in all the course of time. In 663, they destroyed the Mongolian dynasty of the Tukuhun, which held sway in the region of the Koko Nor, and soon their empire extended from Lanchow to the gates of Badakshan. They entered into relations with the caliphs of Bagdad, who at one time allied themselves with them against the Chinese, at another with the Chinese against the Tibetans; they repeatedly captured Singan, the capital of China, and would perhaps have succeeded, in the eighth century, in breaking up their suzerain's empire, if he had not provoked an almost general coalition of Asia against his dangerous neighbours.

I have explained elsewhere how, for nearly two centuries, they had been the more or less irregular and disputed masters of Chinese Turkestan and how, in the course of the ninth century, their kingdom became dismembered in consequence of the legendary rivalries between the civil power and the clergy. The lamas, fed, protected and loaded with favours by royalty, rewarded its benefits, so soon as they felt strong enough, by trying to expel it from the home where it had made room for them. It is the everlasting story. The kings defended themselves and one of them, Langdarma, signalised his reign by a relentless persecution of the clergy. He was no other, if we may believe the chroniclers, than the devil incarnate: he had an incipient horn on his head and he carefully concealed this deformity, which would have revealed his true character to his people. Only those to whom he entrusted the care of his beard and hair were able to see the accusing sign, but they had no opportunity to be indiscreet, for they were put to death so soon as their task was done. At last, an ascetic saint, who, by dint of ruining his health in contemplation, had acquired the gift of second sight, came to know of the existence of the horn and realised that his duty was to rid the sacred land of Bod of this unclean monster. He succeeded in penetrating secretly into the monarch's palace and killed him with an arrow.

In the tenth century, the clergy was restored to its privileges. Kublai Khan recognised as the chief of the Tibetan clergy the superior of the convent of Saskya* and conferred temporal authority upon him under his own suzerainty; and, since then, China has not ceased to support the clergy. The power of the monks as against the lay monarchy declined together with the strength of the emperors and again resumed its vigour at the same time as they. Tsongkapa, the great reformer, triumphed with the Ming dynasty; his successors were eclipsed by the secular kings, who were supported by the Ili Mongols so soon as the Ming dynasty had lost its ascendant, and recovered their pre-eminence so soon as the Tsing dynasty was established; and, lastly, when the lay prince tried once more to seize the authority, the Emperor Kienlong, who raised the Chinese power to its topmost point, ordered him to be condemned and executed and awarded the royal title to the Dalai Lama and the functions of viceroy to another lama in 1751. The consequence of this good

* The predecessor and uncle of the famous Pagspa.

understanding between the Tibetan clergy and China was that the latter was able to dispense with sending a colony to Tibet, kept up a much smaller number of officials and soldiers in Tibet than in Turkestan and, nevertheless, exercised a much greater influence over its civilisation, so that, generally speaking, everything which, in the civilisation of Tibet, is not of Indian origin may be said to have derived its source from China.

CHAPTER IV

MATERIAL LIFE: HABITATIONS, CLOTHING, FOOD, HYGIENE AND MEDICINE

Tents—Houses—Clothing—Food—Climate, hygiene and medicine.

I HAVE already, in the first part of this work, given some details concerning the different subjects which are treated in this chapter. Also, Mr. W. W. Rockhill has handled these questions with remarkable accuracy in his *Notes on the Ethnology of Tibet*, which are abundantly illustrated from nature. I refer the reader to this book and will content myself here with very briefly summing up my own observations and information, which confirm the work of the celebrated American traveller without adding greatly to it.

From the point of view of dwellings, Tibet may be divided into two regions: the region of tents and the region of houses. The latter does not extend further north than the itinerary of Nain Singh by Rudok, Ombo and Senja Jong. East of the Nam Cho, Nagchu, Jyerkundo and the villages of the La Chu Valley present the last specimens of stone houses. Beyond those limits, tents mingle with the stone houses, more numerous than the latter at first and then less numerous, without, however, disappearing entirely, except in a few districts specially favourable to agriculture and unfitted for grazing. Thus, in Ladak, from Lake Pangong to Leh and from Leh to the Karaul Pass, there are no tents. Although tents are pre-eminently the dwellings of the herdsmen, there are, nevertheless, a certain number of Tibetans, as, for instance, the inhabitants of Nagchu Jong, who, while living solely on their cattle, live in houses.

The Tibetan tent *(gur)* is quite different from the Mongolian tent. It is made of a coarse black web of yak-hair, greatly inferior in every respect to the Mongol felt; is quadrilateral instead of round; and is held up by one horizontal and two vertical poles, which are fixed and strengthened by a large number of ropes stretched outside, passing over little stakes at some distance from the tent and then pinned into the ground. It is never pitched on level soil, not only because Tibet has hardly any flat surfaces, but also because the natives avoid the low ground and take shelter on the slopes of the mountains in order to escape too much moistness in spring and, generally, to protect themselves better against the brigands. The tent rests most often against a thick wall of dried ox-dung, which serves at the same time as a stack of fuel and as a screen against the wind and snow; it is usually surrounded, at some distance, by a little stone or mud wall, very low and insignificant in Central Tibet, very high in those parts of Eastern Tibet where brigandage is frequent. This enclosure is called the *rawa (raba*, the *yenchu* of the Chinese*)*; and this is the name which I have always heard given to the Tibetan tents; the enclosure, in fact, has a capital moral importance: it is the limit of the domain of the household gods and the stranger who has crossed its threshold at once becomes the owner's guest. Inside the tent, at the back, is the *cella*, the cupboard of the gods, before which, on the ground, in the place of honour, lies a great block of wood, one or two yards long by eight or ten inches high and badly squared, on which he who is admitted to the place of honour puts down his cup of tea. In the middle is the hearth. The dried dung burns either in a little iron apparatus consisting of three hoops placed one above the other and supported by three legs, or else in a stone furnace, long, narrow, breast-high, with a hearth at one end and a transversal channel with room for several stewpots to boil upon. The smoke escapes through the hole contrived in the top of the tent or most often spreads through the interior, black, acrid and sticky, contributing in a marked way to bronzing the faces of the natives. To the right of the entrance, near the canvas, stands a row of small bags containing the provisions; to the left, the strips of felt and the blankets that serve for bedding are piled up with saddles, iron-ware, pots, pans, cups, a lump of stone for pounding the tea, a churn, a number of mutton-bones, sometimes one or two live lambs and a heap of dried dung. The furniture of the houses displays the same simplicity, except in towns of some importance: the furnace is similar to those in the tents and the chimney is also reduced to a hole in the ceiling.

The Tibetan houses *(khangpa)*, built for the most part of stone slabs, have generally several storeys, two or three, the ground-floor serving as a stable. The roofs are flat, the windows sparingly contrived and, as often as possible, looking out on the court-yard; most of the rooms are lighted merely by narrow slits: only the state-rooms admit the light by wide windows fitted with paper panes and thick shutters of red wood. Every respectable house has, on the first or second floor, a verandah, which does not stand out, but which consists simply of a room of which the outer wall has been removed. The poor houses have a yard at the front or back, while, in the rich dwellings, the buildings are arranged around an inner court or *tsom (khyams)*. The tsom is sometimes on the first floor, the ground-floor being entirely covered over, in which case there is nothing resembling it in European buildings: the tsom becomes a large open-air upper hall. According to the somewhat summary descriptions which the annals of Tang give of the houses of Tibet in the seventh century, it would seem that the architecture has not changed since. These houses, though more solidly built than those of Turkestan, are, on the whole, less convenient and are arranged in an odd and awkward manner, but they are pretty well-suited to serve as a refuge against an armed aggression or as a base for an attack. Like the tents, they exhibit a marked preference for sloping ground, preferring to look down upon the passer-by rather than to see him from below.

The Tibetan dress consists essentially of a very wide gown, 5½ feet long, with very long sleeves, tightened in at the waist and gathered up so as not to fall below the ankle of the men of quality or the townsmen nor below the knee of the common people, who have much walking and work to do. Thus gathered up, the gown puffs out at the breast, forming a huge pocket. At night, the wearer lets it fall and is thus wrapped up from his ears to his feet as in a bed. The women wear the same gown, but never raise it above the ankle. This garment is called *chuba*, the same as the pelisse of the eastern Turks *(juba, jua)*. Among the herdsmen of the north, it is made of unlined sheepskin, sometimes adorned with wide edgings of panther-skin or coloured woollen stuff. In the towns, they wear the same gown in indigo-blue or dark-red wool. The latter colour is the most popular. A woollen gown of the first quality costs at Lhasa as much as 400 *tanka*, or £15. The ceremonial dress of the chief lamas and officials is the Chinese silk costume with the *makoatso*. Trousers are not a national garment; neither the lamas nor the majority of the nomads use them. Delicate people wear drawers of the Chinese pattern. As for shirts, these are worn only by the refined: they are made either of calico or of a sort of very coarse Nepal silk called *buré (buras)*, which I have always seen grey, but I have never been able to discover its original colour. There are two sorts of boots worn: Chinese boots and native boots, which latter have undressed yak-skin soles and stuff uppers with coloured bands. The chief lamas also wear white boots, which are made at Lhasa.

Perhaps there is no country in the world where one sees a greater variety of head-dresses than in Tibet: slender red turbans; little Chinese felt hats with narrow, turned-up brims; huge fur caps with ear-flaps, with or without wide ribbons; tall hats for the summer, with narrow crowns and very wide brims, fastened under the chin by straps; and straw hats of the Tyrolese shape. Some are worn at the same time in the same places; others are peculiar to certain districts, certain tribes or certain groups of tribes. Thus, the shape of the fur caps of Ladak differs greatly from that of the caps in common use at Lhasa. The Goloks and the Zachukkapa have a special round cap, fitting close to the head behind and forming a peak in front; the Panaks wear a round cap, ending in a point, but quite low. Many of the nomads are content to cover their heads and ears with a strip of sheepskin like a peasant-woman's kerchief. Lastly, a large number go bareheaded, which offers no inconvenience, because the Tibetans allow their hair, which is thick and tangled, to grow freely. They are in the habit of twisting the hair at the top of the head into a plait, so as to reconcile the national way of doing the hair with the Chinese, and they adorn this plait with an ivory ring and a narrow band of stuff, in which they fix turquoises or corals. In the towns, the hair is dressed in the Chinese fashion, but not so carefully as among the inhabitants of the Middle Kingdom.

The Zachukkapa, the Goloks and the Panaks are exceptional in having their heads shaved.

The Tibetans, like all nations still in a state of barbarism, delight in showy and massive jewels. In the Jyerkundo district, there are scarcely any men but wear in their left ear a large, heavy silver ring, set with a coral or precious stone. One of the officials who came from Lhasa to the shores of the Nam Cho to meet us wore, by way of an ear-drop, an oblong sapphire not much smaller than a pigeon's egg. As for the women, they wear regular jewellers' shops on their heads. Among the nomads, their hair, arranged in innumerable small tresses that involve more than a whole day's work, is decorated with three great bands of woollen stuff or red silk strewn with rupees, shells, artificial pearls, corals, turquoises, amber beads, red agates, gold, silver or copper reliquaries and the rest. The head-dress of the women of Ladak is more modest. The women of Lhasa, I was told, wear their hair like the women of Chinese Turkestan, gathered into two plaits hanging down their back.

The dress of the women varies more according to the districts than that of the men. In the east, they wear, in addition to the chuba, a sort of petticoat striped blue, green, yellow and red. At Leh, they cover their backs with a sheepskin shawl fastened at the throat with a brooch. This shawl is indispensable at all ceremonies or visits; the rich women line the sheepskin with silk or English cloth, bringing the gold letters of the trade-mark well in view on the shoulder. There has been much spoken of the custom general among the Tibetan women of coating their faces with catechu and much discussion of the reasons for this odd custom. The real reason is the wish to protect themselves against the chaps which would otherwise be caused by the wind and the cold. When the women go into society, as we should say, they remove this coating and are very proud to be able to show a fresh, pink complexion.

The Tibetans, especially the nomads, generally carry on their persons a host of accessories : a knife, a needle-case, a tobacco-box, a pipe, a powder-horn, a tinder-box. The tinder-boxes are similar to those of Turkestan and Altai. A man rarely goes out unarmed, at least in the districts which I visited. Usually, he is content with a sling and with a sword with a straight, strong, two-edged blade, stuck slantwise through his belt, like a dagger. When he is fully armed, he carries also a long rapier in his belt ; in his hand, a lance six feet long, with an iron head and a light, but solid shaft ; and, slung across his body, a long matchlock, with a slender butt-end and a wide and thick iron barrel, furnished with a forked rest.

The food of the Tibetans has been described too often and in too much detail for me to dwell upon it here. I will only make a few remarks. Tsamba, which consists of barley-corns grilled and ground, is not, as some have said, the staple food of the people. It is a very expensive commodity, chiefly among the nomads, and they are as sparing with it as possible. A man eats little more than one or two handfuls of it a day ; on the other hand, he is continually drinking innumerable cups of tea beaten up with butter and salted and he cannot do without this for long, for there is nothing that he dreads so much as a dry stomach. This, with dry, morcellated cheese, forms the real basis of Tibetan food. They add to it a very respectable quantity of meat supplied by the dead animals of the herd, beasts killed when hunting and a few yaks and sheep slaughtered on great occasions. They are in the habit of carefully preserving a certain bone (I forget which) of each animal eaten and this is why we see long rows of bones arranged in the tents. At Lhasa, yak-flesh is mostly eaten. As a rule, the animals intended for food are killed at the end of autumn, when they are well fattened; they are cut into quarters, which are hung up to dry; and, during the rest of the year, the natives eat this raw meat, which they cut into thin shreds. Pork and poultry are absolutely unknown to the nomads and are found only in the southern towns. A change of diet is supplied to the herdsmen of the north-east by a root (*toma?*) which grows freely up to an altitude of 14,500 feet; it is almost black, the size of a small red radish and, when cooked, tastes not unlike salsify. At Lhasa, they have cabbages, potatoes of the European kind, onions, carrots, turnips, peas and beans. They eat a fair quantity of wheat-meal and rice. The rice is usually boiled in the Chinese manner and served with different meats in a sauce, after the Kashmirian style. They also know pilau and different Chinese dishes. But the Tibetans are not at all dainty in their food and set no store by variety. They are naturally large eaters, although many of them are obliged to go on short commons. A Tibetan who had travelled in all the neighbouring countries and who stayed some time with us expressed surprise at our abstemiousness and told us that he had never seen any but the English eat as much as his fellow-countrymen. They have a very pronounced weakness for alcoholic liquids; they drink large quantities of their national beer (*chang*) and of brandy, of which one kind (arak) is manufactured by themselves and another is supplied to them by the Chinese. One may be sure that, if a Tibetan has brandy within his reach and money to buy it with, he will get drunk. But his poverty sometimes mounts too strict a guard over him.

The very severe climate of Tibet is healthy because of its dryness, which is not so extreme as in Turkestan, and of the ordinary purity of the atmosphere. Its chief danger lies in the great variations of the temperature. We observed daily variations of 27 degrees, in December and January, on the shores of the Nam Cho and at

Nagchu, and of 24 degrees, at the end of May, at Jyerkundo. At Lhasa, the thermometer fluctuates most probably between −30 degrees in the winter and + 35 degrees in the summer. The thaw also presents drawbacks owing to the moisture which it produces; but, on the whole, the climate is not favourable to illness. I cannot say as much for the habits of the natives. They have, it is true, the advantage of living much out of doors; but, also, their houses are dirty, as they were thirteen centuries ago, and full of draughts; they sleep immediately over the stables; the court-yards are poisoned with rubbish of every kind and dung-heaps. Among the nomads, whole families are crowded promiscuously in tents which are always too close and sleep in greasy beds eaten up with vermin, in an atmosphere tainted with smoke and with the emanations of the herds gathered around. Neither the men nor the women take any care of their persons. They wear their clothes very long without changing, brushing or shaking them, keep them on even at night, use them as dusters and towels and take them off only when they drop off of themselves. They never wash their bodies and only in quite exceptional circumstances wash their faces and hands. However, to protect themselves against the bites of the wind, they cover themselves over with butter, the most rancid that they can find, preferring to eat the other; and this is very efficacious, for the dust, sweat and morsels of cattle-dung, settling on this greasy layer, form an outer covering which, fortunately, doubles or trebles the consistency of the already thick skin allotted by nature to the Tibetans. Thanks to this process, the people of the country give out a characteristic smell, not so much agreeable as penetrating and persistent, from which the greatest personages are not exempt. They neglect their hair as much as the rest of their bodies and comb it no more frequently to-day than they did thirteen hundred years ago. They content themselves with, from time to time, buttering their hair to drive away the fleas. One is inclined to ask what their plight would be if they did not take this precaution.

In these conditions, it is not surprising that illness is extremely frequent, as well as infectious and contagious diseases of every kind, such as cancerous ulcers *(lhogpa)*, leprosy *(mdzé)*, plague *(nyan)*, syphilis and malignant smallpox. The cold causes many cases of rheumatism and gangrene. Cases of ophthalmia are also very numerous, because of the dirt, the smoke and the glare of the snow. Medicine, of Hindu origin, is practised exclusively by lamas, who use mainly Chinese remedies. I have spoken of this in the first part of the present volume and need not return to it.

CHAPTER V

THE FAMILY

Solidity and extension of the Tibetan family, compared with the Turkic family and the Mongolian family—Marriage; polyandry: Tibetan polyandry is only a form of patriarchism—Condition of the women—Amusements.

FAMILY ties are not nearly so much relaxed in Tibet as they are in Turkestan. Individualism has made but little progress and Tibetan society is to this day essentially a communistical society. It is based upon the idea of the *gens*,* of a group of persons who can go back, by an uninterrupted chain of generations, to a common ancestor. Every Tibetan traces his pedigree to a very remote stage and all those who are united in blood have not only vague duties of courtesy towards one another, but precise and serious obligations. All are bound collectively to assist their kinsman in his need, to come to his aid with money when he marries his children, to pay his debts, to see that he is ritually buried and, in case of murder, to exact the price of his blood. The difficulty of gathering information in Tibet prevents me from fixing this solidarity exactly, but everybody admits it, proclaims it ; and if, probably, it has grown weaker with time, it is nevertheless a very living thing still and reveals itself in every action of life. When an individual is guilty of a crime of high

* *Gyud (brgyud)*, a word which also means cord or, as we should say, chain.

treason, it often happens that all his kinsmen, to a very remote degree, are included in the punishment inflicted on him. It seems that, among the nomads, the tribes are only so many large families, all whose members look upon themselves as springing from a common origin. In fact, it is customary for them all to bear the same name, adding to it, to distinguish themselves, a surname usually borrowed from Buddhic nomenclature. Lastly, the Tibetan nation as a whole is regarded as a yet more extensive family ; to denote it, the same expression is used as indicates the series of generations issuing from a common ancestor *(bodkyi migyud)*; and the king is sometimes given the title of the father of the family.

So far, we have seen nothing that does not exist also, in different degrees, among the Chinese, the Mongols and the Turkomans. Pursuing our analysis and passing from the family in the wide to that in the narrow sense, we shall find that the principles upon which it rests are, at bottom, the same among the Tibetans as among the Turkomans, with the exception of one point, a very important one, it is true, and so strong that it has caused the points of resemblance to be unduly forgotten. The father of the family is the sole and absolute master ; his wife and children owe him an entire obedience, possess nothing in their own right and are not even able, at least in theory, to dispose of their persons. The sons thus remain minors until the day of their marriage ; but, on that day, the father, contrary to the Chinese usage, keeps of his patrimony only so much as is necessary for him to live on and to provide for the cost of his funeral and constitutes his sons the owners of the rest. It is here that we see the difference between the Turkic and the Tibetan custom. Among the Turkomans, each son receives his distinct part *(inchi)* at the moment of his marriage ; among the Tibetans, the eldest son alone receives the whole and becomes the head of the family: the younger sons pass under his authority, fall to his charge and remain incapable minors under his guardianship, even as they were under that of their father. This is primogeniture driven to the utmost point. Are we to behold in it two radically different customs, or to consider that one is derived from the other? And, in that case, which is the older of the two? I am content to put the question, knowing no fact that will permit me to solve it. I will only observe that, among the nomads of the north-east, there is a very marked tendency to divide the herds among the children, although this is not the general custom. It may be contended that this is a survival of the old usage, the nomads being more faithful to tradition than the settled population; but, on the other hand, it would be urged, with, perhaps, greater probability, that non-division, being more in accordance with the principle, which is being impaired, of solidarity in families, was the original rule and that the nomads modified it, as time went on, because they felt its drawbacks and because it is neither difficult nor detrimental to divide herds, while the husbandmen persevered in the errors of the past because they found it inconvenient to portion out houses and fields and because they considered that, by dividing and subdividing among the children and the children's children lands which do not increase of themselves like herds, they would end by turning a large and rich family into a collection of small, poor households, incapable of keeping up the honour of the ancestor's name.

In the matter of marriage, we notice the same analogies and the same differences. Marriage, among both the Turkomans and the Tibetans, has as its object and its effect to hand a woman on from one family to another, to submit her not only to the authority of her husband, but also to that of her husband's family. The bond which attaches her to that family is so strong that it is not broken even after the husband's death ; she then remains under the guardianship of the brother or the nearest kinsman of the deceased, becomes his property and, what is more, his wife, without that this entails any new ceremony. The nuptial rite performed by the first husband has given his relations rights over the woman married which each of them may be called upon to exercise in turn on the death of the last holder. The brothers-in-law of a Turkic woman are thus her deputy-husbands, whose rights are only suspended during the principal husband's lifetime. In Tibet, there is no suspension : all the brothers collectively become the husbands of the same woman so soon as the rite is accomplished. There is therefore an exact correspondence between the rule of marriage and that of property. Among the Turkomans, each man has his own portion, takes up his residence in a separate tent with his wife, of whom he is the sole owner in the same way and within the same limits as of his herds. In Tibet, the land being undivided among the brothers, the wife shares this quality; or rather, for these terms "undivided" and "non-division" are full of confusion and errors, the eldest brother is the sole possessor of the land and the sole husband of the wife. In the nuptial ceremony the younger brothers have absolutely no part: as incompetent minors, they can enter into no valid contract except through the medium of their elder ; they have not the power of making a marriage on their own account, even as they have not that of inheriting from their father in equality of right with their elder.

The Tibetans look upon the family as a group of such absolute unity that there can be only one individual of full age, who is the first-born of each generation. He alone has power of attorney and lieutenancy over the land of his ancestors; he wields authority over the persons of the family and administers the patrimony; he is the living link of the chain at once mystic and real that is formed by the dead ancestors and their unborn descendants; he has the duty of providing for the continuation of that chain after him by begetting sons and of keeping for them the property which he has received from his fathers. The first-born son is henceforth the depositary of the rights of the ancestors and, when he has grown to man's estate, when he is capable of acting for himself and of fulfilling the duties that devolve upon him, his father retires before him, marries him and, in consequence, emancipates him, for his marriage is in itself an act of majority, since it enables him to fulfil the essential office of the head of the family, which is to ensure the succession of the descent. The father has solidly forged his link in the chain; his task in this world is done; he retires superannuated and has nothing more to do than, with the little estate which he has kept back for himself, to wait for the hour to strike for him to go and join his ancestors under ground. It is the emancipated son who is now the real and sole master: he alone is charged to continue the family cult; he alone is responsible and able to act and speak in the name of the ancestors whom he represents; he alone is master of all that the patrimonial house contains: the women who enter it are his, the children who are begotten in it are his. But his younger brothers, born of the same line, hold a sort of natural proxy of his powers: when he is dead, his junior will become, *ipso facto, sui juris;* he will be the master of the wife, of the children under age and the goods of the deceased, within the same limits as the latter was, that is to say, subject to the duty of retiring, when the time comes, in favour of the first-born son, whether it be his own or the dead man's. During the elder's life, all his brothers have the faculty of taking his place in all the actions of life; they are really his substitutes. They, for their part, enjoy the paternal property, which they own virtually, without being able to administer it; and, if their elder, for a time, cease to enforce his rights over his wife, they may, thenceforward, enforce theirs and the wife has towards them the same obligations as towards the head of the family, of whom they are the born helpers in his task of perpetuating the race. They are not allowed to take a wife for themselves, since no strange person may be introduced into the paternal home, which must be single, according to the Tibetan idea, except by an act of the father of the family, the only major, and any woman introduced is necessarily the wife of the master; on the other hand, the latter is not entitled to refuse the co-operation of his juniors, for he would run the risk of compromising the continuity of the family, which only the birth of a considerable number of sons can ensure for certain. Although he has the right to refuse his wife to his brothers, even as he has the still graver right of expelling them from the home, nevertheless, if he reserved to himself the sole exercise of the husband's prerogatives simply from aversion for the sharing system, he would be universally and severely blamed. This sharing system is in no way repugnant to Tibetan ideas, for not only do the relations of the woman with several brothers issuing from the same ancestor fail to impair the purity of the descent; but all other considerations disappear before the legal conception that everything that shoots, grows or is born in the paternal house, whatever its origin, belongs to the master of the house. Legal conceptions of this kind have, in general, a much greater hold upon the minds of barbarians than upon ours and it is not always true to say that primitive or very ancient nations are nearer to nature than ourselves. Nevertheless, if one wife be not considered sufficient, the eldest brother can marry a second and a third, without being limited save by his wishes and his means ; and there is nothing, then, to prevent each brother from having practically a wife to himself: it is a question of friendly arrangement. This leads me to think that the idea of limiting the population has not contributed at all to the establishment or the continuance of polyandry.

To sum up, the principle of Tibetan polyandry lies in an extremely strict conception of the privilege of the first-born and the unity of the genealogical line, which must not be broken and scattered into numberless divergent branches. It is closely connected with the rule of property, which is concentrated in one hand and settled by primogeniture because it is necessary that the possessions, which the ancestor made sacred by his ownership and bequeathed to his posterity, should be preserved in their integrity. This connection is peremptorily shown by the fact that, when one of the brothers leaves the paternal roof and settles down apart to live on his industry and his work, he can introduce into his new home a lawful wife, who belongs to him alone and over whom his brothers have no rights, for she does not live on the property of the family ; and, at the same time, he retains his rights over the wife of his brothers as over the paternal inheritance, of which he continues to enjoy the usufruct to the extent of his share. Among the nomads, who sometimes divide their patrimony, polyandry ceases when property no longer remains undivided. If it be true that, at a prehistoric period, the Turkomans and Mongols lived under the system of non-division, it is probable that polyandry prevailed among them also. The custom which I have mentioned above seems to be a vestige of it and, besides, we know, from the annals of Liang, that, in the sixth century, a Turkic horde, that of the Hoa or Yeptalites, was still practising polyandry in the same manner as the Tibetans, that is to say restricted to the sons of the same father.

The custom of polyandry is considerably reduced in practice, among the rich families, where the sons have many opportunities and facilities for settling down apart and, consequently, for having each his own wife. Orazio della Penna observed this correctly, but he made the mistake of believing that polyandry was only an abuse introduced by the laxness of morals in the poor classes *(tra le persone non molto comode)*. It is among the rich, on the contrary, that the primitive custom has altered and then only in practice, for the theory remains unchanged. What led the Italian monk to think that polyandry was not authorised by law *(non ordinato della legge)* was that the over-strict lamas do, in fact, censure it; but it had penetrated so deeply into the morals of the nation that Buddhism has always been powerless to extirpate it and, to-day, the members of the clergy accept it without taking any steps to contend with it and are satisfied with replying to travellers who ask their opinion that every country has its usages. The brother who separates himself from the community to found a new family may take as many wives as he pleases and it is only poverty that compels him to content himself with one. To sum up, there are four kinds of regular households in Tibet, namely, in order of frequency, those in which there are several husbands and several wives; those in which there are several husbands and only one wife; those in which there are only one husband and several wives; and those in which there are only one husband and one wife.

Tibetan marriage is exogamous: marriages do not take place within the fourth degree of consanguinity and the nomad chiefs have to marry outside their clan.

Conjugal union being a family affair and not a matter of personal inclination, the wishes of the young people interested are in nowise consulted; the marriage is usually arranged upon the birth of the children by the parents of the two parties. I will not dwell upon the ceremonies that accompany it; they resemble in essence, if not always in form, those in use among the Kazaks and the Kirghiz. The negotiations are conducted and the betrothal concluded by brokers (*barmi*) sent by the suitor's father, who pays a *kalyn* (*p'yosma*, pronounced *choma*) to the father of the affianced bride; but the latter, instead of returning only an insignificant present according to the Turkic custom, sends back almost the equivalent of what he receives and the kalyn or choma does not represent the purchase-price of the wife.* The marriage-rite itself is divided into three parts: the ceremony by which the young girl is parted from the gods of her family; the transfer to the bridegroom's house and the sham struggle between his friends and the friends and relations of the girl, which typifies the old wars in consequence of which the clans obtained *jus connubii* among one another; lastly, the introduction of the bride to her husband's domestic hearth, the purification which she is made to undergo and the partaking of tsamba, butter and milk (this is the *confarreatio*). She then receives a new name, for she is as a new-born child to her husband's family; next, she takes between her teeth a piece of wood, which her husband bites between his, and twists a rope out of a few strands of wool which he holds in his hand. The whole thing ends with a great banquet and with part-songs, executed

* The wife is considered to have always belonged to the family which she enters by the marriage-rite. Her father, who has provided for her maintenance until the wedding-day, is like a foster-father whose expenses are refunded with the kalyn (*Cf.* "A Scientific Mission to Upper Asia," Vol. II., p. 114).

alternately by the girls and the young men:* he who stops short when his turn comes to improvise a distich or quatrain has to pay forfeit.

The matrimonial bond is indissoluble in principle and it seems, if my information be correct, that there is no legally organised divorce. However, the husband has the right to put away his wife for a grave reason, such as adultery. When the husband dies, the wife continues to be bound by marriage to the brothers of the deceased ; but, if she have no children, she can resume her liberty, provided that she have taken care to announce her intention before the decease of the eldest: if he agree, he holds one end of a thread of which she holds the other, both pronounce the words of the separation and break the thread by burning it. This rite having been performed, when the decease of the first husband takes place, the widow is at liberty to return to her own family. It must be remarked that the husband must obtain the consent of his brothers in order to repudiate his wife against her wish. If the younger brothers refuse to part with her and the eldest persist in his decision, it may be expedient to divide the patrimony, the younger brothers taking their share and keeping the wife whom the elder has rejected. This proves the exceptional seriousness of the marriage-bond and shows that the younger brothers are not only, as has been contended, slaves and authorised lovers of the wife of their elder brother, but that they possess private rights, derived from their ancestors, which rights, for all that they usually remain latent and slumbering, are capable of being revived in certain circumstances.

It is important that we should not confuse the solidity of the marriage-bond with conjugal fidelity. There is no fixed connection between these two terms.

* The same custom prevails among the Kazaks.

Tibetan husbands and wives, though united by a very strong chain, as a rule observe none too strictly what we should consider their first duty. True, adultery is esteemed to be a grievous fault, because it affects the purity of the descent; but it is not a mortal crime: as a rule, the husband contents himself with correcting his wife and exacting a light penalty, four or five rupees, from her accomplice. From the point of view of family law and domestic religion, it is the judicial notion : *Is pater est* who obtains control ; the essential thing is not so much the material reality of the filiation as the legitimacy of the wife, the recognition of the child by the father and its solemn initiation into the family cult. It is for this reason that the Tibetan who is unable to have a child by his wife or wives sometimes introduces a stranger into his house and charges him to perpetuate his line in his place and stead. In reality, this stranger becomes a conventional brother, having the same rights as a brother born. In the same way, since hospitality, among primitive peoples, consists of the accession of the guest to his host's family, it follows that he can lay claim to the favours of the lady of the house. This is what takes place in Tibet, although the privilege is reserved for intimate friends or for distinguished persons who deign to honour their host of the moment by looking upon themselves as belonging to his family. I remember one Tibetan who was extremely proud that the head of the embassy of Ladak had shown his esteem for him in this way. This custom implies polyandry and, in some nations, survives it.

The Tibetan women enjoy a freedom of demeanour unknown to the women of China and of Moslem countries ; but the Chinese authors and many European writers after them have greatly exaggerated the superiority of their condition and their influence upon the family and in society. They are perpetual minors, under the wardship first of their father, then of their husband, lastly of their son. They attend to all the duties which are most repugnant to their weakness or which the men refuse: they work in the fields, fetch water from the river in heavy casks, gather the dung along the roads, carry the loads of the caravans in the difficult places. The Chinese authors, often more given to argument than to good and faithful observation, have given out that they are stronger than the men. This allegation is utterly incorrect, although, in truth, I need hardly say that they are less feeble than the Chinese women and, in general, more robust than the pale scribes of the Imperial Legate, the firmness of whose wrists does not equal the elegance of their pencils. If they carry things with a high hand in household matters, this is due more especially to the idleness of their husbands; besides, they would not be women if they did not know how to profit by the plurality of their lords and masters in order to stir up rivalries between them, play off one against the other and thus attain their ends. There are some who have one of the brothers as their favourite and make the lives of the others so miserable that they drive them to a division of the property or to exile. But it is a far cry from this to laying down the principle that the Tibetan woman is the mistress in the house and, as a matter of fact, she is not a little despised and harshly treated. I gave up counting the number of times that Tibetans expressed to me their surprise that England was governed by a queen and it was beautiful to see the air of pity and contempt with which they spoke of it as though I were personally responsible for the fact:

"With us," they would conclude, "the female line is the inferior."

However, I rose again in their esteem when I explained to them that, if a woman was then reigning in

London, it was only because the last king had left no male posterity. The Tibetan nuns stand far below the monks in the general opinion and are hardly superior to the laity. The murder of a woman is settled by a compensation half as great as that exacted for the murder of a man. Tibetan polyandry has no kind of relation with matriarchism: it is only a form of patriarchism no less absolute in its principle than the Chinese or Roman forms. Those who imagine that polyandry marks a transition between matriarchism and patriarchism might lay stress, in support of their theory, on the fact that, in Tibet or, at least, in several parts of that country, the consent of the brother of a girl's mother is required before she can be given in marriage. But patriarchism has never implied the suppression of all relations between an individual and his mother's family; marriage breaks only the judicial and religious bonds that connected a daughter with her father: it allows the natural bonds to subsist; the parents of the girl continue to be her protectors after her marriage: they have the right to make representations to the husband if he behave badly, to take back their daughter if she be ill-treated, abandoned or become a widow, to see to it that her interests are respected; and this protection may, in certain cases, extend to the daughter's daughter without there being any need to seek an explanation in the hypothesis of a primitive matriarchism, which there is nothing in the case at issue to justify.

The Tibetan families are moderately prolific: more so than the French, less than the Chinese. Our own investigations agree sufficiently well with the information which the prefect of Nagchu gave us concerning Gyangtse and Lhasa to permit us to state that a polyandric family numbers, on an average, seven or eight viable children, say about three children for two parents. The monogamous households procreate less absolutely, more proportionally. Girls are a little less numerous than boys, at the rate of seven to eight, according to the prefect of Nagchu, which is the exact ratio which Sir Alexander Cunningham gives for Ladak. It cannot, therefore, be said that the insufficiency of daughters was the cause of the institution or the reason for the continuance of polyandry. On the contrary, there are too many women in Tibet to-day and many of them do not get married for these two reasons, that, on the average, there are a few more husbands than wives in the Tibetan families and that a host of men are devoted to religious celibacy. Some of them become nuns, a larger number abandon themselves to prostitution. In all the towns and in the smallest villages, there are unmarried women who ostensibly keep small businesses and particularly drinking-bars ; but brandy and beer are the least important things that they sell. Lhasa is no less renowned for the multitude of its courtesans than for the multitude of its monks ; and a Tibetan who was not apt at glossing over the truth told me, one day, that, like the majority of his countrymen, he went there on pilgrimage more from the first motive than the second. In the main, the Tibetans are very immoral, from our point of view, and they are too coarse to attach much importance to the matter.

In the eyes of a passing traveller, the interior of the Tibetan families seems devoid of light and joy, so wretched is the appearance of things : outside, an icy cold prevails and the whirling snowstorm rages : inside, a poor, smoky, stinking, almost useless fire burns ; the tent or house is dirty, uncomfortable, cold and bare, with its felts too much worn to soften the hardness of the ground ; the clothes are neglected and full of vermin, the food insipid and dull, the duties rough or mean. And yet none loves his country and his home so fondly as the Tibetan: to him his sullen and obstinate country is the finest in the world; for him outside his dilapidated house, outside his tattered tent, shaken by the wind, there is neither peace nor mirth. He finds means of being gay oftener than sad; he has a fine time of it and enjoys himself at a cheap cost. A cup of buttered tea or a pot of beer, with a good pipe of tobacco; a noisy talk, seasoned with spicy jests; a lively game of dice or huckle-bones: that is all a Tibetan asks to make him happy. I did not notice that their amusements were very much varied: what matter, if they always find a new pleasure in them? In this connection, I will point out a mistake made by Mr. Rockhill, who is usually such a safe observer: he maintains that the Tibetans do not indulge much in games of chance and that, in particular, the game of dice is unknown to them. Now there is no people more smitten with the passion for gambling than the Tibetans: they outdo the Chinese themselves and would wager their very shirts, if they had any! The game most commonly played with them is just this of dice: they use three cubical dice *(cho)*, marked, on the opposite faces, 1 and 6, 2 and 3, 4 and 5.

But, of all amusements, those which occupy the first place in their opinion are singing and dancing. They have strong voices and do not raise them in so shrill a tone as the Turkomans; their songs and also their dances are less gay and less lively, but not devoid of grace. Although the slowness and monotony of the voices and movements seem sad to us, the Tibetans are convinced that nothing could be more joyous. Their musical instruments are the Hindu guitar *(piwang)*, the guimbard or Jew's harp *(khapi)*, the bamboo pipe with six or seven holes (*lingbu*) and the tambourine. They love double choirs of men and women, drawn up in opposite rows, replying to each other in alternate verses and moving slowly forwards and backwards in time to the music. They indulge in these musical exercises especially in the spring and always surround them with a certain solemnity: the date is settled beforehand and the men and women who are to take part in them must have made their ablutions and donned clean garments, as if for a religious ceremony. It would be unbecoming to dance at random and out of due form, merely for amusement. The Tibetans have the habit of singing when going through the different labours of agriculture: ploughing, sowing, reaping. In Turkestan, Cherchen is the only place where I observed the same custom. In 1892, at Leh, we were present at a dance similar in every respect to that at which Bogle assisted at Jikatse in the last century: a large number of men and women dancing very slowly in a circle, with a few men cutting extraordinary capers in the middle.* The women who took part in this dance all belonged to the nobility; for only ladies of high degree are permitted to dance before the king: it is their duty and their privilege. In this case, the king was represented by the vizier of the Maharajah of Kashmir.

* C. R. Markham: *Narrative of the Mission*, &c., p. 92.

CHAPTER VI

SOCIAL ORGANISATION

Aristocratic organisation of society, stability of social conditions, hereditary character of the professions—Nobles and commoners.

TIBETAN society is essentially aristocratic, with hardly any of the compromises that have been introduced into the social systems of China or Turkestan. There is an hereditary nobility, which concentrates in its own hands all such wealth, power and influence as the lay element has preserved. As for the clergy, I will not mention it here; its communities are neither more nor less than collective nobles more powerful than the others.

The hereditary principle rules everything and makes itself felt everywhere. Each man is very solidly, if not indissolubly linked to the profession and condition even as to the house of his father. The constitution of the family is excellently designed to perpetuate in one and the same line the possession of the same lands and, as far as possible, to prevent the property from being parcelled out and passing from hand to hand. Not only do the sons succeed to their fathers' estates, but they succeed also to their callings. The son of an official is an official; none is an administrative secretary, a farmer, a painter or a tinker, if his father have not followed the same profession before him. A few exceptions are met with, but their rarity confirms the rule. The protonotary of the prefecture of Nagchu exhibited profound astonishment when I asked him what his father had been: truly, it would have been a wonderful thing if they had ventured to profane the corporation of protonotaries by the introduction of people who could not have qualified with a respectable number of quarterings of protonotarial nobility!

There is something in all this that recalls the Indian castes, with less rigour and complication, however. It does not appear that there is anything to prevent a man from passing from one to another equally honourable profession, and Tibetan society is not, like that of Hindustan, divided into a host of small and strictly exclusive clans. I should look upon it rather, in so far as I was able to ascertain the state of things, as divided into different classes between which were barriers difficult to overcome: nobles, burgesses, plebeians, serfs, pariahs. The last all belong to certain despised trades which are followed by none but pariahs from father to son, such as the smith's, the corpse-carrier's, the currier's and the butcher's, all of which imply religious defilement. I do not think that we must look here for an effect of Buddhism, for the smith's occupation is not blamable from the point of view of the doctrines of Sakya Muni. If a person belonging to an honourable class of society be deprived, through hard times, of every means of existence, he will beg rather than take to one of those derogatory professions. There are degrees among the pariahs themselves: the smith despises the currier and the latter the bearer of the dead. The trades which are accounted honourable are not either all on the same footing and a tinker, for instance, is less esteemed than a maker of religious statuettes. As a general rule, the arts connected with religion confer a special dignity upon those who practise them and place them apart among all the workmen; this favoured treatment they evidently owe to Buddhism. What makes it very difficult in practice for a man to change his trade in order to rise in the social scale is that the employers take no apprentices from among the sons of the profane. When, however, a pariah succeeds, by way of exception, in following a decent trade and making money at it, he is none the less exposed to the scorn of respectable people, who treat him as an intruder, and, at the same time, he loses the esteem of the pariahs, who spurn him as a traitor. Everybody refuses to accept him as a son-in-law and should, at last, a decent, but poor man be found who submits to stoop, for the sake of a little money, and to give his daughter to the pariah's son, the original stain remains attached to the latter and also to the issue of this mixed marriage and will not be wiped out until the second generation.

It is still more difficult, not to say impossible, for commoners to enter the ranks of the nobility. They may succeed when, by chance, a needy noble consents to give his daughter to a wealthy commoner ; in time, the descendants of the latter may be looked upon as noble, if they always manage to marry girls of noble birth during several generations ; but this is not easy, for it is a debasement for a nobleman to allow his daughter to pass into an inferior class. As for the aspirant to nobility, his position is an embarrassing and ambiguous one. I was given the instance of a man of Ladak who, having acquired a considerable fortune, succeeded in allying himself by marriage to an aristocratic family : during his lifetime, he was able to command more or less respect by virtue of his money ; but, after his death, there was none to attend his funeral : neither the nobles, who had never looked upon him as one of themselves, nor the commoners, whom he had disowned and who now disowned him in their turn. Class prejudice is stronger than religion itself. The Buddhist king of Ladak and the little Moslem kings of Baltistan consent willingly to enter into mutual matrimonial alliances, but they agree to no match between their family and that of a correligionist of inferior rank. As, on the other hand, there are but few opportunities of self-enrichment, since big business is almost unknown and trade is in its infancy and almost entirely in the hands of the government and of the lay or religious aristocracy, it follows that, even as there are great obstacles opposed by manners to the change of class, there appear but few aspirants to any such change. The stability of social conditions is therefore very great. The monarchy has done nothing to impair it; for the purpose of government it has employed the nobility, in whose favour it has reserved all the important public offices, so that official and noble are synonymous terms. The government delivers no patents of nobility; only, it may happen that a commoner, thanks to exceptional merit or singular good fortune, rises to one of the highest places in the State: should his descendants succeed in maintaining the position, they will end by taking rank among the hereditary aristocracy.

Apart from the private domains which they have inherited from their ancestors, the Tibetan nobles receive from the State, by way of fiefs, lands of more or less considerable extent, which constitute the salary attached to the office which they fill; they exercise rights of justice, taxation, requisition and base service over these lands in the place of the government. In return, they owe the latter a certain annual fine and a certain military contingent in case of need. The population that inhabits these seigniorial domains is in a state of serfdom which my imperfect information does not allow me to define with exactness. It appears that, by law, no man is bound to the soil and that all are free, at any time, to leave the master's service; but, in practice, they remain hereditary servants of an hereditary master, in consequence of the very great difficulty of finding the means of livelihood elsewhere. These serfs are called *miser* or *yog (gyog)*; they are husbandmen, herdsmen, artisans, office-clerks, domestic servants and secretaries and they give their work for a certain salary or a certain share in the profits of their work. The State, on its side, possesses private domains, organised and administered in the same manner, and it may be said that the State, or rather the King, is only a great noble, richer than the others, but possessing, besides, like our own mediæval kings, a conspicuous right of property over all the land of the kingdom. In addition to their born serfs, the nobles have around them some men who have taken service with them of their own free will, in the hope of obtaining a decent post through their protection and of making their fortune: these dependants are usually younger sons who were not comfortable under the elder brother's roof. Lastly, let us add to these different social classes that of the freeholders, of the small landed proprietors, who, though plebeians, are able to dispose of their goods at their pleasure and owe nothing to anybody, with the exception of the taxes, military service, forced labour and requisition due to the State.

The territories of the nomads of the north-east, which are not within the jurisdiction of Lhasa, have a social organisation similar to the above, but simpler and, probably, older. Each of the different kings is surrounded by a court of hereditary barons, who divide the chief offices of State among themselves and receive perpetual concessions of land, of which the inhabitants are their serfs. Under them are the chiefs of tribes, also hereditary and invariably the largest land-owners of their respective tribes, and, next, the chiefs of clans, who form the lowest degree of the nomad nobility. The monarchy is a comparatively modern function which has been set above the two essential and primitive groups, the tribe and the clan. These appear to be, in the first instance, more or less extensive families, whose heads possess not only political power, but also all the authority of the father of the family and all the prerogatives of the landowner. The Tibetans have no other surname than that of their tribe* and the titles which they give to their chiefs are the same that serve to denote the relations between master and servant and between landlord and tenant.

To sum up, the great mass of the lay society of Tibet appeared to me to be divided into two principal classes: that of the very powerful and highly honoured lords and masters on the one hand; and, on the other, that of the menials and serfs, whose condition is a pretty wretched one, except in the case of those possessing the master's confidence. Almost all the men whom we met were dependent on the great landlords, had charge of only a small part of the latter's property, had heavy burdens and but little profit, did not own the right of disposing of a single sheep and were concerned only to live from day to day with the least possible toil. As for what might be called the independent middle-class, it seems unimportant and uninfluential; the small owners of land and herds are generally over head and ears in debt, to the greater profit of the nobles and, especially, of the monks, who lend to them at a high rate of interest, allow their obligations to mount up, suddenly exact payment when they know their debtors to be insolvent and then have the goods of the unfortunate borrowers seized and sold at a contemptible price. However, these are questions which are as yet very obscure and which would require long, careful and patient study made on the spot. I am fully aware that my observations are incomplete, but I shall be satisfied if I have succeeded in attracting the attention of an intelligent traveller to a few important points.

*The annals of the Soei (sixth century) show that this was also the case among the Tanghiang.

CHAPTER VII

ECONOMIC CONDITIONS: CATTLE-BREEDING, AGRICULTURE, MANUFACTURES

Social conditions of economic development — Physical conditions — Agriculture—Cattle-breeding—Hunting—Mines—Manufactures.

THE family and social organisation which I have just sketched is very unfavourable to the good economic management of the contry. It discourages the spirit of initiative and enterprise. Everyone is certain of finding all that he needs in the paternal house, which is common to all the sons ; everyone is confined to the condition and profession of his father, without having the means of raising himself. Those, however, who are too cramped in the too-crowded family home ; those who dislike their father's calling ; those who aim at issuing from the obscure station in which their birth has placed them : all those, in short, who, among us, form the most powerful lever of the progress of the public wealth go to swell the numbers of the dependants of the nobles or the countless army of the monks, who live at the cost of the industrious population and accumulate ever-increasing capital, whose economic activity is accompanied by a great waste of strength. A few useful trades are considered vile and are reserved for the pariahs ; a man of decent station who lapses into poverty prefers to beg rather than follow a derogatory profession. The serfs have no interest in improving the cultivation of the soil or the breeding of cattle, because they would gain much less by it than their masters; the small landowners are crushed by the great proprietors and the convents, who bear them down under the weight of taxation, ruin them by usury, prevent them from improving their condition by disposing of their property, monopolise the produce and fix the market prices; the large individual or collective landlords are not stimulated by competition to keep on developing their output. And so, from top to bottom, routine reigns side by side with neglect and all efforts towards improvements are banished, for they would be almost always useless and sometimes dangerous. To these general facts, common to the whole of Tibet, must be added, in the eastern portion of the country, political troubles, struggles between the different tribes, local brigandage and lack of security for life and property.

Bad physical conditions join with bad social conditions to make Tibet one of the poorest countries in the world. We have read how naturally scanty the vegetation is. Spread throughout the whole of Tibet are great spaces covered with snow and rocks and occupied by rugged slopes on which nothing grows. The spaces that are not absolutely barren produce, in the greatest portion of the country, only an herbaceous vegetation which is anything but luxurious. In 1892, 1893 and 1894, we travelled in Tibet without seeing any timber. The forests do not go beyond a line drawn about N.E. by E., starting a few miles to the north of Lhasa, passing through Batsumdo, to the north of Dergyeh, and ending at Ltasen Gompa, at the bend of the Yellow River. To the north of this line there are only in certain specially favoured spots a few shrubs or bushes which could easily be counted. In Ladak, the juniper-tree *(chugpa)* and the tamarisk *(ombu)* are the only trees that grow naturally; on the northern banks of the Nam Cho, a few juniper-trees appear; and, in the basin of the Upper Mekong, at about Lat. 33°, there are a few dwarf willows *(changma)*. In the south, the same species exist, but the willows are taller; one also comes across the pine and the fir-tree *(somching)*, which are by far the most wide-spread species, the holly-tree, the birch and, in small quantities and only, I believe, in Eastern Tibet, the cedar, the oak and the elm. Nor, for that matter, is the absence of variety made up for by plenty, for the wood is nowhere sufficient to provide fuel for the natives, who use dried horse or cow-dung in all parts of the country. The crops, which, in Western Tibet, reach as far as the foot of the Karaul Davan and the western extremity of Lake Pagong and, in Eastern Tibet, as far as Dam and Labug Gompa, are not at all extensive, nowhere form large, continuous fields and are only like so many small spots of mould on the huge skeleton of the Tibetan mountains.

Generally speaking, the ground and climate suit only barley, which does not require a very rich soil nor great moisture and which is sown in May, when the winter frosts are over, and gathered in September. This cereal grows up to a level of 15,000 feet in Ladak and of 14,450 at Dam. It might, perhaps, be possible to grow it in a few districts at present entirely uncultivated, such as, for instance, certain cantons of the basin of the Upper Mekong which are below 14,700 feet; but it is evident that there are no great hopes to be based upon this possible extension of the areas fit for cultivation. The price of barley in the places where it is reaped is more than double that which it costs in Chinese Turkestan, varying from 1½ to 1¾ rupees the bushel. Wheat, which is rarer and of inferior quality, grows at a highest level of 13,000 feet in Spiti and of 12,450 feet in the Jyerkundo country. The yield is very small, does not often exceed the proportion of five to one and reaches ten or twelve only in the very best, warm and low valleys. They say that rice is grown at Lhasa at a height of over 11,500 feet, but the information which I received varies in this respect. In any case, Tibetan rice is very bad and hard, more or less red in colour and formed of small and irregular grains; and the well-to-do send to China for the rice which they consume. In the matter of vegetables, those which grow best and in the largest quantity are onions *(tsong)*; they are found wild, in the uninhabited districts, at a height of 17,400 feet. Turnips and pease are also very common. As for fruits, the first place, in point of quantity, is occupied by nuts *(starka)* and apples. I have stated elsewhere all the fruits and vegetables grown at Lhasa. As rain is scarce, they generally resort to artificial irrigation. Agricultural implements are few in number and clumsy and this shortness of tools aggravates the ill effects of the thankless soil. The plough *(chol)*, which is of Indian origin, consists of a piece of bent wood with a sock at the lower end: this machine is drawn by a yak and does no more than scratch the earth. The Tibetan husbandmen use also the spade and the hoe and they reap with the sickle. I do not know if there are any harrows outside of Ladak.

The chief resources of Tibet at the present time lie in the pastures and herds. There are no natural meadows and, so to speak, no artificial meadows except a few fields of lucerne. The food of the cattle is supplied solely by spontaneous common pastures, indifferently rich in consequence, but at least very wide. The grass is very nourishing, but hard and rough and is suited only to specially adapted cattle. Sheep and yaks are the most numerous and the most valuable kinds. Everybody knows the yak *(gyag)*,* the *kutas* of the Turkomans, a

* The initial *g* is quiescent, like many initial letters in Tibetan; the final *g* is pronounced very hard, according to the general rule: that is why we transcribe it with a *k*.

very large, grunting ox, with long, black (sometimes grey, or even white) hair: it is used as a pack-animal; it gives hair for the manufacture of tents and coarse stuffs, meat which is savoury, although a little tough, and hides for export; the female, moreover, gives excellent milk, similar in every respect to that of the cow, of which the Tibetans make butter and cheese. The butter is white, of moderate firmness, and has an insipid, but not at all disagreeable flavour; it is very much like Russian butter. This commodity plays a leading part in the life of Tibet, which is the real land of butter: it forms the staple food and serves as pomade, cold-cream, vaseline, lamp-oil and a material for modelling different religious figures on certain festivals. The price of a good pack-yak varies between 15 and 20 rupees at Nagchu and Jyerkundo; the beasts intended to carry burdens are naturally exceptional animals and an ordinary yak is worth, on an average, only 10 to 12 rupees.

The sheep supply meat, furs for the winter and wool for export and for the manufacture of the native stuffs. In Western Tibet, where the yaks are less numerous, sheep are used for the purpose of carrying loads. The Tibetan sheep is less fat than the Kirghiz sheep and the sheep of Ladak, a country with but little pasture-land, is smaller than that of Eastern or Central Tibet. Its flesh is less delicate than that of the Khotan sheep, the fat more plentiful; the wool is less fine, is thick, hard and rather coarse. The price of the wool is about the same as at Khotan, 26 to 28 rupees the hundredweight; only, it must be remembered that, the cost of living being dearer in Tibet than in Turkestan, the Tibetans in reality derive less profit from the wool of their flocks than the Turkomans. A fat sheep which you could buy at Polur for a rupee or a little over generally costs 2½ rupees in the Tibetan pastures. Tibet supports only a small number of goats, the inhabitants caring for neither the flesh nor the skin, which is reserved for people of the lowest class. It seems that they do not know how to shave the goats' wool, except in Ladak. This very dry and rocky country is well-suited for breeding goats; it contains over 80,000, all very small in size; their wool, amounting to 360 hundredweight at 300 rupees the hundredweight, is sent to Kashmir, where it is employed for the manufacture of shawls, together with the superior quality of wool which comes from Turfan.

The horses are few in number, small and indifferent, excepting on the shores of the Koko Nor, where a host of horses, of Mongol breed, graze: these are rather short-legged and stubby, with short, stout bodies, thick necks, short, wide heads and low cruppers. They differ sensibly from the Kirghiz horses and are exactly similar to those of Polur. Excellent ambling-horses, good trotters on occasion, they are, above all, resisting, sober, gentle and patient; they cover very long distances without stopping, drinking or feeding, in the deep sand of the desert or on the hard rocks of the mountains, under the burning sun of summer or in the snow and the icy winds of winter, content to wait until the halting-place for some brackish water and a little grass of the consistency of pen-holders or pencils, always even-tempered and ready to start again at the first signal. A few of them, by way of exception, are big and long in the body; I have even seen some of the size of our Norman beasts. An ordinary saddle-horse, of suitable age, fetches 80 rupees at Lhasa and only 50 at Sining: these prices must be doubled for an animal fit for the service of an official. The grazing-grounds of the Koko Nor, which are probably the best in Tibet, feed oxen and cows similar and not inferior to those in Switzerland. The crossing of the cow with a yak gives a special product called *dzo (mdzo).*

Donkeys are found only in Ladak; at Lhasa, they know of that animal's existence, but hold it in great contempt; and we once greatly shocked a worthy Tibetan by offering him one of our donkeys as a present.

Side by side with the domestic animals, the wild animals form a resource that is not to be despised. The nomads are good hunters; they make long journeys, sometimes lasting for months, in search of game and penetrate to distant, uninhabited and very inhospitable regions. They go to the north of the Nam Cho as far as the 34th parallel, rarely as far as the 35th. An astonishing number of animals find the means of supporting life in the icy and barren solitudes of North Tibet. There are three kinds which are met with everywhere: the wild yak, which is called *dong (brong)* and resembles the domestic yak, but is bigger; the wild ass *(equus hemionus)*, called *kiang (rkiang)* by the Tibetans, *kulan* by the Turkomans and Mongols, which has the fawn colouring, the size and the appearance of a mule; and the antelope *(kiik* in Turkic, *chawa*, *goba* or *tsod* in Tibetan). There are five different kinds of antelopes, of which I know only the Turkic names: the *yurga;* the *sarygh tekkeh*, which has very long, straight, grooved horns and is perhaps the *tsod* of the Tibetans; the *aka;* the *djura;* and the white *kukmet.** Nowhere are there so many of these different animals as in the upper basin of the Yellow River, to the north of the Golok country, where they wander by thousands in the fine pastures, forsaken by men, which extend over the wide valleys of this region. It is the most wonderful hunting-ground in Asia. The Tibetans hunt the yaks and the wild asses for their skins, the antelopes for their horns, which the Chinese pharmacopœia regards as possessing the most

* There are two other varities of kiik which are not met with in the mountains: the *bugu*, or deer, and the *djiran*, or gazelle.

marvellous tonic and restorative properties. Hares abound in the remotest and wildest districts; but superstition protects them against the hunters. The brown bears are more fastidious than the animals already named: although we established their existence all along our road between the Nam Cho and Jyerkundo, they appear not to frequent the deserted portions of the high table-lands. The wolves penetrate a little further: they are small-sized and not feared by men. We camped more than once near a lair of wolves, but no one thought of taking any special precautions; they are dangerous only to the sheep and dogs, which are very frightened of them, except the huge red-haired mastiffs of Lhasa. Foxes are very common in both the south and north and avoid only the most inaccessible and the coldest regions.

Lastly, there are other animals which are met with only further south, beyond the roads which we followed: such are the small monkey, which, in Eastern Tibet, comes as far as Nyarong, at Lat. 32°, the lynx, the squirrel, the otter and the panther. The skin of this last animal is especially esteemed and the fashionable Tibetans love to trim their clothes with it. A panther-skin costs at least ten rupees at Lhasa and a fine one quite double the money. On the whole, Tibet is far from supplying so many or such valuable furs as North Mongolia and Siberia. The wild animal most profitable to the hunter is the musk-deer, *moschus moschiferus*, known as *laba (glaba)*. I will only just mention the various birds: partridges, which are very common on the shores of the Nam Cho; wild geese, frequent in North-eastern Tibet; cranes in the same parts: the Tibetans do not care to waste their powder on them. Although many lakes abound in fish, as, for instance, the Nam Cho, and we caught small trout in the basin of the Mekong at a height of 14,750 feet, fishing does not seem to be in favour nor to constitute an appreciable resource for the population, at least in the districts which we visited, except at Chuchul on the Indus, south of Leh.

It is difficult to give a valid opinion on the mineral wealth of Tibet. This is probably important. Auriferous ground is found more or less in every direction, especially in the valley of the Do Chu or Takiang, where gold costs only fifteen times its weight in silver, and in the province of Chang; there are copper-mines, silver-mines and mines of precious stones, such as turquoises and lapis lazuli; sulphur, sal ammoniac and borax are plentiful. The Tibetans carefully conceal their lodes of metals and gems from foreign travellers, because they suspect the latter of having no other object than to steal their underground treasures: a serious thing, for, if a profane hand were laid on the riches buried in the bowels of the earth, the incensed divine dragon would at once cause them to disappear and would spread poverty through the land. This superstition makes the Tibetans very cautious of exploiting the subsoil; but, even if it did not exist, the rudimentary condition of their industries would not allow them to make a great profit from the extraction of mineral matters.

The Tibetans display an uncommon ignorance and awkwardness in the most usual and every-day trades. The smiths, whose stock of tools is often confined to a small anvil, a bad hammer of Chinese origin and a bellows resembling those used by the Soudanese, do the little that they know how to do with the greatest clumsiness. We were never able to use a steel axe made at Lhasa: a prehistoric flint axe would have been preferable; and yet it was the master-piece of the best workman in the capital. In the matter of wood-work, the Tibetans, who, in the parts which we visited, have no other instruments than the axe and the adze, make hardly anything themselves except churns, buckets and, in Dergyeh and at Lhasa, stools and wooden cups or basins, which latter are the principal and only indispensable piece of native table-ware. In the east, the framework of the houses is almost always built up by carpenters from Sechuen. The rosary-beads, the bamboo tea-strainers and many of the wooden basins are of Chinese or Hindu origin. The pottery is of native make, but they use the Chinese wheel. They do not know how to cut or set their precious stones. The art of the armourer and of the worker in copper, which have always been in favour throughout Asia, are less neglected than those which I have mentioned. Lhasa and Dergyeh are the two most important centres that I know of these two industries, some of whose products are not to be despised either for their solidity and fitness or for their ornamentation; but the daggers, swords, gun-barrels, tinder-boxes and copper tea-pots that are turned out by the little Tibetan workshops are far from satisfying the local consumption. I may also mention, in particular, the metal-workers, who make trinkets, mostly of solid silver and a little coarse, but not without a certain artistic stamp; at the same time, it must be noted that the most skilful silversmiths in Lhasa are natives of Nepal.

Apart from and above all the manufactures must be ranked that of wool-weaving and the arts necessary to religious worship, which are comparatively flourishing because of the special encouragement which they receive. The religious arts are generally practised by the lamas, who print books, paint frescoes on the walls of the convents, cast copper-gilt, bronze and silver statuettes and make sweet-smelling sticks out of sandal-wood, powdered juniper, musk and incense. The production of woollen stuffs is very considerable everywhere and, although they are very greatly used, is sufficient for local consumption and, to a certain extent, supplies the foreign trade. At Lhasa or in the surrounding districts, they make very thick, warm and stout blankets which are perhaps the best of all travelling-rugs. In the tents and houses, all over Tibet, one steps on felts which are rather indifferent and very inferior to the Chinese or Kirghiz felts. The nomads, in the long leisure hours of their pastoral life, weave a large quantity of wool and themselves make it into very coarse stuffs, probably similar to those which their ancestors manufactured in the sixth century. In the villages of Eastern Tibet, the inhabitants weave woollens of a little superior quality, streaked with green, red, blue and yellow stripes and adorned with little crosses. But the best fabrics, known by the name of *tug (prug)*, are manufactured in certain towns between Lhasa and Tachilhunpo and especially at Gyangtse, which is the chief centre of the industry. They are dyed in one colour, blue, yellow, or dark red, this last shade being by far the most sought after. The piece, which is ten good fathoms (about twenty yards) long and only twelve inches wide, is sold at a price that varies according to the quality: the more indifferent kind fetches 6*s*. at Lhasa; for £4 you get a very fine cloth; and for £6 (about 20*s*. the square yard) you can buy one of the marvels of human industry, a stuff thinner than cloth, but supple, strong, warm, smooth and glossy, very different from the poor specimens which European travellers have brought back with them so far. This industry belongs to the government, which obtains the necessary wool in the pastures of the north on the score of taxation and distributes it among the inhabitants of the midland districts with orders to weave it free of cost for the government; this forced labour takes the place of all taxes in the houses subject to it. The State sells a portion of the produce to the trade at a rate settled beforehand; it sells another portion to the population through the medium of special commissaries, who themselves usually hand over the retail transactions to the local officials; in that case, the government overcharges the prices in accordance with the needs of the treasury, the commissary adds his commission, the prefect allots himself a small profit, the head of the canton pays himself for his trouble and the ratepayer is charged twice as much for the wool as it is worth. It is certain that, if weaving were free, the prices would fall noticeably, while individual activity, at present fettered, would have an excellent opportunity of displaying itself. We thus see that the most important two industries in Tibet, weaving and the religious arts, are, in fact, almost wholly monopolised by the two great official powers in the country, the government and the convents.

CHAPTER VIII

ECONOMIC CONDITIONS *(concluded)*: COMMERCE AND ROADS

The Tibetan's small capacity for commerce—The great trade is in the hands of the monks and the chief land-owners; organisation of trade—Roads to China; to India—Tibet's trade with China—The markets of Likiangfu and Tongking—Tibet's trade with British India; with other countries—The currency.

TRADE affords an even smaller outlet for private enterprise. It is, in fact, almost entirely in the hands of the State, the lamas, the grandees and foreigners; and there is not, so far as I know, a private individual who makes trade his regular and exclusive profession, except in Ladak, but only among the Moslems. Yet the Chinese look upon the Tibetans as endowed in a high degree with the spirit of traffic and brokerage. To tell the truth, they deal in all sorts of things so soon as the occasion presents itself; and, should the occasion not present itself, they readily bring it about, offering to all comers every manner of thing in exchange for something that seems to them worth more. It is not easy to strike a bargain with them, still less to come off best at it. Where there is anything to be made, the Tibetan displays a resourceful, suspicious, crafty, cunning and tenacious spirit; he scrutinises with the greatest attention the object that is offered him in exchange for his wares, handles it, smells it, weighs it in his hand and tosses his head, discovers all the flaws which it has and ascribes to it all those which it has not, looks at you out of the corner of his eye to fathom your views and to see the effect produced by his words, gauges your commercial capacity, measures the degree of your generosity or your avarice, sounds and flatters your vanity, tries your patience, for the rest makes no firm offer, uses vague circumlocutions and beats about the bush indefinitely, shows the greater disinclination to conclude the transaction the more advantageous it appears to him, does not bind himself until he is certain that he will never obtain better terms and, if, nevertheless, he thinks that he has gone too far, comes back to declare that he has consulted his wife and that she refuses to ratify the bargain and makes you a humble bow, putting out his tongue and scratching his ear.

But this is not the way in which a real trader acts. Commerce demands more liberty and breadth; and the Tibetan, unlicked highlander that he is, with his ingenuous cunning, is too much afraid of being taken in and too eager to take in others ever to do much business. Besides, he is domesticated to excess, like all primitive peoples and particularly nomads; he does not want to see anything new; and, when, by chance, circumstances make him come out of his hole, he is uncomfortable, bewildered, and thinks only of returning home at the earliest possible moment, incapable as he is of altering his habits in the smallest degree or of accommodating himself to unaccustomed surroundings. At bottom, he is a husbandman and a herdsman and is only an occasional dealer. He does not settle down to business as a merchant; all the shops and warehouses in the country are kept by Chinamen, Nepalese, Kashmirians, Moslems from North-west India, Ladak and Baltistan. The drinking-establishments *(changkang)* run by native women cannot be considered an exception. The business of the home trade is done either in the bazaars of the town (*krom*, pronounced *tom*), or in the periodical, generally annual fairs which are held near the villages or the monasteries. People go to these fairs from many hundreds of miles around; there are herdsmen who travel 400 miles to go and sell their produce at Nagchu Jong. There, private individuals, shepherds or farmers, exchange their respective wares among themselves or sell them to the professional traders, who are the foreigners above-mentioned, or to the representatives of the great nobles and the monasteries, who, together with the State, are the only merchants on a large scale. They alone, in fact, dispose of important funds, consisting of their properties, their benefices, taxes, perquisites, more or less voluntary gifts and bequests, which are paid, to a good extent, in kind, and the produce of the manufactures which they carry on, or cause to be carried on for their benefit. Thus, the Lhasa government, the heads of the several principalities, the officials, the convents accumulate considerable stocks of goods, collect in a central point the produce of the surrounding country and fit out large caravans to carry it to places at several months' march and to bring back foreign goods, which they sell off, at the best possible profit, at the most favourable time. For the rest, princes, lords and lamas all abuse their power to increase their gains: if the buyer does not turn up of his own accord, they hunt him down and sell him at a very high price something for which he has no use; they oblige the villein bound to labour and service to work for nothing or at a ridiculous wage, force him to sell at a loss everything that he possesses and condemn him, for the least fault, to pay a fine consisting of so many bricks of tea, furs or pieces of stuff.

The great lay or religious nobles who do a foreign trade keep, in the places where this trade is centred, at

Tongkor, Darchedo,* Likiang or Leh, their responsible agents, called *tsongpons*, that is to say overseers of commerce, who remain constantly at their posts, superintend the warehouse in which their employers' goods are kept, receive and lodge the caravans dispatched by the latter and attend to the operations of buying and selling. These tsongpons, some of whom have small armies of servants and inferior agents under their orders, are men of importance, confidential persons, sometimes relations of their masters, government officials or lamas of mark. They are not the same as our agents or managers of branch establishments, for they are bound to their principals not only by commercial obligations, but also by social duties; they are their subordinates in the capacity of subjects, obediential monks, dependants, serfs or domestic servants, before being so in their capacity of business-agents.

The roads being long, difficult and sometimes dangerous, consignments of goods are not made often: it is more profitable to fit out the largest caravans possible, in order to diminish the general cost, to travel only at the best seasons and to be better protected against the brigands. Thus we met, on the road from Nagchu to Jyerkundo, a caravan dispatched by the chief lama of Tachilhunpo that numbered no fewer than 800 horses and 90 men. These great convoys are led by tsongpons who are similar to those who live abroad and who are more or less high in rank according as he who sends them is himself a more or less great person. The tsongpon has supreme authority over all who accompany him; he can, as a special favour, permit private individuals to join the convoy with a limited number of loaded animals, on condition that they submit to his command and pay a certain fee. On the journey, he has the right to requisition animals and food everywhere and

* The Tibetan name for Tasienlu.

in the same measure in which his master possesses it; if he be a monk, he receives hospitality in all the convents of his order, if a royal or ministerial agent, from all the officials, if the agent of a minor noble, from all those who keep up relations of hospitality with his employer. This organisation of the foreign trade goes back to the remotest antiquity; in former days, China knew no other and the imperial and royal caravans were no different from the political embassies. In the same way, the commercial expeditions dispatched periodically to Peking by the Maharajah of Nepal and the chief lamas of Lhasa and Tachilhunpo and to Lhasa by the King of Ladak or, in his stead, since 1842, by the vizier of the Maharajah of Kashmir to this day assume the character of a political mission.

The means of communication are extremely inconvenient and difficult and are no more encouraging to trade than are the lack of resources of the country and the aristocratic organisation of society. What is known as a road, *lam*, or even a high-road *chalam (rgyalam)*, is a mere track that crosses valleys deeply set between mountains, tumultuous torrents seldom supplied with bridges and not always fordable and rugged passes over 16,000 feet high, on whose slopes the snow lies heaped to a thickness of several feet; the ground, full of dents and holes or encumbered with blocks of stone, seldom offers a space wide enough to allow two loaded animals to pass abreast; sometimes the road consists only of a ledge of a few inches wide jutting out from the perpendicular wall of the mountain, a ledge covered with ice or sticky mud and hanging over deep precipices. The yak is the animal best-suited to roads of this sort: its weight breaks the ice and it hardly ever slips; its huge mass and its short legs give it a wonderfully firm balance, which enables it to pass everywhere and to extricate itself from the worst scrapes. It is not necessary to carry fodder for the yak, which contents itself with such grass as it finds, hard though the grass may be; and this quality is particularly valuable on the desert roads, devoid of all resources, such as that from Nagchu to Jung. But the yaks are lazy, undisciplined, fond of feeding and ruminating at their ease; they can only go short stages and carry tolerably light and not easily breakable loads, for, instead of marching with even steps, in a regular file, like the horses and camels, they go in a troop, promiscuously, shaking from side to side, jumping, trotting, knocking one against the other. In the mountains, they cover only nine or ten miles a day; over flat country, as between Tsaidam and Sining, one can get as many as sixteen miles out of them. Horses go twice as far in a day as yaks and they are sometimes preferred, although they are more expensive and more difficult to feed.

The high-roads of Tibet may be divided into five groups. The first group joins Lhasa with Sining (Ziling in Tibetan) and Lanchow. The most westerly of the roads of this group, which is also the longest, but the most frequented, because it is the only one that is safe from the incursions of the Golok brigands, goes through Nagchu Jong, the Lugrat and Chumar Rabdun fords and Jung in Tsaidam. This road, which was followed by Huc, has been gone over by no Europeans south of the Do Chu. It is 1,160 miles long, or only 1,130 to Tongkor, where the Tibetan agents reside. The yaks take 108 days to cover it: 20 days from Lhasa to Nagchu, 88 from Nagchu to Sining. It passes through populous districts for only 56 miles from Lhasa until a little beyond Pumdo Jong and 92 miles from Sining to Tongkor Gompa: between these two narrow belts, the traveller comes upon only two small villages, those of Nagchu and Jung, in the distance of 1,060 miles, of which over 500 are uninterrupted desert, that separates those two localities. At any rate, the region which it crosses, being very near the sources of the big rivers, does not, as yet, present any very deep erosions nor, consequently, great marching difficulties, notwithstanding the lofty altitude. Another road, which was used in the last century, has been abandoned because of the Golok robberies. It is straighter than the former, from which it parts a little to the south of the Chumar Rabdun fords, to make for Lakes Kyaring and Ngoring, between which it passes, and then for Tongkor: it measures 1,060 miles to this last town, of which 800 are in the desert, and therefore offers no appreciable advantage, even if its safety were restored. The road which we were the first to reconnoitre and which runs past the sources of the Mekong, Tachi Gompa, Jyerkundo, the Stongri Cho and Tongkor Gompa is not perceptibly longer (1,110 miles) and is uninhabited for only 360 miles between the Za Chu and the neighbourhood of Tongkor Gompa. Still, from the commercial point of view, it does not compare with that which leaves it at Labug Gompa and, passing through Archung, Ltasen Gompa, Lhabrang Gompa and Hochow, reaches Lanchow, which is the real commercial centre of this region. It goes almost wholly through inhabited country and the journey is only 1,275 miles, as against 1,315, the length of the road used to-day. But the Goloks who occupy it allow none save the Lhabrang Gompa caravans to pass, even as they leave the Kyaring Cho road open only to the chief lama of Tachilhunpo, when, every three years, he travels to Peking, and the road from Jyerkundo and Tongkor only to the caravans of the monasteries around Jyerkundo.

The second group of roads connects Lhasa and Tasienlu (Darchedo). These roads are three in number and, by a strange chance, the first Europeans to see them and travel by them have all been Frenchmen.

The most southerly, the most direct and also the most difficult is that which passes through Gyamdo, Lhari, Chobando and Chamdo and has been followed so far only by Huc and Gabet: it is 1,030 miles long and takes the yaks three months and a half. M. Bonvalot and the Orleans prince inaugurated the middle road by Sog Jong and Chamdo, which appears to be little used. Lastly, we ourselves were the first to trace out the north road through the sources of the Mekong and Jyerkundo, the portion which joins this last point to Tasienlu having been covered by Mr. Rockhill in 1891. This third road is more frequented and is not much longer than the former (1,140 miles, as against 1,100). The reason for the preference which many give it over Huc's shorter road is that the latter is detestable. The description which the famous missionary gave of it cannot be far removed from the exact truth: several of the details were confirmed to us by Tibetans who had followed it and notably that relating to the pass which the yaks can descend only by sliding from the top to the bottom of the frozen slope. Nevertheless, the Imperial Legate of Lhasa never takes any other road, because this is the most inhabited and the best supplied with resources. To this group we may add the road of 540 miles which goes from Songpanting to Chamdo through Zogchen Gompa, with a branch road to Jyerkundo, but which is not open for regular purposes of commerce and is used only by the Songpan smugglers, who are good friends with the Manchu bandits.

The third group joins Lhasa and Likiang in Yunnan. The distance between these two towns is 950 miles, passing through the valley of the Sampo-Brahmaputra as far as Chum Jong, through Po Jong, either Kiangka or Dayul, Tseku and Wisi. This is the least-known district of Tibet.

The fourth group comprises the roads which connect Lhasa with India. The most practical of these is closed to commerce by the Tibetan government, acting in concert with the Chinese government. It is 325 miles long and takes a mounted man in nine days from Lhasa to Darjeeling, the terminus of the English railway. The open roads reach India through Bhotan and Nepal. Tasisudan, the capital of the former country, is only 250 miles from Lhasa; Khatmandu, the capital of Nepal, is 530 miles, going through Gyangtse, Tachilhunpo, Saskya, Lasikar Jong and Nilam. A fourth road goes from Lhasa to Assam through Chetang, Dirang Jong and Odalgari, but the traffic on it is insignificant.

The fifth group is composed of the two roads that lead from Lhasa to Leh, one through Tachilhunpo, Gartog and Rudok, the other through Senja Jong, Ombo and Rudok. The first, although the longer of the two (1,340 miles as against 1,175), is the only one that carries any considerable traffic, because it passes through much more populous districts, the most populous, in fact, and the most flourishing of Tibet. This is the road taken by the mission of the vizier of Ladak. The traders make the journey in four months with yaks and in two and a half with horses, while the official messengers, who travel day and night and change horses at each station, do it in eighteen days, thus covering about 75 miles in twenty-four hours. I will not speak here of the roads that lead from Lhasa or Tachilhunpo to Chinese Turkestan, because these have no commercial importance.

One would naturally expect that Tibet would have more active relations with India than with any other country; but history and politics have decided differently. The greatest part of Tibetan trade is carried on with China and finds an outlet at Tongkor, Tasienlu or Likiang, the towns where the tsongpons are settled. At Tongkor, the Tibetans buy Mongolian horses, leather, saddles and harness, boots, felt hats, a few silks for the lamas, a few cottons which the Panaks are almost the only ones to use, flour, tobacco from Lanchow and Singan, paper, iron pots and different articles of hardware, swords and fire-arms. They sell wool, furs, musk, joss-sticks, rhubarb and, moreover, saffron, sugar-candy, dates, shells and amber which they have bought in British India. The value of the turnover does not appear to exceed forty thousand pounds.

Much more important is the Tasienlu market, although the roads that lead there are no shorter and, indeed, if we look upon the real commercial centres, namely Lanchow and Chingtu, as the termini, we find that the former is less far than the latter from Lhasa (1,310 miles and 1,210 miles as against 1,360 and 1,250). But the districts passed on the road to Tasienlu are more thickly populated; while Kansu is poor, Sechuen is one of the richest and most populous provinces in China and produces almost everything that China produces. Tibet depends politically upon Sechuen, and Tasienlu has the monopoly of the tea-trade with Tibet just as Sining has the monopoly of the same trade with Mongolia and Turkestan. Now tea is the article that is sold in much the largest quantities to Tibet and at much the highest profit. According to the official accounts of the *likin*, Tasienlu sells every year to its Tibetan customers over thirteen million pounds of tea, fetching, according to the quality, from 4d. to 6d. per pound at Tasienlu and from 11d. to 1s. 7d. at Lhasa: a respectable figure to which must be added all the tea that is smuggled, principally by way of Songpan. This trade is a source of great profit to the Chinese houses at Singan, which have obtained from their fellow-countryman, the Viceroy of Sechuen, the exclusive privilege of selling tea on the Tibetan market. The absence of competition enables them to charge a very high price for very bad material. This export tea contains more wood than leaves in the bricks of inferior quality; it is often damaged and the best is not calculated to flatter our European tastes. But the Tibetans are used to it and like it. They have a fixed prejudice in their minds that any other tea is adulterated and dangerous. Even in Ladak, subject to British authority, where they can obtain tea from India of a better quality and at a lower price, they obstinately insist upon drinking that awful tea from Tasienlu, declaring that the tea sold by the English is a poison capable of giving the consumer every sort of disease. Merchants, government and lamas—often, for that matter, one—are all alike interested in encouraging this popular prejudice, the merchants because of the material profit which they derive from it, the government and the lamas in order, as far as possible, to prevent commercial relations with the English.

One might write a curious chapter on the influence of prejudice in commercial matters. We have just seen, in regard to the tea-trade, that prejudice can be stronger than personal interest. The saffron-trade affords a no less singular example of the same fact. China gets her saffron from Tibet, which itself is obliged to buy it from India. The road is bad and long, the carriage costly. In order to make up for the consequent increase in price, the goods are adulterated and the Chinese buy under the name of saffron an ingenious and abominable mixture. It would evidently be to their advantage to have this article sent straight from India by sea: they would then have it cheaper and of a better quality. But the Chinese are persuaded that Tibetan saffron is the best of saffrons and they will not exchange their persuasion for the truth.

Besides tea, Tasienlu exports to Tibet cottons in small quantities, cotton tents, silks to a somewhat important value, brocades, katags (a sort of coarse silk scarves, which the Tibetans give to persons whom they wish to honour and which perform the functions of our visiting-cards), expensive furs, saddles, porcelain, turquoises finer than those of Tibet, fire-arms, hardware, drugs, tobacco, Japanese matches, which are used all over Tibet, wheat-meal, rice, black sugar, vinegar and preserved provisions for the Chinese functionaries and officers. The Tibetans bring in exchange woollen stuffs and blankets, hides and furs, musk, joss-sticks, gold-dust, antelope-horns, rhubarb, borax and Indian goods. They buy much more than they sell and make up the difference in rupees, which they obtain through their trade with India, where they sell more than they buy.

The Likiangfu market seems to have been important before the revolt of the Moslems of Yunnan. But, in consequence of the war which unsettled that province from 1855 to 1873, Likiang was ruined and has never completely recovered itself. This town is the centre of the rather slender trade which Tibet carries on with Yunnan; and musk passes through Likiang on its way to Tongking. It is the natural outlet for the products of South-eastern Tibet and of the comparatively rich and populous valley of the Mekong to the south ot Yerkalo. There is no doubt that, being without the tea-trade, this market is in a condition of decided inferiority to Tasienlu. Still, it occupies a fairly good geographical position: situated at seven days north of Talifu, which itself is the meeting-point of the valleys of the Mekong and the Red River, it is nearer to Lhasa than any other Chinese town and, what is more, the Tibetan capital is, by way of Likiang, hardly any farther from the Tongking frontier than from Chingtu. It is therefore not impossible that, if the proximity of our Indo-Chinese colonies give new life to the trade of Yunnan, Likiang will profit by this and supply us with the means of establishing lucrative relations with Tibet. We would buy sheep's-wool, goat's-wool, hides and furs, meat, cattle, Mongolian horses, gold and musk, all of them things which, in this part of Asia, are hardly to be procured except in Tibet. We would give in exchange glossy cloths, in plain colours, by preference red or blue, wrought and set precious stones, amber, arms, telescopes, spectacles with smoked glasses, clocks and watches, musical-boxes, metal plates and dishes, ornamental paper-weights, broad-nibbed steel pens, strong, unglazed writing-paper, mirrors, thread, needles, large scissors, knives. In the houses of the great people and especially in the convents are rather curious collections of European objects from all parts. The Dalai Lama and the Pangchen Rinpocheh have little museums of our arts and industries. It is quite certain that, if only our merchants and manufacturers succeed in planting their economic influence in Yunnan, this influence will be able to spread over Eastern Tibet and it will then do so quite naturally. But we must cherish no false ideas: the radius of Tongking's commercial activity is very limited and extends only to inhospitable lands whose scattered and poverty-stricken inhabitants are unable to buy much of us and, what is worse, are not disposed to be satisfied with the costly and rubbishy articles that are too often offered them. In this respect there is even much less to be expected from Tibet than from Yunnan. Only if Tongking becomes an industrial country, which it is quite capable of becoming, can it hope to be a considerable centre of attraction. In that case, Yunnan and Tibet, which are now insignificant and not very hopeful customers, will be useful to the development of the colony through the metals and wool with which they will supply it.

At present, Tibet buys in British India almost all the European goods that it requires. But this trade is not encouraged by the Tibetan and Chinese authorities and suffers greatly from the prohibition against the import of Indian tea, which might compete triumphantly with the Tasienlu tea. I have said that, the Sikkim road being kept strictly closed, there are no direct dealings between Tibet and India, except through Assam, an exception of no importance. India trades with Tibet mainly through Nepal; next to that, through Ladak; lastly, to an almost inconsiderable extent, through Bhotan. Tibet sends to India across its southern frontier woollen blankets and stuffs, raw wool, hides and furs, gold, silver, borax and salt, musk, *karvi (zira)*, or cumin, and medicinal plants; and it receives inferior cloth-stuffs, a few silks and flowered cottons, brocades, indigo, spices, sugar-candy, coral, pearls, amber, shells, arms, knives, scissors and needles, copper kitchen-utensils, a few metal plates and dishes and different European knicknacks. The greater part of the rice consumed by the Tibetans comes from Nepal, Sikkim and Bhotan; Bhotan also supplies them with much-appreciated tobacco and Nepal with the cloth known as buras and with jewellery.

To Leh, Lhasa sends principally tea, woollens and religious objects. The inhabitants of Ladak use no other tea than the brick-tea from Tasienlu, which costs them 3*s.* per lb., more than double the price at Lhasa, while the Indian dealers offer them good tea at one rupee the pound. Leh also receives from Western and Central Tibet and sends on to India gold from the mines of the province of Chang, turquoises from Lhasa or China, salt, borax and sulphur from the northern uplands (Changtang), sheep's-wool and goat's-wool from the provinces of Chang and Ngaris (to the value of about 250,000 rupees), musk, rhubarb and various medicinal plants. It imports from Kashmir, to send on to Western and Central Tibet, shawls, brocades, English cloth, indigo, saffron and spices of every kind, sugar-candy, a little barley and rice, copper dishes, cutlery, jewellery, coral, artificial pearls, &c. The total value of the trade between India and Tibet is very small. The inevitable insufficiency of the English statistics does not enable me to estimate it with exactness, but I do not think that it amounts to two million rupees. Between 1891 and 1893, the fluctuating trade with Ladak averaged 53,500 rupees and 169,000 rupees with Tibet through the intermediary of Ladak. During the same period, India did business to the extent of 38,500 rupees a year with Tibet through Sikkim, of 2,815,000 with Nepal, of 49,000 with Bhotan. The trade between India and Tibet, therefore, amounts to 261,000 rupees, *plus* the undecided amount, very much greater, however, than this figure, of the business done through the intermediary of Nepal and Bhotan.

The increase of this traffic depends upon the throwing open to commerce of the road between Darjeeling and Lhasa by the Chumbi Valley. The attempts made by the Anglo-Indian government to secure this opening ended, in 1893, in a commercial treaty of which I shall speak later, because at present it offers only a purely political interest. But, even if trade were entirely free on this side, neither India nor, still less, England could expect to find in Tibet a very important market for disposing of their produce; only, from the day when the Himalayan region is given up to British activity and is dependent, at least from the economic point of view, upon the Indian Empire, it will supply that empire abundantly and cheaply with the things in which at present it is most lacking: salt, hides and, above all, metals and wool, which, in India, is of very inferior quality. India will then definitely be what it is already on the way to becoming, one of the greatest manufacturing Powers in the world.

Leh is at present as important a commercial position as any commercial position can be in the midst of poor or indifferently rich districts. It is not a centre of production and consumption, for Ladak is one of the most barren and thankless countries of Tibet and its population does not exceed 178,000 souls; but it is still the necessary point of transit between India, Baltistan, Badakshan, Turkestan and Tibet. The roads which run to it from Lhasa are prolonged to Srinagar and Rawal Pindi, to Yarkand and Khotan by the Karakoram Pass, to Badakshan and Bactriana by Iskardo and Gilgit. This last route, nowadays of no great importance to Tibet's foreign relations, was famous in the middle ages and was the great connecting-road between Balkh and Lhasa. From Leh to Iskardo is ten days' march (185 miles) along the Indus; from Iskardo to the Baroghil Pass, thirteen days (250 miles) down the Indus, up the rivers Gilgit and Yasam and across the Darkot Pass. Beyond the Baroghil Pass, the road joins, at Sarhad, on the banks of the Ak Su, the routes from Kashgar, goes down the Ak Su as far as Ishkashim, crosses the Sardab Pass and, through Zebak, runs down to Feyzabad, which is twelve days from the Baroghil Pass and nine from Balkh. This town, therefore, is twenty-one days, or 440 miles, from the Baroghil Pass; forty-four days, or 475 miles, from Leh; and 2,200 miles from Lhasa. This is the road which the Tibetans used in the seventh and eighth centuries when they went to occupy Wakhan and to spread themselves as far as the extreme western limit of the Arabian Empire. Since then, the Tibetan race and language have receded as far as Baltistan and the relations between Tibet and the region of the Upper Oxus have became almost insignificant. The yak-oxen of Tibet carry to Wakhan a little hashish bought in

Chinese Turkestan and, in the Iranian dialect of the Wakhan, the hashish and the yak-ox have kept their Tibetan names, *bang* and *dzo*. Tibet receives a small quantity of rubies and lapis-lazuli from Badakshan and a few dried fruits, especially apricots, from Baltistan.

The very small trade done between Tibet and Chinese Turkestan uses almost exclusively the Karakoram Road. Leh imports from Yarkand, either for local consumption or for export to Tibet—I am not speaking here of what is destined for India—a little tobacco, hashish, of which the Western Tibetans have, unfortunately for themselves, acquired the habit, dried fruits, Kirghiz horses and Ili horses, which latter are known in Tibet as Yarkand horses and are sought after for their relatively larger size, felts and rugs, especially Khotan saddle-rugs, a few sable and otter-skins and a little Russian leather. I am not aware that Tibet sends anything to Chinese Turkestan in return, except a few turquoises and some musk, which has become famous in the writings of the Moslem authors under the name of Khotan musk. The Karashar Mongols, who go to Lhasa by the Ambalashkan Pass or the Angirtakshia Pass, take a few of their native horses to the Tibetan capital and bring back some religious objects and a few woollens; but this is unimportant.

Among the European goods sold in Tibet, German or Austrian goods occupy the first place after and a very long way behind those of English origin. Cutlery, drugs, fancy goods, needles and thread are the articles that most often bear the mark "Made in Germany" or "Made in Austria." Imitation jewellery commands no sale at present, for the Tibetans are not stupid savages and buy, in respect of jewels, only such objects as can be sold, when necessary, at not too great a loss. A very small quantity of Russian goods finds its way into Tibet through Yarkand or Lanchow. I, for my part, saw no

Russian imports except some Okh horses, a little Russian leather and a few pairs of Russia-leather boots introduced by the Mongols. Certain travellers have established the presence, in several districts of Eastern Tibet, of a number of pieces of Russian cloth; but, at Leh and in the Lhasa territory, I have never seen any but English cloth. Of French trade I need not trouble to speak, for it cannot be very interesting to point to the stock of claret and champagne which our resident at Leh keeps in his cellar nor the dozen boxes of sardines which the Hindu grocer at the same place offers to sell to the rare tourists passing through; and yet it would be unjust not to mention to the reader a box containing six cakes of scented soap, which were the only specimens of soap that could be discovered within the radius of Lhasa in the month of January 1894 and which their purchaser was delighted to sell to us after having had them for forty years in his shop.

The commonest coin within the limits of the kingdom of Lhasa is the tangka,* a silver piece struck at Lhasa by the Dalai Lama, larger, but much thinner than our franc and containing a considerable quantity of alloy. It is worth one-eighth of an ounce of silver, two-fifths of a rupee, or 8½*d.* There is no smaller money and the tangka is cut into two, three or four pieces as required. This Lhasa coinage is not looked upon with favour outside the States of the Dalai Lama and ceases to be current at a short distance from the frontier or is accepted only at a loss of one-third of a rupee or one-ninth of an ounce.

On the other hand, the Chinese silver ingots and the Anglo-Indian rupee *(gormo)*, which sometimes serves to ornament the hair of the women, passes everywhere without undergoing depreciation. Still, the rupee is not

* This is the same word as the Turkic *tenga*, which denotes a coin having exactly the same value.

accepted by the Tibetans on the shores of the Koko Nor. The Chinese ingots occur less frequently, because they are not so convenient to carry ; but the ounce of silver *(srang)* is considered from one end of the country where the Tibetan tongue is spoken to the other as the real monetary basis. The silver ounce does not vary, whereas the rupee and the tangka are subject to slight fluctuations. The former was quoted, in 1894, at ·3125 ounce, the latter at ·125. The value of the currency has not been affected by the fall in the price of silver and the price of commodities has remained stationary. Only gold has gone up in price, but not so much as in Turkestan ; it still costs only eighteen times its weight in silver at Lhasa and fifteen times at Jyerkundo or Batang.

CHAPTER IX

RELIGION : SURVIVAL OF OLD FORMS OF WORSHIP—THE PONBOS

Dogmatics of Buddhism in general and of Tibetan Buddhism in particular—How the original principles of Buddhism have become degraded and distorted—Cult of the dead, of ancestors and of the domestic hearth—Remains of the old worship of natural phenomena; gods and demons—The Ponbo sect, which has remained faithful to the primitive religion—True character and role of Buddhism in Tibet.

WITH the exception of the people of Baltistan, who are Shiite Moslems, and about half a million Ponbos distributed over every part of the country, all the Tibetans are Buddhists. But, though I have only to say that the inhabitants of Chinese Turkestan are Moslems for the reader to know what I mean, explanations are necessary to point out precisely what must be understood by my statement that the Tibetans are Buddhists. The religion of the Tibetans is very different from the doctrine which the Enlightened One preached in India in the fifth century B.C. This doctrine conceived the world to be a mere collection of attributes which are not attached to any real substance; the universe is composed only of appearances, is an immense illusion; nothing exists in itself, for everything ceases to exist at the very moment at which it is, everything lapses in a perpetual evolution. Happiness is, therefore, not possible, since it would be destroyed at the very instant when it was attained; life, an aggregate of indefinitely changing modalities, is necessarily imperfect, devoted to evil, suffering and death. Death, in its turn, is only a speck in the universal evolution, a passing from one form of life to a new form; for so great is the power of illusion that the elements that constitute the appearance dissolved by death retain in the depths of the unconsciousness the desire to enter into the composition of a new appearance and, like a blind man who does not see the vanity of things, they wander through the empty night, allowing themselves to be led by karma, the effect of all their former actions, and to be flung into the mould, whether superior or inferior, which the latter assigns to them; * the form having been

* The Buddhist conception of the metempsychosis is very different from the vulgar conception. It is not the continuation of the personality of each individual after death, the passing of the soul into another body. The first Buddhists and the profound Hindu philosophers upon whom they based their teaching, the philosophers who invented, five or six centuries before Christ, almost all the ideas which the German philosophy of our own age thought that it had discovered, were far from entertaining any such childish notions. To them the soul is only a series of psychic attributes and acts, in the same way as the body is only a series of physical facts. When the whole of the facts that constitute the corporeal appearance is dissolved by death, it does not disappear any more than does the whole of the psychic facts that constitute the moral personality, for nothing is lost, nothing is created. The acts subsist and continue to influence the entire life of the world by entering into new combinations. If an individual have led a bad life, the bad effect of his acts will make itself felt after his death by entering into the formation of new moral beings, who will have the same qualities of covetousness, of vain attachment to the things of the world; and the evil of the universe will be increased by it. On the other hand, he who has led a good life, who has stifled desire within himself and suppressed activity, will, by that very fact, have suppressed the causes of future evils, will not have contributed to the motion of the wheel of life that engenders wretchedness; and, if all living beings follow his example, that fatal wheel will at last come to a standstill, rest will succeed action and perfection and the cessation of existence, those two indissoluble terms, will reign alone. The reward or the penalty of a good or a bad life is, therefore, not individual happiness or unhappiness in the world to come, but general happiness or unhappiness.

This theory was too lofty for the universal egoism to follow: each wished to keep the benefit of his efforts for himself, instead of placing it in the public money-box; and the Buddhists, with the exception of the most distinguished teachers, ended by accepting childish and popular opinions on the soul and the life to come.

recovered, consciousness returns and, after it, successively, sensation, the desire for life, the love of the good things of the world, the transmission of existence to an heir, suffering and death. The wheel thus turns without end ; and we cannot escape from this circle of wretchedness save by the knowledge of the truth that shows the falseness of things and the irreparable evil of existence and by the abolition of passion and desire, which are the causes of life. By realising absolute apathy, we avoid the law of becoming, we enter into the perfect, immutable state, from which consciousness, feeling, joy and suffering have disappeared. This pessimistic philosophy excludes all theodicean speculation. God is superfluous, since everything in the world is rigorously determined. He cannot exist as a perfect, distinct Being and master of the universe ; for either existence cannot be conceived without action and movement, whereas action and movement derogate from absolute perfection, or else existence is conceived abstractly, stripped of all its modalities, in which case the perfect, immutable Being, without thought or will, without anger or love, incapable of acting or of thinking of acting, without limits and, consequently, indistinct, without attributes in short (for attributes are relative and therefore incompatible with perfection), becomes lost in Nirvana, that is to say in the cessation of existence, which differs in nothing from the absolute.

This severe doctrine, reserved to the initiated few, was soon corrupted and was invaded by the mythologies of Brahmanism and Shivaism, by popular superstitions and by the metaphysics of the theologians. The deterioration was especially perceptible in the countries of the north, which adopted the teaching of the school known as that of the Great Vehicle, or Mahayama, because, making the greatest allowance for human weakness, it boasted that it carried more men to the shores of salvation.

The Enlightened One, the Buddha, who, they say, under the name and form of a small prince of the north-west of India, was the first to preach the good rule, became a god and was considered as the universal soul in place and stead of Brahma. He was the first principle, the sole being, eternal, incorruptible, manifesting himself in three persons without affecting the unity of his essence: the first is the transcendental Buddha, the personification of Nirvana and of the Supreme Law; the second proceeds from the first, of which it is the reflection and the representation in the celestial world, where conscious and active life develops itself with all the splendour and all the perfection of which it is capable, an intermediary world between that of the absolute and that of humanity; lastly, the third, which proceeds from the two others, is the Buddha made man.

Later, but still in very remote ages, each of these three persons was multiplied by five; each of the five metaphysical Buddhas (Dhyani Buddhas) and of the five celestial Buddhas (Bodhisattvas) was subdivided, in accordance with the Shivaistic conceptions, into two principles, male and female; and, above this ramification, was recognised a supreme and primordial Being (Adi-Buddha or Togmai Sangyeh), of whom all the others are only emanations in the first, second or third degree. It was a desperate effort to pass through a degradation of subtle shades from illusion to truth, from movement to repose, to bridge over the space between miserable, lying, transient man and the true eternal, infinite, immutable, impassive being, the Nirvana-God, by ascribing to that Motionless One an eternal evolution, begetting throughout eternity a conscious and active, but wholly spiritual manifestation, which, in its turn, begets an active and carnal hypostasis. Buddhism thus became a form of monotheism deeply impregnated with pantheism and Nirvana was transformed into absorption into the bosom of the divinity or of the universal soul, of which each individual soul is a detached atom.

This view seems to have prevailed among the Tibetan people, who were unable to understand the theory of primitive Buddhism. They generally speak of Sangyeh without an epithet, as of a sole God, notwithstanding his different names which denote his numerous manifestations. They send up prayers to him and believe him capable of interfering in the affairs of this world and even of modifying the effect of karma; or, rather, each pious invocation goes to increase the assets of him who utters it and entitles him to a better life in the next world. Many ascribe to Sangyeh a creative power similar to that which the old Hindu mythology attributed to Brahma. By an effect of his will and the power of his meditation, he is said to have formed out of pre-existent chaotic matter the Rirab Gyalpo, or King of the Mountains, which, stretching its prodigious mass of gold, rubies, sapphires and crystal from the depths of the abyss to the summit of the skies, was to be the axis of the universe; then he brought forth from the bosom of the primitive waters a first world which was successively destroyed and reconstructed, for an incalculable number of times, under different forms. Sangyeh, according to the same people, is interested in the universe and in men in particular: he is a god-providence. Originally, men were superior beings, who looked at Sangyeh face to face, whose bodies were illumined by an inner light, performing the office of the absent sun; they enjoyed extraordinary length of days, were exempt from the ills and maladies that distress modern mankind and had no need to work to live. But, in time, they became perverted; their bad actions weighed down their good deeds; and, losing their privileges, they descended (probably by successive regenerations) to the level of the men of to-day and were plunged into darkness in consequence of the loss of the divine light that formerly shone from their bodies. Then, Sangyeh created nine suns, whose excessive heat liquefied all that existed, and the world became no more than a mass in a state of fusion, in which the King of the Mountains alone subsisted. Next, by the force of his meditation, he provoked the formation of a sort of protoplasm, which, solidifying, increasing and subdividing, constituted a new world, with its four real or fabulous continents, its stars, its gods, men and beasts. Men, trusting the subtilty of their intellect, will become perverted again until, despising the supreme and eternal law which Sakya Muni preached, they will, in the pride of their apparent power, come to make war upon the last of the faithful and upon the terrestrial incarnation of Buddha, the Dalai Lama, who, under the name of Gyaser (?) Gyalpo, will have to mount his white charger and draw his sword in defence of the truth. Then, the end of time will be at hand; and, when the universe has been destroyed by the will of Sangyeh, he will fashion another in a later period. Note that the world in this conception does not cease to be an appearance without reality: it is the product of the power of illusion of Sangyeh and as it were a dream of the Divinity, the only really existing thing. This essentially Shivaistic doctrine does not, perhaps, agree with the teaching of the majority of the Tibetan doctors, except the conclusion, which presents anew the legend of Krishna, recalls that of the Antichrist and is an article of faith; but, as no great importance attaches to these questions, it is possible for even Gelugpa lamas to hold these ideas without being treated as heretics.

Apart from Sangyeh and his celestial and terrestrial emanations, who make only one with him, Tibetan Buddhism recognises a host of secondary divinities borrowed from Hindu mythology and from the old local religion. These divinities, good and bad alike, receive a regular worship and enjoy special attributes and independent power. The Tibetans are very much afraid of their whims and their anger and are more anxious not to displease them and to appease them or to force their favour by ceremonies, forms and sacrifices than to follow the mystic road that leads to the final deliverance. Therefore, Buddhism is atheistic, monotheistic, pantheistic, polytheistic, according to the view which one takes of it. The disciples of Gautama are not at all embarrassed by what we are inclined to look upon as monstrous contradictions. Anyone who is more or less accustomed to metaphysical speculations knows how easy it is to pass from one to another of those categories by almost imperceptible shades and how frail are the barriers that separate them, barriers set up by the prejudice or the limited logic of the philosophers or theologians. At bottom, Tibetan Buddhism bears a strong resemblance to Hinduism in its metaphysics, save on a few important points, in its doctrine of karma, of the transmigration of souls, of the renunciation of the good things of the world, of the absorption into the universal soul; in its mythology, worship and ceremonies. Buddhism, originally devoid of worship, has taken to itself almost the whole of Hindu worship, with its array of idols, formulas and complicated rites. It has also borrowed some details from the Christian liturgy, through the intermediary of the Nestorians established, in the middle ages, in China and Mongolia; but it appears that this influence has been exaggerated, many of the things which were believed to be taken from Christianity having since been found to exist in the religions of India.

Moral perfection and indifference to the outward illusion, necessary to obtain salvation, have been relegated to the background and the coarse, popular conception of religion has gained the day. The divinity has ceased to be inactive, insensible to the prayers of men and to their efforts to please it; it has become a king whose wrath is to be feared, but whose favour can be skilfully captured; it has again fallen under the domination of rites and formulas. Prayer is no longer a simple homage, but solicitation and even, in certain conditions, a means of effective compulsion. Works have assumed an excessive importance and by works we must understand not morally good works, but acts of material devotion, intended to circumvent the divinity, to force his attention, to tire his resistance, to oblige him, by special favour, to bend the impassive law to the will of his courtiers. Buddha, who laid down the principle of the renunciation of the vanities of the world, Buddha, who set up for an object the annihilation of the personality, is asked to grant wealth, health, the satisfaction of covetousness and pride, is constrained by a ceremony more solemn than any of the others to distil the elixir of long life. His devotees pray for the dead as though the dead could escape the fatal consequences of their acts. If Buddha refuses to be moved, they apply to one of the thousand gods that surround him, each of whom has his particular role, his special power, his own horrible or amiable shape, his personal harsh or benevolent character, a host of courtly chamberlains, graceful maids-of-honour, generals, fierce defenders of the faith, dread duennas, not to speak of the diabolical animals that go about in the purlieus seeking whom they may devour. The supernatural world is a court where they distribute good and bad seats for the life to come, spiritual graces and temporal goods, calamities and miseries: to obtain the former and to be dispensed from the others, the Tibetans exhaust themselves in measures, in solicitations, intrigues, gifts. They build thousands of temples; make tens of thousands of statues; prostrate themselves; sing hymns; mutter endless prayers; grind out an even greater number by water-power or by hand; say their rosaries; celebrate solemn services; make offerings and give banquets to all the gods and all the devils; wear amulets and relics; write talismans; wave streamers covered with prayers or lucky emblems, which the breath of the wind sends flying through space; pile up numberless heaps of stones with pious inscriptions; turn around all the objects which they regard as sacred: mountains, lakes, temples, heaps of stones; go in processions and on pilgrimages; swallow indulgences in the shape of pills made by the lamas out of relics; drink down with compunction the divine nectar *(dudchi)* composed of the ten impurities, such as human flesh and worse; practise exorcism, witchcraft and magic, even to obtain spiritual blessings; perform pious mysteries and dance strange and frenzied sarabands to drive out or shatter the devil: and thus is Tibet made to spin distractedly, without rest or truce, in religion's mad round.

I will linger no further on the dogma or ritual of Tibetan Buddhism. Mr. Waddell* has treated this subject lately with much greater accuracy and detail than I could do from my unaided memory. I will content myself with giving a few notes on a matter that particularly attracted my attention in the course of our journey, namely the remains that still survive of the old local religion. What I have already said shows that the spirit which animated this religion of former times is deep-rooted in the Tibetan soul, has grafted itself on the Buddhic stem and made it bear fruits which it was not intended to produce. Much more, a certain number of forms, rites, divinities of the old religion have remained, if not untouched, at least recognisable. Such is the cult of ancestors, although Buddhism was of all religions the least disposed to leave a place for that, for it does not

* L. A. Waddell: *The Buddhism of Tibet*. London: 1895.

admit that the living can do anything for the souls of the dead nor the latter for the living. Their destiny is rigorously determined beforehand; they do not remain in the tomb, but are condemned to come to life again under different shapes, in new combinations of matter, without retaining the memory of their former states. Nevertheless, the lamas have been compelled by the force of popular superstition to make serious concessions on this point. They come themselves to recite prayers and litanies by the bedside of the deceased, in order to send his soul to the western paradise; they celebrate religious services in the temples for the repose of the dead; the family bestows lavish alms upon the clergy and the poor in the belief that this will be useful to the defunct in his future life. Above all, the lamas, giving him a scarf of honour, are careful politely to recommend the deceased not to return from the other world, to understand that he is dead and that he must not come back to trouble the living; they give him very precise directions as to the road which he is to follow, for fear lest he should take it into his head to lose his way and find himself once more, by mischance, where he has no business to be. When they take him to the place of burial, they turn to him from time to time to beg him not to give them the slip, for he must be good and feel that they are thinking only of his welfare. The dread that the spirit of the dead man will escape from the lower regions to visit the house which he has left holds sway over the Tibetan mind. The nomads of the north-east, when a man lies dying, ask him if he intends to come back after his death: if he answers yes, they suffocate him; if no, they let him die in peace. On the day of the funeral, the relations assemble and take a meal together in honour of the dead man, who receives his share of the dishes. When the funeral is over, they dress up a block of wood in the dead man's clothes and place on the top a piece of paper which is supposed to be his portrait; and, every day, they offer him food to eat. We know from Tibetan books that this was a general custom in the seventh century; nowadays, the ceremony is limited to forty-nine days, by the end of which period the spirit of the dead man has necessarily found a place in a new body. But they continue to show him worship. The ashes of the burnt portrait are mixed with earth and made into little cones *(chacha)*, which they carefully preserve on the domestic altar. They also place a few in rough monuments raised in the country. Throughout Tibet one comes across these chachas, which are sometimes said to be representations of Buddha; this is only a manner of describing their sacred character. The relics of important persons, of chief lamas, are placed in more imposing monuments called *chorchen (mtchodrten)*, that is to say receptacles of offerings, altars. Nowadays, these very numerous chorchens are oftenest only empty tombs or cenotaphs; but it was not the same in former days, as may be concluded from their old name of *dungrten (gdungrten)*, receptacles of bones. The Chinese authors tell us that, in the seventh century, tumuli were raised over the tombs of the dead kings and even great buildings to which people came to do homage and to present offerings to the spirit of the prince. Here we have the prototype of the Islamised mazaars of Turkestan. Again, the shades lived in the tomb a life similar to that which they had led on earth, for with the king were buried his pages, his horses, his clothes, his jewels and his arms. Nowadays, the Tibetans celebrate a commemorative ceremony one year after the death of their kinsman and, every year, in summer, they offer libations to the shades of their dead ancestors. Before every tent one sees a cord, stretched horizontally, to which are fastened streamers, generally nine in number. They reproduce the *somos* of the Altai Turkomans, which represent the souls of nine ancestors, whose duty it is to protect their descendants; but, in modern Tibet, these protective streamers are covered with Buddhist inscriptions with wishes for happiness.

The cult shown to ancestors is not only a token of pious memory, is not only a provision served out to them to save them from starving in the next world, but is also a homage shown to divine beings, to superior powers, in exchange for their protection. The ancestors receive the title of gods (*lha*). It is from their ancestors that the Tibetan sorcerers, like the *kams* of the northern Turkomans, derive their power and they are necessarily hereditary. The grand official sorcerer of Tibet, who resides at Nechung, always invokes a special demon called the king (*gyalpo*), from whom he himself is descended and who came from Mongolia. The lama summoned to a sick man to exorcise the demon that possesses him has recourse to his own tutelary genius, who is very probably, in that case, the Buddhic form of the ancestral genii, the natural protectors of their descendant. A certain number of gods or devils, honoured by the Tibetans, are considered to be the shades of heroes or heroines whose cult has spread from their own family to a wider circle. Thus the *spamos*, or fairy huntresses, are the ghosts of ancient queens. It is contended that the most terrible of all the devils, the *duds*, are the spirits of the old persecutors of Buddhism. But the fact that proves beyond doubt that they are divinities of an earlier date than the religion of Sakya Muni is that offerings of swine are made to them, although sacrifices of live animals are forbidden by that religion.

The cult of ancestors is complemented by the worship of the household gods, which stands towards the former in a correlation which my insufficient information does not enable me to state with precision. Every house has its divinity *(nanglha)*, which ordinarily occupies the hearth, although, at certain times, it is installed in other parts of the home. This god does not love strangers, who, for this reason, are admitted into his presence only with certain precautions. Every morning, the members of the household offer him water, wine, milk; they light a lamp before him and take care to revive the fire in the hearth with a branch of juniper, which is a sacred shrub to the Tibetans, as it is to the Turkomans. At night, they again burn a branch of the same plant and carry it through and about the house in order to drive away evil spirits; for fire itself is regarded as a divine being and as the natural protector of those who keep it in. It might be worth finding out if this domestic fire was not originally confused by the Tibetans, as it is by the Turkomans and the Mongols, with the domestic divinity and the divinities of the dead ancestors. Be this as it may, the community of domestic worship forms the link that binds together the members of one family and is able to take the place of real relationship. All the Tibetans are organised into little mutual burial-societies, composed of neighbours and friends who are not related by blood, but who all have the same god and who, consequently, are assimilated to descendants of the same ancestor *(ruspa chigchig)*: they are called *paspon*, or cousins, and it is their duty to provide one another with burials; and none but a paspon can show the last honours to a deceased person, for the shades reject the homage of any stranger to their family and cult. Consequently, the soul of one who dies far from his paspons and who is interred without their aid will be for ever miserable and will roam the earth to the great terror of the living. To allay the irritation of the shades that have not received regular burial, the lamas go from time to time and fling pellets of tsamba into the rivers and wells, inviting all wandering spirits to come and share the feast. In the same way, two Tibetans who propose to conclude a compact of friendship similar to the *andalaku* of the Mongols solemnly sacrifice an animal and drink its blood, the essential vital fluid, in order to bring themselves in intimate communion with the divinity to whom the victim has been offered and who has become infused by consecration in the animal's veins: in this manner, the contracting parties have within them the blood of the same god, that is to say of the same ancestor, and are brothers.

Side by side with the remains of the domestic religion, we find a large number of remains of a religion of nature absolutely similar to that of the ancient Turkomans and the ancient Mongols and to that which is still in vigour, in spite of some modifications, among the Chinese. The Tibetans behold a divinity in every natural phenomenon, in every external object that attracts attention by its peculiarity or its size. Many lakes and mountains have a divine character and are the object of worship: such are the Nam Cho, the Iki Namur, the Koko Nor, the Samden Kansa Mountains, Mount Tiseh near the sacred Lake Mansarovar, the Amnyeh Machen, the sacred mountain of the Goloks, whose name means the August Ancestor Ma and seems to point to a connection with ancestor-worship. I could prolong this list indefinitely. There is a god who makes liquids to ferment; another who causes illness; a third who causes death: whenever a decease takes place, a special ceremony is performed to drive him away. There is a goddess who looks particularly after little children *(tumlhamo)*; a god who presides over the chase. Each canton, even each inhabited valley has its special genius *(jidag)*. On the rocks and in the caves live mischievous gnomes *(tsan)*; the depths of the earth are occupied by legions of jealous and spiteful demons *(sadag)*, of gloomy and hideous aspect, who fly into a rage when men dig the earth in search of hidden treasures or for other reasons and who kill them or spread misery and disease in the neighbourhood; the sources and rivers are guarded by so many man-snakes *(lu)*, who remind one of the naiads and have been assimilated by the Buddhists to the *naga* of the Vedic mythology. Above these particular divinities reigns the celestial dragon *(dhug)*, the personification of the clouds and, perhaps, more generally, of the gloomy sky, who makes the storm burst forth, sends down the gentle rain, causes floods, the plague and contagions. He is the exact same as the dragons of the Mongols and Chinese. His earthly enemy is the red tiger *(tsagmar)*. The latter is often represented in five-fold: one, yellow, in the middle, personifies the earth; and, in the four corners, the blue one is wood, the red metal, the white fire and the black water. These are the five sacred elements, which are revered also by the Turkomans, the Mongols, the Chinese and the Annamites. The divine tiger has been turned by the Buddhists into a protecting genius of the true faith. As for the five elements, although the Tibetans still know them and speak of them as sacred things, their worship has lost its importance and its precision. Traces of them survive in the five flags carried by the official sorcerers when accomplishing their rites, in the five colours with which the Saskyapa lamas paint their convents and, especially, in the successive groups of five hypostases in which Buddha is manifested. With the worship of the five elements are also connected the two crossed sticks, a symbol of the sacred fire, and the feast of water, which is celebrated in September: at that time, water is considered to be gifted with supernatural properties and everybody bathes in the rivers, thinking thus to obtain a long life.

Another ancient god, having also the form of an animal, is the Wind-horse (*lungsta*), who is depicted on innumerable streamers waving in mid-air. This Tibetan Pegasus, whom the Buddhists have laden with the three precious jewels of the good law, appears to be a personification of the wind galloping through space and breathing good and bad luck by turns. When a hurricane gets up, the lamas send a host of sheets of paper, with the effigy of the Wind-horse, flying in the air, so that the god, accepting the homage, may be appeased and cease to endanger the lives of travellers.*

The celestial bodies play a smaller part in the religious preoccupations of the natives, although the latter believe in their influence over destiny; but their astrology, which is widely practised, is of Chinese or Hindu origin. As in China, a sacred respect is shown to the hare, which the hunters never touch; this animal is probably connected with some lunar cult. In the month of December 1893, we assisted at the feast of lanterns, or rather of lamps, which is known in China as in Tibet. The poor herdsmen on the shores of the Nam Cho lit, at night, in their tents, all the butter-lamps which they had at their disposal; this ceremony, in its humble simplicity, showed us better than any sumptuous festival in a big town could have done the depth of superstition of which it was a manifestation. Its object is to ask for the return of the sun and to pray for the triumph of the light threatened by the winter darkness. The lamas have made it into the feast of Tsongkapa; but the example of China proves that its origin is much older.

At a later period, an attempt was made to put a little order into this chaos of primitive deities by arranging them all under two categories, each with its supreme head. The terrestrial gods were subjected to old

* Huc, describing this ceremony, distorts its real meaning.

Mother Earth, dressed in yellow, mounted on a ram with great horns; an ugly, gloomy and fierce goddess, the guardian of the gates of the infernal abyss, which, if they opened, would spread terror and death among the race of mankind. We have seen that she was worshipped by the inhabitants of Chinese Turkestan before the introduction of Buddhism. The gods of the sky and air received for their master Namlhakarpo, an old white-haired man, dressed in white and riding on a dog. He, like Zeus, represents the clear sky that distributes light. These two higher divinities of the sky and earth have their equivalents in the Turkic, Mongolian and Chinese mythologies; they were the chief objects of Tibetan worship in the seventh century and their cult most probably dates back to that prehistoric period in which the four nations were neighbours in the mountains north of Mongolia and formed only one ethnical group.

The Tibetans thus live in the midst of a formidable swarm of gods and demons* whose rustling they hear, whose breath they feel, of whose vague forms they catch glimpses in the darkness. They have a heavy task to conciliate, to avoid offending or to appease all those fantastic beings, jealous, susceptible, powerful and always ready, like savages, to abuse their strength. Hence come the innumerable practices to which the natives devote themselves and to which Buddhism has only added. Some of them, of course, are of earlier date than the introduction of the religion of Sakya Muni. For instance, the nomad, before drinking, dips the forefinger of his right hand into his bowl and sprinkles a

* God is *lha*, demon *deh (hdreh)*. This latter word seems to have a very general meaning uniting all the categories of demons. We must not translate *lha* by good genius and *deh* by bad genius; the lhas, at bottom, are no better than the dehs; but, as genii of the air and light, they have more benefits to bestow, whereas the others are subterranean and tenebrous genii.

few drops towards the four cardinal points, while reciting a prayer: this is a libation in honour of the genii of the air and the ghosts of the dead that may be wandering in the neighbourhood; in the same way, they are offered the remains of each repast. The traveller does not fail to pay homage to the special divinity of the canton through which he is passing, for fear lest it should play him some trick. The mountain-passes are supposed, because of their height, to be more particularly frequented by the gods and the Tibetan, on reaching the summit, mutters a deprecatory formula and throws a stone on the little pile heaped up by those who have come before him and almost always surmounted by a few ragged streamers. These heaps of pebbles (*obo* in Mongolian, *dobum* in Tibetan), which resemble the old Kirghiz tombs, are sacred monuments and not mere land-marks to show the road.* The people often turn around them, which among most of these nations constitutes a pious act. These pious turns (*skorba*)† are certainly not of Buddhic origin, for we know that the ancient Turkomans employed the same method to show their veneration for the holy places and for their dead in particular. It is worth noting that this ceremony is performed by keeping the object of worship on the right, that is to say by turning in the same direction as the course of the sun; and this leads one to think that it was originally a form of sun-worship: indeed, we know that the sun, especially the rising sun, filled a great place in the primitive Turkic religion.

There subsist a few traces of the old animal sacrifices banished by Buddhism. To drive away the ghosts returning from the other world, the Tibetans sacrifice animals in effigy. On the last day of the year, the lamas,

* The obo is the analogue of the *ansab* of the Arabs and the *cippi* of the ancient Romans.

† The *tawaf* of the Arabs.

dressed up as skeletons and as hideous demons, perform the dance of the red tiger, the most extraordinary of the ceremonies of Tibetan Buddhism: they cut into pieces and pretend to eat a puppet in human form representing the enemy of religion and of the country. This festival is evidently the survival of that at which the Tibetan chiefs, meeting on the first day of the new year, took the oath of fidelity under the auspices of the priests, who immolated a number of criminals and divided their flesh among those present.* The Tibetan sorcerers are very like the sorcerers of the Mongols and Turkomans; like these, they indulge in frenzied and convulsive dances and in horrible yells, addressed either to their own ancestors or to the earth and sky. The first among them, the grand sorcerer of Nachung, who is one of the principal persons in Tibet, contends that his ancestors were natives of Mongolia. It is very possible that he is descended from the high-priest of the old Ponbo religion. He who is said to be his first ancestor is that same white god of heaven who is the first divinity of the Ponbos and the tradition which declares that his ancestors were Turkic and Mongolian kings suggests the idea that the clergy of the ancient Tibetans was perhaps of the same stock as that of the ancient Turko-Mongols. The almost entire similarity in the religion of these peoples, as opposed to the characteristic differences of language and customs, would thus be explained of itself. All the sorcerers *(nagpa)*, to whatever category they belong, are lamas; they foretell the future,† point out which practices should be fulfilled in order to remedy

* Hence the accusations of cannibalism of which the Tibetans have been the victims.

† Some of their methods of divination are purely Chinese. Others are Turko-Mongolian, such as the pebbles arranged in a certain order, corresponding with the *kumalak* of the Kazaks, and the consulting of the shoulder-blade of a sheep *(sogpa)* put to the fire, which is especially useful in discovering lost or stolen objects.

present evils and ward off evils to come, conjure up and exorcise devils and cure the sick. There are some who make a specialty of causing the rain to fall or cease; they correspond with the Turkic *yadachi* and, like these, employ a stone to which they attribute supernatural virtues, calling it the water-crystal *(chuchel)*: it is probably jade. However, the orthodox lamas have recourse to a simple offering in honour of the divinities of the waters *(nagas)*, accompanied by an appropriate form of prayer.

Not only has the old religion left a deep impression on the soul of the Tibetans who profess Buddhism, but it has also retained to this day a large number of adherents, who are called, as in former times, Ponbos. They are to be found in every part of Tibet, but especially in Eastern Tibet and in the province of Chang, which they look upon as their cradle, or, at least, as the seat of their most revered sanctuary. The Buddhists having brought their efforts to bear mainly upon Central Tibet, in other words upon the richest district in the country, one meets with but very few of the votaries of the old faith there. On the other hand, Eastern Tibet having never been subject except in part and superficially to the Lhasa government, the Ponbos are still strong there and their number amounts to not far short of half the population. All the Tibetans living along the high-road from Nagchu to Jyerkundo, between the Chachang La and the Damtao La, are Ponbos, as are also many of those who live in Dergyeh and in all the country to the north-east of Chamdo. The Ponbos are said also to predominate in Poyul. Zogchen Gompa is the most important of their monasteries in the north-east; it is there that most of their books are printed. Hating the victorious religion, they have nevertheless felt its influence and, prompted by fear, they have tried to lessen the dogmatic differences, so as to be able to pass for heretical Buddhists and not for infidels. Thus they ascribe the foundation of their sect to an incarnate divinity whom they assimilate to Buddha and call Chenrabyungdung (Gchenrabsgyungdrung). Nevertheless, they recognise none of the human hypostases of the Buddha whom the orthodox revere and they treat the Dalai Lama as an impostor. He whom they look upon as the true and only incarnation of Chenrab bears the title of Ma Rinpocheh. They say that the first head of Buddhism in Tibet, who pretended to be a god made man, maintained a long controversy with their high-priest. The latter proposed to his adversary, in order to settle the quarrel, that they should together attempt the ascent of the great ice-mountain, Gangrimocheh, the sacred and inaccessible mountain said to be situated in Chang. The proposal was accepted and then the Ponbo high-priest had recourse to powerful enchantments, which enabled him to rise in the air and to arrive without difficulty at the inviolate summit of the mountain, amid thunder and lightning, while his rival was struggling to climb the lower slopes. The orthodox accept this legend at least in part; but they declare that the infidel magician was struck by lightning while flying through the air, thus leaving the victory to the protagonist of the true faith.

The Ponbo lamas are not compelled to celibacy and they wear their hair long; some of them live in convents, others are distributed among the lay population, from whom they are distinguished neither by their manner of life nor by their appearance. The Ponbo priests are often hermits, leading isolated lives in remote mountains: the more solitary they are the better are they able to influence the powers of heaven and earth. At a place called Zama, in the dark gorge of the Charrong Chu, we passed not far from the tent of a Ponbo hermit, much revered as a priest and feared as a magician, and the terrified Tibetans who accompanied us hastened their steps. The institution of convents is, no doubt, borrowed from Buddhism. The primitive clergy of Tibet does not seem to have had a monastic organisation. It was none the less very powerful, as may be conjectured from the important part which it played in the most solemn act of Tibetan politics, the taking of the oath; from the vigorous struggles which it maintained against Buddhism; and from the high position retained in modern society by the official sorcerers, who are certainly the successors of some of the Ponbo high-priests, if not their descendants.

The Ponbo lamas are, before all, sorcerers and necromancers and exactly resemble the *kams* of the northern Turkomans, the *bos* of the Mongols and, lastly, those whom we call *shamans*. When exercising their magic functions, they wear a tall, pointed, black* hat, surmounted by a peacock's feather or merely a cock's feather, a death's head and a pair of crossed thunderbolts; they have a drum formed of two human skulls, which is as essential an object to them as is the tambourine to the Siberian shaman. Different from the orthodox lamas, they sacrifice animals and especially cocks, whether because they attribute a sacred character to this bird or because it has this advantage for the worshippers, that it is not expensive. They throw spells in the same manner as our mediæval sorcerers, by sticking pins into a little figure representing the person upon whom the spells are cast. To cure diseases, they employ the same method as the Mongols: they put the sick man's clothes on a clay figure upon which they write his name and throw it away in a distant and desert spot; the spirit of death takes this little statue for the patient himself and, believing him dead, troubles about him no longer. If the patient be a notable chief, a man plays the part of the

* It is probably the colour of their hats which has caused them to be vulgarly called black lamas.

statue for a small sum of money: he has to leave the camp or the village and go away as far as possible, without returning so long as the chief is alive. These customs are perhaps not quite unknown to the orthodox Tibetans.

The principal divinities of the Ponbos are the White God of heaven, the Black Goddess of the earth, the Red Tiger and the Dragon. They profess a profound veneration for an idol called Kepang, made of a mere block of wood dressed in bits of stuff. I was not able to ascertain what it represents, but they say that it is the same divinity that, under the name of Pekar, inspires the orthodox sorcerers. The most sacred symbol of the Ponbos is the gammadion cross, the *svastika* of the Hindus, but turned from right to left. This emblem is a remnant of fire and sun-worship: it represents the solar wheel and the two sticks (the *arani* of the Hindus) which, when rubbed together, produce the sacred fire. The presence of the name of this symbol, *yungdung*, in the name of the mythical founder of the Ponbo religion shows the predominant importance of fire-worship in the primitive religion. The Buddhist Tibetans also possess a similar emblem, except that the brackets are turned in the opposite direction; they, however, ascribe a less value to it than do the Ponbos. For the rest, we can apply to the latter all that I have said concerning the survival of the old native creeds among the so-called Buddhist Tibetans. Their religion, which is a coarse naturalism combined with ancestor-worship, is the same as that practised from time immemorial among the Turkomans, the Mongols and the Chinese; and that is why it so greatly resembles Taoism, which is no other than the primitive religion of China, covered with a varnish of Hindu metaphysics.

The religious practices of the Tibetan Ponbos do not differ essentially from those of their Buddhist brethren:

both recite endless litanies made up of invariable formulas, unwearyingly spin their praying-wheels, erect *manis** and *obos*, wave pious streamers, turn at every opportunity around the religious monuments, temples, manis and sacred lakes and mountains. But the Ponbos are distinguished by small details of form. Instead of employing as a prayer the Buddhist formula "*Om mani padmé hum!*" they use the formula "*Om maté muyasaledo!*" of which I do not know the meaning. Instead of turning their praying-wheel inwards, from right to left, with the sun, they turn it outwards, from left to right; and again, while the orthodox Buddhists, in describing the sacred circle around the objects of their cult, always keep them on the right, the Ponbos always keep them on the left. This is the capital difference between the two sects, the only one which each takes account of; and the mills that turn to the right abominate the mills that turn to the left. In the old religions, we often find the two ways of turning and the two svastikas employed concurrently, those which go with the sun being considered divine, the others demoniacal and suited for magical operations. The Buddhists having preserved only the first, the Ponbos attached themselves solely to the second, from a spirit of contradiction and also because their religion bore a strongly accentuated character of black magic.

And so, in this citadel of Buddhism which is Tibet, the population either is very hostile to the religion of Sakya Muni, or else adheres to it only with its lips and in form, while neither men's hearts nor their minds have, at bottom, changed. The lamas allow the infidels to live around them, even as they let false opinions live in the minds of their faithful. The real fact is that Buddhism, whose expansion has sometimes been compared with that of Christianity and Islamism, is a religion

* The *mani* is a heap of stones covered with pious inscriptions.

of monks and initiates that is not made for seculars or the vulgar. There is no genuine Buddhist save him who has known the vanity of the world and who has renounced it absolutely. Without that there is no salvation. The monks, who have taken vows of poverty and chastity, who are plunged in meditation and who are not concerned with the cares of this world below: the monks alone are within the pale of the church; the laymen, the black men *(minag)*, as they are called, poor people with dim minds, chained to falsehood, steeped in the flesh, eaten up with desires, are necessarily without the fence: they are definitely those who do not follow the way of truth. That is why the lamas deeply despise the laymen, the more so as the latter are unable to allege any excuse, to claim any indulgence, seeing that the inferiority of their condition is the consequence of the inferiority of their conduct in their previous existence.

Christianity also, no doubt, preaches indifference to the world and one need not stretch greatly certain passages in the Gospels to deduce a theory of renunciation as absolute as that of Buddhism; but beside those passages there are others which make allowances for the necessities of active life and which make room in the house for all men of good will. If the tendencies towards perfect renunciation nearly prevailed at the beginning, when men were enclosed in a narrow circle and believed the end of the world to be at hand, the practical side of Gospel teaching soon gained the ascendant when the community had spread. As for Islamism, this is an entirely practical religion, which does not stray into the indefinite regions of the ideal and which, therefore, is, even more than Christianity, a religion of laymen, of men engaged in the business of the age; and, whereas, in Christianity, the priest preserves a marked spiritual superiority over the layman, he has none in Islamism.

Such are the reasons for which these two last religions have always exercised an incomparably greater social and moral influence than Buddhism.

The Tibetan lamas trouble hardly at all about the people, except to extract their sustenance from it and to keep it under their temporal authority. For this reason, they solicitously foster its superstitions instead of crushing them and nurture its belief in their superiority, which is inaccessible to any layman, and in their power over divine beings, demons and nature. They pass for the necessary intermediaries between mankind and the divinity. "There is no god without lama," says the proverb; and the clergy has constituted itself the distributor of temporal as well as of spiritual benefits, has given a fillip to Buddha to compel that impassive god to trouble himself a little about the affairs of this world, has infused new life into all the popular deities whom the Enlightened One flung back into their nothingness, has monopolised them and made itself their commissioner on earth. The necessity for strengthening their credit with the common people that supports them has obliged the monks to modify their original character as well as alter their doctrines: they have had to diminish their isolation, to step down from the tower of ivory in which Sakya Muni meant to enclose them, from contemplative to become militant, to combine with their monastic profession the functions of priests and sorcerers. They have purely and simply taken the place of the Ponbo priests of old and resigned themselves to rendering the people the same services in order to receive from them the same wage. Shrewd dealers in religious commodities, they supply all articles in demand after the desired pattern; and, more eager to satisfy their customers' tastes than to impose their own, they have opened more departments in their shops than Buddha ever expected. To tell the truth, some of these wares are of a quality so inferior that the lamas do not stoop to use them for themselves: such, for instance, are the ceremonies intended to guide the souls of the dead in their passage from this world to the next; but, since the vulgar herd likes them and is willing to pay a good price for them, they let it have as many as it asks for.

On the whole, Buddhism has but very little improved the manners of the Tibetans. It has added to their superstitions without removing any in return; it has kept alive their distrustful and crafty highland ways; it has done nothing to inspire them with a deeper sense of virtue and honesty. From the religious point of view, it has not inculcated a more wholesome conception of the divinity; and of all its beautiful metaphysical and moral doctrines only one has pervaded the whole people: that of the transmigration of souls, but spoilt and debased to such a pitch that the Tibetan employs it to silence his scruples and, with a safe conscience, to cheat his neighbour, whom he presumes to have been capable of cheating him in a previous life. Still, we must honour Buddhism for abolishing human sacrifices, for spreading the respect for science and books, for setting a noble moral aim before a few chosen souls, for kindling a flame of ideality, feeble though it be, on the mountains of Tibet, which, but for that flame, would have remained dark and devoid of glory.

CHAPTER X

THE ORGANISATION OF THE CLERGY

The monastic hierarchy—The number, power and wealth of the monks —The different religious orders; the real position of the Dalai Lama; the Dalai Lama is not a pope.

THE influence of Buddhism has been, above all, material and political, thanks to its clergy, which has obtained an unprecedented temporal power and ended by holding universal sway, by bending all men's minds to passive obedience and imbuing them with a certain gentleness, which has been very wrongly attributed to the theories of Sakya Muni. The clergy of Tibet owes its social and political mastery to several causes and, first of all, to its powerfully-organised hierarchy and to the inflexible discipline to which all its members are subjected. At the head stands a general, whose jurisdiction, which comprises rights of life and death, extends over all the convents and all the monks of his order spread over the whole surface of the countries where the Tibetan tongue is spoken. In each district is a provincial appointed by the general; at the head of each convent an abbot *(kanpo)* deputed by the provincial and sanctioned by the general.

Under the abbot, in each monastery, are two classes of dignitaries, spiritual and temporal. The spiritual dignitaries are the *lobpon (slobdpon)*, or director of studies; the *bumdzad (dbumdzad)*, or minister of religion; and the *chochimpa (choskrimspa)*, or prefect of discipline and ecclesiastical judge. When the first dies or resigns, he is regularly succeeded by the second and the latter by the third. This last is chosen by lot before the sacred images by three lamas appointed for that purpose by the principal dignitaries. It often happens that the lobpon is the same as the kanpo, but this depends upon the wishes of the provincial. The administration of the temporal goods is confided to a *shadso (pyagmdzods)*, or treasurer, who comes immediately after the bumdzad in rank and who has under his orders a *nerpa*, or bursar and coadjutor of the treasurer *con spe successionis*, who is himself assisted by a *nerchong*, or under-bursar, nominated by the treasurer. The under-bursar is the ordinary agent of the convent outside its walls; he looks after the workmen, the husbandmen, the herdsmen of the convent. Different inferior functions, some profitable, some honorary, are distributed by the spiritual and temporal heads, who thus keep up among the monks a spirit of emulation beneficial to good order and discipline.

The monks are divided into two classes: the *gelong (dgeslong)*, who are monks in the full enjoyment of their functions, and the *getsul*, or deacons, who have received a solemn initiation, by which they become the husbands of the church, and who spend twelve years in passing through different stages. Below these two classes of monks are the *dapa (grapa)*, or novices, and, lastly, the simple candidates for the noviciate, who are subject to discipline without having any privileges. Not every one is allowed to present himself as a candidate: the more important convents receive only the sons of good families; all accept only children of decent birth and endowed with good physical and mental constitutions. The monasteries skim the cream of the population for themselves; they take the most robust and the most intelligent individuals. As, on the other hand, the clergy is usually better fed than the laity—excepting a few of its members who practise maceration—the expression "as fat as a monk" is as current in Tibet as it used to be elsewhere; and, as they have leisure and are obliged to study, they maintain and increase their intellectual superiority over the rest of the nation.

To the powerful organisation of the monastic body and the superior quality of its members must be added the extraordinary number of the latter. There is no instance of any ancient or modern country containing so great a multitude of monks, for they number, on the average, one to every four laymen. There are certainly in Tibet at least 500,000 monks, without counting Ladak and Sikkim. All the superfluous children who would grievously overcrowd the paternal house, all those who, though of poor birth, are ambitious and feel that they have the intelligence and the will to succeed go to swell the army of monks. To people of low origin to enter the religious state is the only way to rise above their condition: by this means, they may hope to attain the highest positions, with great difficulty, it is true, and with a great disadvantage as against members of rich or noble families, who are always preferred and privileged in those homes of poverty and humility, the convents; but still the door is not hermetically closed to them, as it is in the lay state. In this way, not only does the clergy draw to itself all individual men of worth, but again there is not a Tibetan family, noble or base-born, but has several of its members in convents and is thus interested in the prosperity of the clergy. The prefect of Nagchu Jong told us that, in every family, two male children out of five become monks. This evidence was confirmed by several persons and nothing could be more imprudent than for a family to try to avoid paying this human tithe. Moreover, the considerable material advantages offered by the ecclesiastical state and the compromises that can easily be effected with the apparently so strict rule remove any reason for fearing to take the cloth.

The monastic army is not only numerous and well disciplined: it is concentrated in 3,000 monasteries resembling so many fortresses, perched on the mountain rocks, amply stocked with provisions, filled with arms and ammunition, to which the lamas, despite their ministry of peace, are not afraid of resorting. In case of public danger, the sacred trumpet sounds and the monks take down their matchlocks and lances, make trousers of their shawls *(zangos)* and go off to the war. Around these monasteries lie vast domains which are their property, crops and pasture-lands which feed immense flocks. These fields and pastures are entrusted to farmers *(gonyoks)* who work on shares, who hold nothing in their own right, who contract to cultivate the land and watch the herds of the monks and who are bound to supply annually a quantity of butter, wool and barley fixed beforehand by the treasurer. If the herds or the fields entrusted to the farmer produce more, the surplus is for him; in the same way, the probable increase of the cattle is fixed each year by the treasurer and the farmer benefits by any residue. The treasurer makes his calculations strictly enough to prevent the farmer's profit from being more than a slender one and he nearly always takes more than half the gross income for the convent. These gonyoks are not only tillers of the soil and shepherds: they are also manufacturers; they make woollen stuffs, jewellery, pottery for their ecclesiastical masters; they are masons, carpenters, smiths, millers, caravaneers. They are subject to the jurisdiction of the lamas and owe them all the labour which the latter choose to exact, without being entitled to any wages. Nevertheless, they do not entirely escape the authority of the Lhasa government: they pay taxes to the amount of two-thirds of those paid by its direct subjects and are allowed to appeal to its judicial system in certain cases and according to certain rules which I was not able to ascertain with precision.

Over and above their landed and house property and their herds, the convents possess treasures accumulated during centuries: gold, silver and precious objects, sometimes of considerable richness. They receive a host of gifts and bequests: not a Tibetan dies but leaves a good part of his personalty to the nearest convent; every child that takes the vows brings a dower in proportion to his means: every lama gives to the convent a share of his personal gains, for the lama is anything but a worthless asset. He is, according to circumstances, a parish-priest, a fortune-teller, a wizard, a doctor, an apothecary, a painter, a sculptor, a printer, a writer, a reader, a trader or a beggar; he sells little statues, praying-wheels, books, lucky trinkets, rosaries, indulgences in pills, prayers, formulas, charms and amulets against all possible and impossible misfortunes, remedies, incantations and horoscopes. When a man marries or dies, the lamas come in the greatest possible number to assist him, for cash; when he meets with misfortune, they charge for driving away his bad luck; when he meets with good fortune, they charge for offering up thanks; when nothing happens to him, good or bad, they charge again for preventing things from becoming worse. All perquisites remain the monk's own property, except the tithe deducted by the community. If a lama leave a personal fortune at his death, it goes to his family, all but the part which he always bequeaths by will to the monastery. For the rest, the monks support themselves at their own expense. They have a separate house or room in the convent, where they live more or less comfortably according to their means and their piety. The community supplies them only with a certain quantity of barley (about 240lbs. a year in Ladak), with buttered tea three times a day and with a piece of stuff for clothing. Its expenses do not amount to the profit which it derives from its members; and, even then, its burdens are relieved by the offerings of the laity or the rich lamas, who often pay for a round of tea or a piece of stuff to all the monks of the convent. The chief lamas, being personally richer than the others, are, of course, supported at the expense of the community; by virtue of their dignity, they receive plentiful alms from the devout; the treasurers, in the course of their administration, make considerable sums and always have a share, generally a fifth, in the commercial business of the convent.

As the monasteries dispose of most of the capital of the country, they have monopolised nearly all the trade and all the finance and these do not form the smallest part of their revenues. Of the trade I have already spoken; as to finance, the convents undertake to make the money of private individuals pay by investing it in their own business; also and above all, they lend money at thirty per cent. to all applicants, on good security, chiefly on mortgages. If the borrower does not pay at the given time, they show kindness and consideration, let him sink deeper into debt, help him a little and end by selling him up and annexing his fields to those of the monastery. They do not lend to the poor, for that would be giving; and the lama receives, but does not give.

If you care to seek for a comparison in history, you might say that a Tibetan convent is a Roman patrician, great landlord and justiciary in one, having under its orders many agents and many servants, who make of its house and its annexes one large city, producing all the commodities necessary for life, supplied with all the necessary or superfluous manufactures, importing and exporting great quantities of goods. The comparison becomes still more accurate when you consider that the lamas, like the patricians of old, are masters of the auspices, alone possess the formulas that influence the gods and reign over souls as over matter. This moral cause of the strength of the clergy is perhaps no less powerful than all the others put together. It has not converted men's minds to the truth, but it has taught them to respect the ministers of the divinity, some hundreds of whom are gods upon earth,* while a few others are able, by force of meditation, to hold their breath long enough to defy the laws of gravitation and to float in mid-air.

The religion of Tibet consists in its essence of a concatenation of superstitious practices and of a constant veneration shown to the lamas, to whom it would be a namelesss crime to do the least injury. A theft committed on a lama entails a ten times greater penalty than one committed on a layman; to murder a layman is three or four times as cheap as to murder a monk. This does not keep the Tibetans from loving to sneer at their monks, to criticise their greed of gain and their tyranny, to scoff at their hypocrisy and to tell sprightly stories about them. In this they resemble the Italians of the middle ages; but their boldness shows itself only in words and they are all the humbler and more servile in action.

And so, to sum up, the Tibetan clergy possesses all the known elements of dominion: religious authority, territorial wealth, financial and commercial supremacy, armed force, numbers and discipline. Even the spell derived from the principle of heredity has been pressed into their own service by these celibates in a very particular fashion; for those of the lamas in whom the spiritual authority resides are considered as being divine

* The incarnations of Buddha number 70 in Tibet, 76 in Mongolia and 14 in the neighbourhood of Peking.

hypostases, of which not only is the race perpetuated through the ages, but their very persons are reincarnated, ever identically, under successive forms.

Until now, I have presented the Tibetan clergy as a body one and indivisible. This is its first appearance; but, if we prolong our examination, we find that this clergy is divided into several different monastic orders, each of which has its special hierarchy and its own independent general. The Dalai Lama is only the most important general of these orders: the other generals show him the deference due to a person of eminent dignity, but they are in no way subordinate to him from the religious point of view; they owe him no obedience save inasmuch as he is actually their temporal sovereign; and that is why it is quite inaccurate to compare the Dalai Lama with the Pope. Within the order of the Dalai Lama himself there is a person, the Pangchen Rinpocheh of Tachilhunpo, who enjoys no less a spiritual dignity and is his inferior only in temporal power. The Chinese take good care to support him and to keep him in reserve, in case the Dalai Lama should cease to show the necessary docility.

The monastic order of which the Dalai Lama is the head is that of the Gelugpa (Dgelugspa), which was founded about the year 1400 by Tsongkapa, a monk of the Koko Nor district, who may be compared with Hildebrand (Gregory VII.), like himself a reformer of the monastic orders which had lapsed into laxity and forgetfulness of their good rules. He endeavoured to restore Buddhism to its original purity, to rid it of the sorcery and the superstitious practices that dishonoured it and to compel the true believers, that is to say the monks, to display a more austere virtue and a greater respect for their vows of renunciation and poverty. He succeeded in part; and although, since his death, the convents of his rule have gradually degenerated, there are still some in which the greatest austerity and discipline prevail. The monks who drink brandy or have commerce with women are beaten and expelled; and one comes across a good number of unfrocked Gelugpa. It is said, it is true, that punishment reaches only the poor devils who have no money with which to soften the rules and those who apply them; still, we must not put greater faith in the popular tales than they deserve and, though abuses evidently exist, it is none the less true that many chief lamas are above all suspicion. As for sorcery, it was too effective a means of domination to be given up without, at the same time, being replaced by some inferior substitute; and, accordingly, the Gelugpa, while maintaining a certain reserve in this respect, nevertheless number among their ranks the greatest two or three sorcerers in Tibet and the famous convent of Ramocheh, at Lhasa, is a veritable school of magic.

Since the time of Tsongkapa, all the heads of the Gelugpa, called Dalai Lama or Gyamcho Rinpocheh (Rgyamcho Rinpocheh)* have been looked upon as incarnations of Avalokita or Charazi (Spyanrasgzigs), the Creator, the judge of souls, the celestial hypostasis of Amitabha, the Sun-Buddha. Charazi had already been incarnated before in King Srongtsangampo; he is the special patron of Tibet, he to whom the invocation, a million times repeated, "*Om mani padmé hum!*" is addressed. The present Dalai Lama, Tub Chan, born in 1876, is, according to the only authentic list officially recognised at Lhasa, the twelfth successor of the first Dalai Lama, born in 1391.

* Dalai Lama is Mongolian; Gyamcho Rinpocheh is Tibetan. The former title, although couched in a foreign language, is fairly well known in Tibet. Dalai means sea or ocean, as does Gyamcho; Rinpocheh means precious jewel. The title most frequently used, next to the above, is Bang (Dbang) Rinpocheh: His Most Mighty and Most Precious Majesty.

Side by side with the Gelugpa exist some twenty different orders, of which only four deserve mention. The oldest of all and also the most corrupt is that of the Nyingmapa (Rnyingmapa), or the old ones, of which the origin goes back to Padma Sambhava himself. This first apostle of Tibet was obliged, in order to spread Buddhism widely in the eighth century, to make it more agreeable with a host of devilries borrowed from India and from the old local religion, thus fighting the Ponbos with their own weapons. The Nyingmapa have followed in the errors of their patron, to whom they offer an idolatrous worship, and they are to this day addicted to all the practices of magic familiar to the Ponbos. Their rule is not a severe one and does not enjoin celibacy. Their principal convent, where their Living Buddha resides, is that of Tsari; Sagti Gompa, in Ladak, and perhaps Dergyeh Gompa belong to this rule, as does the convent of women at Samding, on Lake Yamtog, whose abbess is an incarnation of a greatly-revered sow-goddess, assimilated to the Indian goddess of the dawn, but probably a relic of the old local creed. The Tibetans believe that the nuns of this convent are sows in human shape and that they resume their real nature when they please. The pig plays a great part in the popular religion of the Tibetans: it is a powerful enemy of the evil spirits and the god of the hearth is represented with the head of a pig. It is probably a symbol of the fecundity of nature. The number of the Nyingmapa monks is considerable and it is not certain that it does not equal that of the Gelugpa.

The reforming movement introduced in the eighth century under the influence of Atisa gave birth to two separate orders, which were subsequently divided into several sub-orders. That of the Kargyupa was not very succesful, because it was an order of hermits; but from it issued the two important sub-orders of the Karmapa and the Dugpa (Hbrugpa). The principal Karmapa monasteries are those of Sutsur, to the north of Lhasa, and of Gyeseh; the centre of the Dugpa is Dejenchu Gompa (?) and their most famous and wealthiest convent is that of Himis, in Ladak. In Bhotan there are no monks except of this latter rule, which is not much severer than that of the Nyingmapa.

The order of the Saskyapa, which received from Kublai Khan the temporal sovereignty of Tibet, still holds sway to this day in Mongolia and North-eastern Tibet. Its living Buddha, who resides at Saskya Gompa, to the south-west of Jikatse,* is also venerated by the Nyingmapa. The *gégen* of Urga, the chief lama of Mongolia, belongs to this order. The monks of Jyergu Gompa and of Tumbumdo are Saskyapa. Their convents are painted in longitudinal white, black, red, blue and yellow stripes, which are the five colours representing the five sacred elements. The lamas of this order are not allowed to drink brandy; celibacy is not looked upon as necessary or obligatory, but only as meritorious.

All orders other than the Gelugpa are commonly spoken of by the Chinese as red lamas, in opposition to the Gelugpa, who are called yellow lamas because of the colour worn by the celebrants in the ceremonies of their religion. All these orders are distinguished more particularly by their rules of discipline, by a peculiar devotion for this or that hypostasis of Buddha, by the choice of a special tutelary divinity. The dogmatic differences do not mean much to us: they are no greater than those which separate the Roman Catholic Church from the Greek Catholic Church. Many lamas

* This incarnation of Buddha can be born again only in Tibet: a trick of Chinese policy, which has thus tried to withdraw the choice from the always considerable influence of the lay princes of Mongolia.

know nothing of them; and the sometimes very keen rivalries that exist between the various orders are based upon temporal rather than spiritual reasons. All, without exception, recognise the Pangchen Rinpocheh and the Dalai Lama as the loftiest incarnations of the divinity; the Gelugpa, in their turn, admit the authenticity of the incarnations venerated by the Nyingmapa or the Saskyapa; and the latter are not subordinate to the former, because both, in principle, represent one and the same god. The Dalai Lama is merely *primus inter pares*: he has no authority over the other orders and cannot reform their rule, which has never been submitted for his approval. As for the people, they care not at all for these divergencies: in their eyes, all the lamas, yellow or red, are equally qualified to influence the supernatural powers on their behalf, to save them from the tricks of the devils and to obtain for them good health, good harvests and a happy transmigration.*

* These various considerations, added to the fact that there are very few real Buddhists outside Mongolia and Tibet, show that any policy founded on "Panbuddhism" would be the vainest of vain illusions.

CHAPTER XI

ADMINISTRATION AND POLICY

Divisions: the kingdom of Lhasa—Central power; taxes; officials—The public forces—Predominating influence of the clergy in the government—The Chinese protectorate and the policy of China in Tibet—The policy of England—The principalities and tribes of Eastern Tibet are independent of Lhasa and directly subject to China.

FROM the political point of view, the whole of Tibet, with the exception of Ladak, Baltistan, Spiti and a part of Sikkim, is dependent on China; but it is far from forming one administrative whole. Since the remotest times, Tibet has been divided into four provinces which cut up the country into longitudinal zones and which are, beginning in the west: Ngaris (Mngaris), the independent region; Chang (Gtsang), the pure country; Bu or Wu * (Dbus), the central country; Kam (Khams), the land. Ngaris includes Baltistan, Ladak and the Gartog and Rudok districts; Chang has Jikatse for its capital; Lhasa is the capital of Bu; and Chamdo may be considered as the centre of Kam, which is the largest of the four provinces. This purely historical division corresponds, at the present time, with no reality and I mention it only by the way.

For the purposes of the Chinese administration, Tibet, in our day, is divided into three parts: the south-west, which is directly dependent on the Viceroy of Sechuen; the north-west, which is subject to the

* The Chinese call it Wi.

authority of the Imperial Legate of Sining; and the remainder, which is under the Imperial Legate of Lhasa. The boundaries of this third division contain the kingdom of the Dalai Lama and various detached principalities.

Let us speak first of the kingdom of Lhasa, which forms the most important and the most populous part of Tibet. Its limits are British India and Chinese Turkestan, the sources of the Chumar, the mountains that separate the Upper Nag Chu and the Upper Chag Chu, the Tachang La, the Nagchu Valley, the Mekong Valley from about Lat. 31° to nearly Lat. 28°. Beyond these limits, certain territories are in dispute, as we shall see; within them, the Pangchen Rinpocheh of Tachilhunpo holds sway over nearly 100,000 souls in the province of Chang and the chief lama of Saskya Gompa is master over his own district. Poyul, which is inhabited mainly by Ponbos, forms an enclave independent of the Dalai Lama and directly dependent upon the Imperial Legate of Lhasa. I estimate the territories directly subject to the authority of the head of the Gelugpa to contain a population of 1,500,000 inhabitants, including 300,000 monks.

The government, in its present form, was organised by the Chinese, who, in 1751, finally abolished the lay monarchy and placed the temporal power in the hands of the Dalai Lama, who, however, has but a purely honorary title from the political point of view: he is only the nominal depository of public authority, nor could he well be otherwise, seeing that, on principle, he is raised to the throne while still in his swaddling-clothes; moreover, he would degrade his divinity by busying himself too closely with the world's affairs. The effective power belongs to a lama who bears the title of *gyatsab (rgyaltsab)*, or viceroy, who appoints or confirms all the officials and who settles all business of high importance in concert with the *kalons (bkablon)*. These, who are four in number, are all laymen : they have the general direction of the administration and are the keepers of the royal seal, but they are bound to report any weighty business to the viceroy. Under the kalons are sixteen or seventeen administrative colleges of two or three lay or religious members, such as the college of accounts *(tsipon)*, the college of the treasury *(shadso)*, the college of public granaries *(nyertsangpa)*, the college of justice *(chagpon)* and the rest. The kalons have around them a court of young attachés *(tungkor)*, all of noble birth, from among whom the lay administrative staff is almost exclusively recruited. The Tibetan territory is divided into 80 (?) districts administered by prefects *(jongpon)*, who, like the Chinese officials, combine administrative, judicial and financial functions.

The Tibetan government raises few taxes in money; most often, it draws from each district contributions in kind according to the nature of the produce proper to the district : butter, hides, raw wool, barley, wheat, horses and so on. Nominally, the taxes amount to about one-sixtieth of the capital (one rupee to five yaks), but the arbitrariness of the officials largely increases the proportion. Moreover, there are contributions in manual labour : the manufacture, on behalf of the State, of woollen stuffs, arms, appliances, tools ; the carriage of baggage ; the building and repairing of roads, bridges, forts and various structures. If, luckily for the tax-payers, the State is not lavish in the matter of public works, it and its agents, by way of retaliation, are constantly sending over the roads all manner of goods and baggage, for the carriage of which its subjects are bound to supply, free of cost, horses, yaks, or, on occasions, the use of their shoulders. Nothing makes them grumble more than this forced labour *(ulag*, from the Turkic *ulagh)*, which often takes them by surprise at the moment when they most need their time and their beasts. Add to this forced sales at exaggerated prices, of which I have already spoken and to which the government resorts more or less according to the condition of its coffers, and free gifts, which are obligatory, for every good and loyal subject—and all subjects are thus defined—is bound to give alms to the State and, when he dies, to bequeath to it a part of his personal chattels. In the main, in Tibet, children inherit none of the personalty of their fathers, all that does not fall to the government going to the monks. The Dalai Lama, for his part, has a special resource in the sale of indulgences, which takes the most unexpected forms, and in that of statuettes, amulets and blessed rosaries. He sends his agents into every Buddhist country, into Tibet proper, Ladak, Mongolia and China,* to sell tea or pieces of wool, in his name, at the most exorbitant prices and to throw in with the goods a quantity of indulgences in proportion to the generosity of the believers.

The officials are paid no salary, but receive, by way of privilege, more or less extensive territories, upon which they have the right to administer justice and to raise taxes on their own account. They have also various sources of profit, lawful and unlawful; they make deductions from the product of the taxes; they requisition workmen free or almost free of cost for their private needs; they exact presents on various occasions: accession-gifts, parting presents and so forth; they pocket the fines in which they mulct culprits; lastly, they receive the fees of the litigants. This last source of revenue is one of the most profitable, for, if the litigant does not bring a few lumps of butter under his cloak, if the money does not chink in his purse, if no

* The Chinese buy objects coming from the Dalai Lama as magic talismans.

sheep bleats behind him, if a few chickens do not pule in his bag, his case is dismissed and he has to pay the costs. The Tibetans know this and comply without reluctance, thinking, with Crispin, that justice is so fine a thing that you cannot pay too dearly for it. The lower orders, in general, display towards the magistrates and the agents of authority a crawling servility which I have never seen equalled in either Turkestan or China. This respect is not instilled into the Tibetan by esteem, but by a state of mind in which are mingled the fear of blows, superstitious terrors and the sense of his own wretchedness and of his weakness in the face of the evils that beset him. The king and his agents, even the laymen, are considered to partake of the divine nature; consequently, the people have the same opinion of them as of the gods, those formidable and malignant beings whom one must carefully avoid irritating and against whom one must protect one's self by means of incantations. No Tibetan goes to law before performing certain rites intended to oblige the judge to decide in his favour.

The public peace is maintained by a sort of mounted police consisting of men called aptuks. There are many hundreds of these under the direct orders of the central government; in addition, the prefect has several at his disposal. The policemen of the central government are fed at the expense of the State, but they all live apart, each with his own family, and receive no salary. They must have their arms and their horse and be always ready to start at the first call. When the father is too old, his son succeeds him. The departmental policemen are not fed at the cost of the administration; they are merely exempt from taxation. It is rather a title of honour, the aptuks all being men of good family and enjoying a certain credit.

There is no regular army, except a small troop at Lhasa which serves as a pretext for the employment on active service of six *dapons (mdadpon)*, or generals, and 156 other officers. The whole population is organised into a militia in the same way as the Mongols, but less severely. Every man capable of bearing arms and of paying the cost of his military outfit is bound to serve as a soldier whenever he is ordered to do so. His keep during the continuance of the campaign is at his own expense. This expense is very heavy, for there are great distances to be covered and the roads are very bad. Under good officers, the Tibetans would make fairly good soldiers, provided that they were not taken out of their country. They are accustomed to marching, make little of crossing mountains that would cause foreigners to hesitate, are easy to feed, do not fear the inclemency of the weather, are practised in the use of weapons and have a profound respect for their leaders, while nothing is easier than to inspire them, by human or supernatural means, with the most absolute confidence in victory. But clericalism has enervated the military spirit and they who have constituted themselves leaders of men are often violent, but timid and cowardly. At the time of the Sikkim business, the government was at great pains to collect on the British frontier 30,000 men, some of whom came from Chamdo, having marched for two months, carrying all their provisions with them : when the day of battle came, the English shelled the chief lamas, who stood gathered on a rising ground and who immediately turned to the right about, having imposed all this labour and almost ruin upon poor people only to treat them to the spectacle of their leaders' shame.

In spite of the absence of a standing army and the weakness of the police, the government is able to make its orders obeyed even in the most remote districts. This is due to the terror inspired by the severity with which it punishes the least offences against its authority ;

to the presence in every centre of any importance of high officials, who are great enough to command respect and too small to venture to attempt anything against the State; to the cunning system of mutual espionage that prevails in every section of society; and to the great number of lamas distributed throughout the country, all of whom are devoted to the government, which works through them and for them. In fact, from the political and administrative point of view, the clergy has reduced the lay element to a small pittance and has left it only so much as could not well be taken from it without exasperating it to the pitch of revolt. It is true that the four ministers are laymen, but they are subordinate to the religious viceroy. In the central government there is an equal number of lamas and laymen; in each district there are two prefects, one religious and one lay, who are supposed to be equal, whereas, in reality, the chief duty of the second is to nod his approval of all the acts of the first. If a layman be placed in charge of a special mission, diplomatic or other, he is always accompanied by a lama, who says nothing, who seems to have nothing to do but tell his beads, but who watches his companion's words, deeds and movements and reports them to Lhasa. The social condition of the clergy, as described in the last chapter, prepares us for this state of things.

Though absolute in theory, the authority of the central power is limited in practice by the privileges of the clergy in general, to whom the greatest deference is due, and by the privileges of the local magnates. At Lhasa, the viceroy is the master only in appearance. Chosen obligatorily from among the members of one of the three more important monasteries of the neighbourhood—Depung (Hbrasspungs), Sera, or Serra, and Galdan (Dgaldan)—he is a tool in the hands of that one of the three to which he belongs and he allows it to enjoy a predominant influence. Moreover, the ecclesiastical authorities of these three monasteries are always consulted in important affairs and each of them assigns a special delegate to every official mission. All three place a large number of their members in the public offices and there is hardly a civil servant but comes from one of them; all three alike are supported at the cost of the State; and it may be said that all that portion of the net proceeds of taxation which is not absorbed by the Court of the Dalai Lama and the requirements of public worship* is employed in pensioning Depung, Sera and Galdan. In conclusion, these three convents are the real masters of the State by reason of the number of their monks (20,000),† of their wealth, of the multitude of their servants, of their proximity to the capital, of the large number of priories under obedience to their abbots and of their relations with the greatest families of the country, all of which number members of the monasteries among their kinsmen. The result is a series of ardent rivalries and intrigues, in which poison and riots play their alternate parts: Sera owes its present pre-eminence to no more laudable means. In the provinces, the government is limited by the landholders, who have certain rights of justice, forced labour and taxation over their serfs, notably by the chief among them, namely the great monasteries, such as Dikung, Mindoling, Tsari, Gyangtse, Mingeh and Lhari. Furthermore, it limits itself by abandoning all or a part of its rights over portions

* The expenses of public worship, ceremonies, prayers and so forth amount to £32,000; of the Dalai Lama and his Court to £8,000 charged upon the taxes, without counting the Dalai Lama's private profits, which are much greater.

† They say that there are 9,000 at Depung, 8,000 at Sera and 5,000 at Galdan. These figures are probably a little exaggerated, but not much. The plain of Lhasa contains 30,000 monks, all of whom, on rising, see the first rays of the sun shine upon the golden roof of the Potala.

of territory in favour of its officials or of the convents, leaving it to them to provide for their administration and to keep a special register of the receipts and expenses connected therewith.

We now see the complex nature of a political situation that hides itself under an apparent homogeneity: two aristocracies, one of which is lay, enfeebled and subordinate, but nevertheless exists; the other religious and itself divided into a score of monastic orders, of which four or five are important. In the first of these orders are two persons who are equal ecclesiastically, although unequal politically; among the dependants of the first of these persons are three convents disputing one another's influence. This enables us to understand how the Chinese government can keep up its authority in Tibet with twenty-one officials and less than 1,500 soldiers. It was the Chinese government that placed the Dalai Lama and his partisans in the high position which they enjoy to-day, because it saw in them the best instrument for bridling the king and the lay aristocracy, ever turbulent and impatient of the yoke; because it clearly saw that an ecclesiastical administration is eminently adapted to humble men's souls, to teach them meekness and obedience; lastly, because, by attaching the principal religious head of Buddhism to itself, it made sure, at the same time, of the fidelity of the pious Buddhists that are the Mongols. Even if the Dalai Lama and his followers were tempted to forget the obligations under which they lie towards the Chinese government, they could not forget that Tibet is unable to resist a Chinese army and that the Emperor, by shifting his good-will to the rivals of the Dalai Lama, could cause the latter the greatest annoyances. Besides, the Emperor does not admit that an incarnation of Buddha can, by virtue of his divine nature, escape in any manner from the imperial authority; and, should the case occur, he arrogates to himself the right to withdraw from circulation the Buddhas who have ceased to please, by issuing decrees prohibiting them from reappearing in human form. And, therefore, the Resident General, who represents the Emperor at Lhasa, enjoys considerable authority in both internal and external affairs; I say considerable and not undisputed authority, for the Tibetans, for all their appearance of gentleness, are not lacking in that obstinacy and that stubbornness which we observe in the devotees of all countries.

This Resident General or Imperial Legate *(kinchai)* has the same rank as the governor of a province (second class of the second rank, with the dark-red button). He is always selected from among the Manchus, as are the Imperial Legates of Sining and Mongolia. He is under the Viceroy of Sechuen, but he has the right of corresponding direct with Peking. He is assisted by a vice-legate, who is also a Manchu, and by fifteen officials, Manchu, Chinese or Nepalese secretaries and interpreters. Moreover there are a commissary *(leangtai)* and a military officer at Lhari, with 130 soldiers; a commissary and four military officers at Lhasa, with 500 men; a commissary and six officers at Jikatse, with 700 men; and an officer, with a few soldiers, at Tingeh, on the road between Jikatse and Nepal. The troops are kept up by the Sechuen treasury; the commissaries are appointed by the viceroy of that province; it is their business to pay the troops and to fulfil the functions of consuls, that is to say, they adjust the differences between the Chinese merchants and between the latter and the Tibetans.

The Imperial Legate alone is qualified to conduct the foreign affairs of Tibet, although he has to consult the local authorities. In the interior, no official, no abbot of a great monastery is appointed without his approval; he has practically the last word in the election of the Viceroy; he has the right to control the public finances. Moreover, he is the equal in dignity of the Gyatsab and, consequently, superior to the ministers, who have only the rank of *taotai* (third rank, pale-blue button), and to all the officials, who, in principle, owe him absolute obedience. But his authority is accepted and respected only on condition that he does not make it felt too severely. He has ulag rights over all Tibet and, like all Tibetan officials, receives, by way of allowance, a certain number of cantons, in which he levies taxes and exercises all the rights of sovereignty. In this way, the canton of Dam and part of the country north of the Damlarkang La are within the jurisdiction of the Imperial Legate. In Tibet, as in Mongolia, the Court of Peking remembers to grant salaries to the chief personages: this is a sign of sovereignty as well as a means of action;* a feeble one, it is true: the Dalai Lama himself and the Viceroy receive a certain sum under this head; the ministers receive £30 a year each, with four pieces of satin, and the convents, in the aggregate, about £12,000.

The Chinese do not seek here, any more than in Turkestan, to profit by the economic resources of the country. They do a certain amount of trade and, as in Turkestan, have kept the tea-monopoly for themselves; but they have done nothing to improve the means of communication, to perfect agriculture, to develop the pastoral industry, which ought to be able to supply the whole of South Asia with wool, or to exploit the different mines in which the subsoil seems

* The dependence of Lhasa on Peking is, for that matter, marked in a more formal manner. The new Dalai Lama chosen by lot must receive investiture from the Emperor, who is free to withhold it. The Viceroy holds his seal at the Emperor's pleasure; the kalons are furnished with imperial patents; the imperial edicts are valid in Tibet, on condition that the local authorities countersign them, which they cannot refuse to do.

to be very rich. Chinese goods are admitted only on payment of a piece of silver per package; the Chinese merchants are not allowed to live in the country nor to enter it for the purposes of trade, unless supplied with a ticket from the Sechuen administration, which is valid only for a year: at the end of that period, they have to go. As for the Chinese women, all of them, even the wives of functionaries and officers actually serving in Tibet, are absolutely forbidden to set foot in the country. And so, whereas, in Turkestan, you find at least a small number of Chinese colonists, you do not see a single child of the Middle Kingdom in Tibet. These measures may be ascribed to a sense of prudence on the part of the Peking government, which prefers to avoid difficulties and unpleasant businesses, and to the national want of tolerance of the Tibetans, who refuse to suffer strangers within their gates. The monks, those representatives of a religion which was able to pass for a religion of universal brotherhood, open their convents and grant orders only to Tibetans, the sons of Tibetan fathers.

The economic and colonial points of view are quite secondary matters for the Chinese; it was, above all, for strategic and political reasons that they annexed these marches of Tibet, so that they might serve them for a barrier against independent and encroaching neighbours. According to the principles which I have set forth in connection with Turkestan,* it appeared to them that the best way for them to hold the country easily and cheaply was to prevent strangers from entering it and thus to deprive them of any temptation to concoct intrigues with the malcontents, under pretext of opening up commercial relations, and excite the people to rise in rebellion. The question has sometimes been mooted whether it is the Tibetans who wish to close their door

* "A Scientific Mission to Upper Asia," Vol. II., pp. 292 *et seq.*

or the Chinese who force them to close it. This is an idle question. The Chinese and the Tibetans sometimes quarrel with each other, but they are quite at one against the foreigners. The lamas, jealous of holding undivided sway over the people that feeds them, fear lest new ideas should enter together with the foreigners, lest the simplicity of their dependants' hearts should be impaired and their numbers decreased. They well know—and the example of Ladak is there to remind them—that, if another Power than China should take possession of Tibet, it would not fail, with the complicity of the laity, to cut down the prerogatives and the exorbitant profits of the monasteries: hence, to whatever order they belong, they feel it to be to their interest to keep the foreigners at a distance, to checkmate their pretensions as far as possible and to make common cause, in this respect, with the Chinese government. Taking advantage of the unbounded credulity of their flocks, there is no absurd legend that they do not sanction with regard to the Europeans, those sinister wizards who are coming to rob Tibet of its protecting gods and to deliver it as a prey to all the devils of the abyss let loose.

However, the government of Lhasa is unable to close the gates of its territory hermetically: it is needs obliged to admit, under close supervision, those natives of India to whom their common religion, or old custom, or a regular treaty gives the right of travelling and trading in the country. Notwithstanding irksome obstacles, the trade between India and Tibet is fairly active: Kashmirian, Nepalese and Hindu merchants live in the principal towns, at least provisionally; the Moslems of Western India have built a mosque in the shadow of the sacred mountain. Through their subjects, merchants, pilgrims and bandits, who move secretly about Tibet, the English are perfectly well-informed of all that occurs among their suspicious neighbours: of the religious dissidences, of the restless factions, of what they may hope to expect. The geography of the country is well enough known to them to enable them, in case of need, to dispatch a military expedition into the country, the present maps being no worse than those which we used to conquer Tongking. Certain signs warrant one in believing that English money has been distributed among influential persons in Tibet to pay for actual or virtual services of a political order. But the system of isolation of the Tibetans has, none the less, the double advantage of fostering the distrust and prejudice of the people against the Europeans and turning it into a vigilant guardian, like a chained watch-dog, and, besides, of preventing the English from freely organising and supporting a party of their own, around which the malcontents and seekers after novelty would be able to range themselves.

Up to the present, the English have displayed little enterprise or decision in their attempts to end this state of things. The last important event was the conquest of Sikkim, which they achieved in 1888 and which was confirmed by the treaty of 1890. This conquest gave them the whole sky-line of the first range of the Himalayas, except, however, the little valley of Chumbi, to obtain which they made fruitless efforts. This valley being the key of the best road leading from Lhasa to Calcutta, the Tibetans attach great importance to its retention.

When, in 1893, we arrived on the shores of the Nam Cho, the English and the Tibetans were just engaged in discussing, at Darjeeling, the terms of a commercial treaty; and this coincidence caused us some difficulty. The Indian government demanded that the road from Darjeeling to Lhasa through the Chumbi Valley should be thrown open to trade and the Tibetans opposed this with all their might. Troops were brought up and we heard that they were ready to close with one another. Finally, everything was arranged and, on the 5th of December, a treaty was concluded between the Chinese and the English stipulating that a market should be established in the Chumbi Valley, seven miles beyond the Jilep Pass, which marks the frontier. The Indian merchants were authorised to go to this market and there to trade under certain conditions. The English thought, perhaps, that, by establishing the market at Yatung, they were at least opening a garret-window into Tibet; but the Tibetans took care to put ground-glass panes to it. This Yatung is an absolutely deserted place, with not a man in it nor a house. The Chinese, it is true, undertook to put up the necessary buildings; the promise may be taken for what it is worth: "*Ah! le bon billet qu'a La Châtre!*" as Ninon de l'Enclos said on a famous occasion. The sale of Indian tea being prohibited for five years, there is no hope, in any case, of doing much business on this market; but the English, no doubt, think that, if no goods are exchanged, there will, at least, be an exchange of blows, which would permit them to send a few Sepoys to restore order.*

If England has succeeded in chipping the frontier of Tibet, she has lost the faculty which she enjoyed in the eighteenth century of keeping up agents there. In 1772, the chief lama of Tachilhunpo having written to Warren Hastings to ask him to withdraw the British troops from Bhotan, Hastings acceded to his request and sent Bogle to him as an ambassador, who was exceedingly well received. In 1782, the Pangchen Rinpocheh having meanwhile died, his successor received the congratulations of Warren Hastings through the medium of Captain Turner. After him, a Hindu, Purungir Gosain, remained at Tachilhunpo as the permanent agent of the

* In reality, this treaty has never been fulfilled (*Note of 1904*).

Viceroy of India and was even received at Lhasa. In 1792, Warren Hastings' successor, instead of assisting the Tibetans against the Nepalese, who had invaded Tibet, took the part of the Nepalese against the Chinese, who had sent an army to drive out the invaders. From that time, the Tibetans ceased to have friendly relations with the English and coalesced against them with the Chinese. We must not, however, attach greater value to this fact than it deserves : the Indian government had had relations of an intimate character only with the chief lama of Tachilhunpo, whose political importance is very insignificant ; since then, there has been no absolute rupture, the Pangchen Rinpocheh is not in the main hostile to the English and there is reason to believe that, if the matter depended only on himself, he would be glad enough to receive their visit.

The Dalai Lama, on the contrary, has always shown great reserve, although things were not so bad at first as they are to-day. In 1810, Thomas Manning, who, it is true, bore no official character, was admitted into the presence of the Dalai Lama at Lhasa and remained in the capital for a year. No European has been so far since, except Père Huc, who was soon expelled. Alarmed at the immense and continuous progress of the Indo-British power, the Tibetans have sat lurking in their lair, have barricaded the entrance and refuse to let the foreigner establish a footing, lest he should soon establish more. I believe that China and Tibet are so firmly convinced of the necessity of keeping their door closed that they would risk a war rather than give way on this point. Now, whatever interest England may have in keeping up untrammelled relations with Tibet, not only would she never undertake a war to end the isolation in which that country confines itself, but she is not even anxious to embark upon a serious diplomatic campaign with this object. As a matter of fact, Tibet, so soon as it had become accessible to the English, would, at the same moment, become accessible to the Russians, who could thus easily push their intrigues as far as the Indian frontier; and England, who can never be sure of the loyalty of the numberless populations of India, considers Russia's intrigues to be more dangerous than her arms.

I am therefore of opinion that Tibet will never be open to Europeans until it is under British protection. The Indian government is in not so great a hurry to extend its territory in the direction of Tibet as in that of Afghanistan, because it has not, on that side, to fear the progress of so ambitious and formidable a Power as Russia. It has, I know, up to the present, been a fundamental axiom of Indian policy to keep China as far as possible; but China has only just enough power in Tibet to prevent herself from being driven out by the natives: she is not capable of taking the offensive and asks only to be left in peace and to leave her neighbours in peace in their turn. Only, should the day come when England would be unable to defend Turkestan against Russian conquest, then it would seem to her necessary to enforce her protectorate on Tibet, not only by way of compensation, but especially in order to establish on her northern frontier a border-state similar to that of Afghanistan and serving to keep at arm's length a disagreeable and dangerous neighbour. This is the same object which she pursues on every side of the Indian frontier; and, when she has attained it, she will be furnished—what with Afghanistan, a portion of the Pamirs, Ladak extended to the edge of the Desert of Gobi, Tibet and Burmah—with a colossal buffer of mountains, behind which she will at last enjoy her repose in her garden, sheltered from the storms that sweep the desert and feeling only the soft and refreshing breezes that blow from her seas. It is a glorious and charming dream, similar to that which China had, but not beyond realising, nor absurd.

One sometimes hears it said that their protectorate over Afghanistan is more embarrassing than profitable to the English and this would be all the more so in the case of a protectorate over Tibet. This opinion does not seem to me to be inspired by a sound acquaintance with Asiatic things. The Calcutta government is ambitious, but it has a clear and accurate view of the conditions under which it can exist and expand. History is there to teach it that a powerful and warlike enemy, having the upper hand in Afghanistan, would soon be master of the basin of the Indus and the plain of the Ganges. To this the examples of the Ghaznevids, of Sultan Baber and of Ahmed Shah bear evidence. Now the case is exactly the same with Tibet. So soon as the English have reason to fear that the influence of so dangerous a Power as Russia will make way in that country, they will be driven to establish their protectorate over it. Let the Cossacks enter Kashgar and Khotan and the Sepoys will enter Tachilhunpo and Lhasa. These two eventualities will depend strictly upon one another.*

---

* I make no alteration in my text of 1898. Since then, the Indian government has been led to interfere in Tibet by the misgivings which it has felt at the attempts made by Russia to establish relations with the Dalai Lama.

A chief lama of Lhasa, Agoan Dordjieff, a Buriat and a Russian subject by birth, went to St. Petersburg in 1900 and 1901 and was officially received by the Emperor. The Russian government, on its side, sent M. Tsybikoff, a Buriat, a graduate of the faculty of oriental languages of St. Petersburg, on a mission to Lhasa, where he remained during almost the whole of 1901. The Tibetans, closing their doors to all the world alike, by that very fact constituted themselves the voluntary protectors of the northern frontier of India and it was to England's interest to respect their isolation. As they now, however, ceased to play

There is another matter : Tibet would be for England an excellent position from which to defend against the attacks of any other nation that basin of the Blue River, or Yangtzekiang, of which she is so jealous and to keep it dependent upon her from at least the economic point of view. If China should show herself definitely unfit to resist both the enemies that beset her on every side and the internal troubles that gnaw at her vitals, if the advance of Russia towards Mongolia and the northern provinces should come to threaten the basin of the great river, the English will feel the necessity, to protect their interests, of spreading to the gates of Sechuen and, by occupying the Tibetan citadel, of obtaining a strong hold on land of the stream which their naval power would not be great enough to guard.

China is quite aware of the precarious nature of her dominion over the kingdom of Lhasa, which is threatened by the English, on the one side, and compromised, on the other, by the lamas, who suffer her only for fear of falling into a yet worse evil. She seeks to remedy this situation not by taking action at Lhasa and endeavouring to substitute her direct government for her protectorate, which would be too difficult and dangerous, but by gradually reducing the extent of the country subject to the authority of the Dalai Lama, by stripping it, whenever the occasion offers, of some morsel of territory, by eating the artichoke leaf by leaf. She would be quite content to leave the Tibetans in

that part, it suited the British government to seek to make its influence paramount in their country. The object has remained the same; circumstances and the means employed have altered.

Russia, separated from Lhasa by many thousand miles of desert and of partly insuperable mountains, is badly situated to offer opposition to the action of the English. Moreover, she can afford to stand aloof, because Buddhism is of but very little political importance, while the influence of the Dalai Lama, which was created by the civil power, can be by it destroyed, reduced or transferred to other incarnations of Buddha (*Note of* 1904).

peace ; but a powerful and rebellious Tibet does not answer her purpose.

In previous centuries, the struggles between the clergy and the civil power were an excellent means of weakening Tibet and, when the Emperor decided to intervene in favour of the representatives of religion and to restore the government to them, he took care to keep a good slice for himself: the portions in the east and north-east now administered directly by the Viceroys of Sechuen and Kansu; so that, if the kingdom of Lhasa came to be destroyed by a national revolt or by foreign conquest, there would still remain a belt of land to serve as a protection to China proper. The successors of Kienlong followed this policy of successive and almost imperceptible encroachments with the continuity of view and the tenacity that characterise Chinese diplomacy. They took advantage of the now latent, now active rivalries between the native princes, the chief lamas, the different sects, as so many constant pretexts for interference ; and, so soon as a landed magnate put forward a violent claim to his independence and showed himself strong enough to maintain it, they explained to the Lhasa government that it did very wrong to undertake to keep so turbulent a vassal in order and that it would be worth much to its peace of mind to shift the burden to China's stronger shoulders.

The Debajong, on its side, made use of every circumstance to try to recover the land that had been snatched from it; and this led to conflicts that were incessantly renewed. The terrible reverses which China experienced after 1860, the Taiping Rebellion, the revolt of the Moslems of Turkestan, Kansu and Yunnan gave Lhasa its opportunity. In 1863, a war having broken out between Menyag and Dergyeh, the Debajong interfered in favour of the latter, upon which it imposed its protectorate, and annexed Menyag in 1866.

The general of the Debajong, a certain Punropa, governed the country for ten years and ground it down, without pity, to provide for the barbaric luxuries with which he surrounded himself. An able politician, he had succeeded in preparing for the annexation of the neighbouring countries of Litang and Batang and had already made secret conventions with the chiefs of those two territories. But the inhabitants had complained to Lhasa of the exactions to which they were subjected and jealousy of the ambitious general's power and successes caused their complaints to fall upon willing ears. Punropa was recalled, on the understanding that he would be made a minister, but he had hardly returned to the capital, when he died, suddenly, in December 1877; a few weeks after, his son, his daughter and all his relations disappeared; and to-day there is not a single member of his family living. Dergyeh took advantage of Punropa's departure to recover its independence; in 1890, Menyag, in its turn, at the instigation of the Chinese, rose in rebellion and drove out the Lhasa functionaries.

In 1887, the Debajong intervened in the country of the Hor Kangsar; in 1894, it entered upon a conflict with the people of Surmang, whom it laid claim to submit to ulag; but, in both cases, its intrigues were baffled by Chinese diplomacy. The Chinese, having got rid of the Moslems, had regained the upper hand in Tibet: Ribocheh and the Hortsi country were detached from Lhasa in 1886, the chief lamas of Jaya and Chamdo received authority to send periodical embassies to Lhasa in the same way as the Dalai Lama and the Pangchen Rinpocheh and their independence towards the Debajong was recognised. At the moment of writing, I hear that a Chinese prefect has been installed in Menyag.

Chinese power does not make all this progress without encountering serious obstacles on the part of the local chiefs as well as of Lhasa. Although the name of the Emperor still carries great weight in those countries and the chiefs prefer the mild and almost imperceptible suzerainty of Peking to the harsher and more imperious sway of Lhasa, nevertheless the efforts made by the Chinese to restrain the jurisdiction of the Debajong have not been free of disadvantages to themselves. They stirred up feelings of independence in the princes near their frontier and urged them to revolt against Lhasa in order to make them subject to their direct authority; but those princes did not shake off one yoke to pass tamely under another and the Chinese felt the difficulty of submitting to their law those whom they had encouraged to throw off discipline. The native chiefs reduced their obligations to a minimum; some even refused to make any act of submission. The Prince of Dergyeh allows no Chinese traders to live in his territory and does not let them travel on the high-road except on payment. The seventeen other Tibetan States of Sechuen—Chagla (containing Tasienlu), Litang, Batang, on the Chando road, Mili, south of that road, Menyag, the five Horpa clans, Toskyah, Somo, etc., in the north—although they have long been direct vassals of China, give the Viceroy great trouble in making them respect the small authority to which he lays claim. The Chinese are installed seriously only at Tasienlu; on the Jyerkundo road, they have only three little posts of twenty men, of which the farthest and the most considerable is that of Hor Kangsar, near the Za Chu. Of their recent occupation of Menyag it is impossible to say anything as yet.

Apart from the Tibetan States that are directly subject to the Viceroy of Sechuen, there are two other classes that are dependent on the Imperial Legates of Lhasa and Sining respectively. The Imperial Legate of Lhasa is empowered to exercise the Chinese protectorate, not only over the possessions of the Dalai Lama, but also on all the independent countries enclaved within them—Tachilhunpo, Saskya Gompa, Poyul—and all the outlying countries that have been detached from them subsequently to Kienlong's conquest, namely, the principality of the Hortsi, Ribocheh, Chamdo and Jaya. The boundaries of the Imperial Legate's influence are formed, on the north, by the Tang La and Damtao La Passes, by the mountains that separate the basin of the Nu Chu from that of the Pam Chu, by a line crossing the Pam Chu and the Za Chu, or Mekong, at about Lat. 31° 40′. Then the frontier reaches the valley of the Blue River, goes down it to about Lat. 29° 30′, from there turns into the valley of the Mekong and follows it until about Lat. 27°. The Chinese keep a small garrison at Kiangka, under the orders of a captain, and another at Chamdo, under the orders of a colonel; but they are not even represented in Ribocheh or in the Hortsi country. This latter country, which lies between the Tatsang La and the Damtao La, comprises the basins of the Chag Chu and the Sog Chu; south of the Tatsang La, the little valley of Duglong also forms part of it. The majority of the population are Ponbos and this was the cause of its separation from Lhasa. All the Tibetans living on the road from Nagchu to Jyerkundo within the limits specified, the Ataka, the Horpongrama, the Sogdema, the Kengkiema, are, without exception, dissenters. This is the case also with their chief, who bears the title of Hortsi Gyabpeko, is a layman and lives in a tent like all his subjects. His residence is at Pachen, two days below Wabeh Sumdo on a little affluent running into the Sog Chu on the left. It may be remarked of the Tibetan chiefs that, like the Mongolian chiefs, they do not care to instal themselves on the high-roads, beside the big rivers, or in the plains; they generally resort to remote places, difficult of access, near the sources of the rivers. Three days below Pachen, in the Sog Chu Valley, stands the monastery of Sogzendeh, whose lamas are independent of the Hortsi Gyabpeko. The latter's dominion extends, from west to east, between the great eastern tributary of the Nag Cho to Bumundo. He has a number of tribal chiefs or debas under his orders and receives a small allowance from the Emperor of China. The kinglet, whose country is poor and sparsely peopled and who wears a simple sheepskin gown, seems to be fairly well obeyed; he levies on each family and each head of cattle a very light tax, of which the Imperial Legate takes a share. The latter has no agent in the country, but, from time to time, sends an officer to Pachen to receive the prince's homage and tribute.

The third part of Tibet subject to China lies within the jurisdiction of the Imperial Legate of Sining, who himself is dependent upon the Viceroy of Kansu. This jurisdiction is bounded by that of the Imperial Legate of Lhasa as far as the sources of the Dergyeh Chu; next, the frontier goes up to the north-east, crosses the Do Chu at 60 miles to the south-east of Jyerkundo, runs to the north of Dergyeh and the Horpa country, crosses the Ta Kinchuen at Lat. 32° and, in the north-east, joins the frontier of Kansu proper, following the watershed between the Hoangho and the River Min. Within these boundaries are contained the States of the Nanchen Gyapo, the four tribes of the Zachukkapa, the States of the King of the Goloks, the Gomi and Panak tribes and, lastly, the district of Ngamdo. The Nanchen Gyapo, a lay king, resides at Pam Jong, on the Pam Chu, north of Ribocheh. The whole region from the Damtao La to the frontier of Mongolian Tsaidam and to the boundaries of the Do Chu basin is placed under his suzerainty. The Tibetans speak of him as a venerable person, but also as a poor fellow who is led by the nose by the lamas. For that matter, in all the principalities of Eastern Tibet, the lamas either are the nominal and real masters or else are completely independent of the civil power and exercise a considerable influence over it. The King of Tasienlu is the only one who has authority over the clergy of his States, for which reason he is surrounded, in the eyes of the Tibetans, with a formidable and mysterious majesty, no less than the petty King of Ladak, with whom nobody in the world is fit to be compared, unless it be the Emperor of China in person. The power of the Nanchen Gyapo is effective only in the Pam Chu Valley, in the immediate neighbourhood of his residence. Elsewhere, the tribal chiefs, more or less encouraged by the Chinese, render him little more than a platonic homage. The tribes known to me are the Dungpa, the Gejis, the Rakis, the Taorongpa and the Nyamcho. The Dungpa extend from the Damtao La to the source of the Mekong. Their chief is encamped at Damsarchawo, near the source of the Dam Chu, three days to the east of the road. The Gejis, who are more numerous and consist of 3,000 laymen and 500 lamas, are distributed over the upper basin of the Mekong, between the Zanak La and the Zeh La. Their chief is encamped at Zamarsang. The Rakis run from the Zeh La to the Serkyem La. The Taorongpa, a much superior tribe to the foregoing, are bounded by the Serkyem La, the Tao La, twenty miles south-east of Jyerkundo, and the watershed between the Do Chu and the Zachu Golok. Their not very large country is comparatively thickly populated and covered with numerous villages; and they are the only one of all the tribes which I have named that occupies itself with agriculture. They are divided into twenty-five clans, each commanded by a lay chief; it would not appear that they have a general chief and their common affairs are settled in the assembly of the chiefs of clans. In reality, the Saskyapa abbot of Jyergu Gompa is the veritable master and the chiefs of clans are, in fact, no more than his agents. He has 3,000 monks in his obedience, distributed over various convents, each owning large properties and having rights of high and low justice over the surrounding cantons. The only parts of the country that escape his authority are the lands and villages belonging to the rare Gelugpa monasteries, which have the abbot of Labug at their head and do not number more than 800 monks. To the north of the Taorongpa are the Nyamcho, who themselves border upon the Mongols of Tsaidam.

In the east, the region of the Upper Za Chu, which is fairly populous and contains crops and villages except in the part which I travelled through, is independent both by right and in fact of the Nanchen Gyapo. It is divided into four cantons, administered by four native chiefs, whose head is the superior of Tubchi Gompa. Next come the superior of Kanar Gompa, the lay chief of Yongka and the lay chief of Chuma. The people of this country are distinguished at first sight by their shorn heads from the long-haired subjects of the Nanchen Gyapo. Also, they carry longer lances, measuring about 11½ feet. These points make them resemble their neighbours the Goloks, to whom they are closely related by kindred. They are particularly turbulent and, if they are a little more cautious in their robberies than the Goloks, this is only because they live in houses and are more exposed to reprisals.

If the subjects of the Nanchen Gyapo give the people of Zachukka a bad name, this does not mean to say that they are much better themselves. Private property is but little respected among them; one often meets small caravans of Tibetans or Chinese that have had their horses stolen by the natives; and the people of Lhasa never travel that way except in numbers and well-armed. As for the cantonal chiefs, for the most part lamas perched in their lamaseries as in sparrow-hawks' nests, it is not uncommon for them to be parties to the pillage and to justify it by invoking the law of reprisals. In fact, everybody, afraid of being robbed by his neighbour, indemnifies himself as and when he may, often enough beforehand, and pays himself by theft for the losses which he has suffered or may suffer in the future. The Kirghiz system of the *baramta* is practised everywhere. When an individual has occasion to complain of a theft, a murder, a rape, an outrage of any sort, on the part of an individual of another clan, instead of running off to his solicitor, he appeals to his own clan, which takes up arms and goes off to plunder the herds of the clan to which the culprit belongs. This is the Tibetan way of serving a writ of caution. Struggles ensue, not always unattended with bloodshed; prisoners are taken and often drowned; and, from reprisals to reprisals, the quarrel can be indefinitely prolonged. It is very difficult to settle a definitive peace that wipes out all the wrongs done and suffered on both sides.

The Goloks,* generally called Sifans by the Chinese, are masters of the whole region lying between the Kyaring Cho and the watershed between the Ma Chu and Min rivers; they extend south to Lat. 32° and are bounded by Dergyeh and the Horpa clans. They are divided into twelve tribes, of which that of the Kengens is the most important. Their king, who bears the title of Archungnurbu Gyapo, resides in the Ma Chu valley, to the south of the mighty chain of the Amnyeh Machen. They are equipped and dressed in the same manner as the Zachukkapa: sheepskin garments, long lances, short

* From Go (*ngo*), face, and *log*, crooked, that is to say rebel. *Ngolog chedpa*, to pull a crooked face, is a current phrase meaning to rise in rebellion.

hair, flat, round caps fitting close to the head at the back and forming a kind of peak in front. They have no houses and live in tents, the lamas and the king as well as the rest. The clergy seems to occupy an inferior position among them, although it is fairly numerous and not devoid of influence. The Goloks are absolutely independent of China, both nominally and in reality. They form a regularly-organised society of brigands. Every summer, they fit out one or more expeditions of 300 to 1,000 horsemen, who ride mostly in the direction of Lhasa, carry off herds of cattle, women and children and plunder the caravans of merchants. These expeditions are commanded by the chiefs of tribes, with the consent of the king, who receives a percentage of the proceeds. They sometimes penetrate within sight of Nagchu Jong and pursue their ends until well within Mongolia. The people of Tsaidam fear them greatly: Naichi, whose pasture-lands were formerly frequented by the Mongols, has had to be abandoned because of the repeated inroads of the Goloks. A void has been made all around the country of those bandits; large and rich pastures are to-day deserted, none daring to venture there and put his head in the lion's mouth: although they never pitch their tents nor drive their herds beyond the Amnyeh Machen Mountains, they permit nobody to settle there or even to pass between these mountains and Lake Kyaring. This is not the policy of the dog in the manger: it is a mere variant of Protection. The Goloks, in so acting, confer upon themselves, by virtue of the right of the strongest, the monopoly of working the salt of the Kyaring Cho; and this monopoly is a very profitable one, for a large part of Eastern Tibet has no salt: the whole country between the Tatsang La and Jyerkundo is without it and the poorer natives use salt red earth instead. The Goloks therefore sell their salt at their own price to the Zachukkapa and to the Horpa, who pass it on to their neighbours. Being practical people, they do not close their doors to all traffic: they have a sort of commercial treaty with the Salar Moslems and with the people of Songpanting, who are allowed to sell their wares freely in the Golok country on condition of surrendering a certain part of their profits to the tribal chiefs and the king. The Salars and the Songpang people, being smugglers, lose nothing by this: they simply pay to the Golok chiefs what they ought to pay to the imperial treasury.

The Goloks are not only shrewd men of business and manufacturers, but also pious people who know their religious duties: they give a free passage through their territory to the caravans of certain convents, such as Labug and Lhabrang, who pay them in indulgences and bills of exchange on the next world. As for merchants unprovided with a regular passport, they are plundered mercilessly and the Chinese officials are spared less than anybody. The idleness and corruption of the Chinese administration have always kept it from employing force for the preservation of law and order. The mandarins, to excuse their neglect, paint a very romantic picture of this brigand-ridden country, representing it as inaccessible, bristling with formidable mountains, intersected with gloomy gorges. As a matter of fact, it is one of the least inaccessible countries in Tibet; the valleys are wide, the passes easy, except, perhaps, those in the Amnyeh Machen. Nevertheless, the Goloks are difficult to catch: living as they do in tents, it does not take them long to break up camp at the first alarm and to take refuge on heights where they are not easily followed; but the principal reason why they are left in peace is that a military expedition in a poor and distant country, amid an untractable population, is a costly and arduous operation involving serious responsibilities. It is evidently much simpler to stay quietly at home and to pocket the money which the Emperor sends for the maintenance of the troops.

There remains but little for me to say of the Panaks, who live on the shores of the Koko Nor, to the south, east and north, the western margin being occupied by Mongols. They wear their hair short like the Goloks and are distinguished from the other Tibetan nomads by their round, peaked caps and their blue trousers of Chinese cotton-cloth. I have already pointed out the peculiarities of their physical type, which indicate an admixture of the neighbouring Mongolian element. Like the Mongols, they always guard their herds on horseback, which is the habit of the people of the plains or of wide flat valleys. Their tents are similar to those of the other Tibetans, except that they are larger, measuring as much as 50 feet by 30. The stone stove is also a little different in appearance. Some of the Panaks have white, round felt tents like those of the Mongols, but this is an exception. The Panaks seem to have but few relations with their Tibetan congeners of the south, from whom they are separated by many days' march, and they would hardly know them, if they did not go on pilgrimage to Lhasa and if they did not see a few caravans from Lhasa and Jyerkundo pass their way. This fact at once becomes evident to the traveller through the disappearance of the rupee, which is replaced by Chinese money. The Panaks are known in Tsaidam and at Tongkor and Sining as incorrigible thieves, though they struck me as decent people enough: they are only pilferers and not brigands like the Goloks. They have no king, but only chiefs of clans; they are more nearly subjected to the Imperial Legate of Sining than the other Tibetans and pay him annual taxes.

It is safe to say that the authority of China is not firmly felt beyond Tsaidam, the chain south of the Koko

Nor, the country of the Gomis and that of Lhabrang Gompa. The Goloks do not trouble about the Imperial Legate, except to rob his agents on occasion, and the Imperial Legate, on his side, pretends to ignore them. In the vast region that stretches between Tsaidam, Chambo and the Damtao La, he has only two representatives at Jyerkundo, mere interpreters of his yamen, knowing the Tibetan language. These modest agents employ their abilities as best they can in persuading the petty local chiefs to keep the peace and their mediation sometimes has good results; but this mediation is of the platonic order, for they have no serious means of .compelling respect of their authority, beyond a threat of Chinese intervention. They have no escort, but only a few dorghas, or native policemen, similar to the aptuks of Lhasa. The few Chinese merchants who trade in the country are allowed to reside only at Jyerkundo and, although this village is subject to Kansu, they have to be furnished with letters from the administration of Sechuen. The Imperial Legate issues letters only for the immediate neighbourhood of the Koko Nor and for Tsaidam; and these letters are valid only for forty days, which prevents the holders from going as far as Jyerkundo. The only reason for this measure is to preserve for the Sechuen administration the whole profit from the Tibetan trade, part of which passes through Jyerkundo. The fiscal obligations of the inhabitants of this district towards the Chinese government are limited to the payment of a tax of one-eighth of an ounce of silver, say one-third of a rupee, per hearth and per annum, to the maintenance of the two interpreters and their dorghas and to the free supply of the animals, straw and fuel which they need for their movements. The Imperial Legate never appears in the countries which he is ordered to administer;

he thinks, very justly, that his majesty gains by not being seen close at hand. Only, every three years or, perhaps, every year, he goes in great state to the first pass affording a view of the Koko Nor and makes his offerings and prayers to the divinity of the lake, who, in return, assures to him the possession of the whole country under the divinity's protection. Moreover, every three years, he sends to Jyerkundo a Chinese official having the rank of a prefect, in order to receive the solemn homage of all the assembled chiefs. This is the same ceremony that was observed in the sixth century and doubtless earlier still. In truth, the Tibetans are one of the nations that have changed least in the course of the centuries and it is greatly to be regretted that they are so difficult of access and so obstinately opposed to enquiries.

THE END